In Pursuit *of* Knowledge

In Pursuit

of

Knowledge

Scholars, Status, and

Academic Culture

Deborah L. Rhode

STANFORD LAW AND POLITICS
An imprint of Stanford University Press
Stanford, California 2006

Stanford University Press
Stanford, California

Printed in the United States of America on acid-free, archival-quality paper

Library of Congress Cataloging-in-Publication Data

Rhode, Deborah L.

In pursuit of knowledge : scholars, status, and academic culture / Deborah L. Rhode.

   p. cm.

Includes bibliographical references and index.

ISBN-13: 978-0-8047-5534-4 (cloth : alk. paper)

ISBN-10: 0-8047-5534-5 (cloth : alk. paper)

1. College teachers--Professional relationships--United States. 2. Education, Higher--Aims and objectives--United States. 3. Universities and colleges--Research--United States. I. Title.

LB1778.2.R48 2007

378.1'2--dc22   2006023422

Designed by James P. Brommer
Typeset by Bruce Lundquist in 10.5/15 Minion

for

J. PAUL LOMIO

and

THE STAFF OF THE STANFORD LAW LIBRARY

Contents

Acknowledgments

This pursuit of knowledge has been immeasurably assisted by the knowledge of others. Faculty colleagues George Fisher, Patricia Gumport, Patricia Jones, Pamela Karlan, Nannerl Keohane, and David Luban gave generously of their time and talents in commenting on early drafts of the project. Lawrence Friedman not only labored over the entire manuscript but also has provided the model for the exemplary academic life to which many of us aspire but few manage to live. Christopher Walker offered valuable research support, and Mary Tye prepared the manuscript with extraordinary skill and endless diligence and good humor. The book is dedicated to J. Paul Lomio, the director of the Robert Crown Law Library, and to his exceptional staff. I am especially indebted to librarians Sonia Moss, Rich Porter, Erika Wayne, and Kathleen Wilko: without their knowledge, my own pursuit would never have been possible. I am also grateful to Amanda Moran, my editor at Stanford University Press, whose insights and support guided this book at every step of the way.

My greatest debts on this and every other project are to my husband Ralph Cavanagh. After three decades of acknowledging his contributions, I still cannot come close to doing them justice. Anyone who knows him will know why. I hope he does as well.

In Pursuit *of* Knowledge

Chapter One

THE ACADEMIC MISSION:
IN PRINCIPLE AND PRACTICE

"The examined life was easily overrated." That was the judgment of the dissolute English professor in John Gardner's *Mickelsson's Ghosts*.[1] And despite our aspirations to the contrary, most academics appear to operate on that assumption. Although we live the "life of the mind," we generally lack opportunities to think systematically and self-critically about what that means on a daily basis, and about the gap between our principles and practices. This largely unexamined life is, of course, not unique to academics. An increasingly secular culture presents ever fewer opportunities to confront unsettling questions about the distance between ideals and institutions. But both the profession and the public have a stake in ensuring a more searching analysis of academic culture, particularly in research universities. These institutions play a crucial role in educating the next generation of leaders and in extending the frontiers of knowledge. That role imposes corresponding responsibilities, and the ways in which universities fall short should be matters of personal as well as public concern.

The foundations for closer scrutiny are already in place. Academics have never lacked for critics. Their character has been the subject of frequent parodies; their culture has been the topic of scathing popular commentary and extensive scholarly analysis. Yet seldom do faculty outside the field of higher education pay much attention to this literature, and seldom are the critiques well informed by multiple disciplinary traditions. This book seeks to engage a broader audience by expanding its lens. By drawing on the best that has been written from literature, education, history, sociology, economics, law, and related fields, the chapters that follow aim to enrich the pursuit of knowledge that they describe.

The chapters are organized around the central roles of academic life: scholarship, teaching, administration, and public intellectual pursuits. Two themes predominate: the gap between principles and practice, and the distortion of the pursuit of knowledge by the pursuit of status. These problems play out in all aspects of academic culture. However, given the diversity among educational institutions, it makes sense to focus on a particular context. The United States has some 4,200 colleges and universities, ranging in size from a few hundred students to over 50,000.[2] Liberal arts, evangelical, technical, and research-oriented institutions operate with vastly different resources and priorities.[3] The discussion in this book emphasizes the nation's 260-some research universities, which confer about a third of all B.A. degrees and three-quarters of Ph.d. degrees.[4] These universities set the standards to which higher education generally aspires and supply much of the knowledge base and faculty for institutions of all types. This is also the culture that I know best. After spending over a quarter of a century as a university professor, I wanted to write the kind of book that I had always wanted to read.

The Culture of Complaint

It is scarcely surprising that academics have inspired extensive critical commentary. The life of the mind has always attracted a disproportionate share of individuals with pompous or eccentric personality traits, which are natural magnets for satire. That is true in any culture, but anti-intellectual undercurrents have been especially strong in countries with populist democratic traditions, such as the United States. Over the past quarter century, the growing size, influence, and cost of higher education also have increased the public's stake in its performance and heightened awareness of how far it falls short.

The result has been a chorus of critics with competing variations on similar themes. Legions of politicians, pundits, governmental bodies, and academic experts have all identified serious challenges, which some consider of crisis proportions. Shrill polemics vie with sober scholarship, usually distinguishable by title: *Going Broke by Degree*, *Imposters in the Temple*, *Killing the Spirit*, *The University in Ruins*, and *Profscam* versus *Academic Duty*, *The Work of the University*, *Liberal Education and the Public Interest*, and *Universities in the Marketplace*. But cutting across this spectrum are shared concerns. Whatever their other differences, most commentators identify a mismatch between public needs and academic priorities. And that disjuncture is, in turn, often rooted in the pursuit of prestige and profit, which has too often hijacked the pursuit of knowledge.

Such criticism, however, needs to be kept in perspective, and should be informed by a comparative framework that popular polemics ignore. Measured against higher education in other nations or other eras, the American academy is thriving. As former Harvard president Derek Bok notes, "most experts here and abroad believe that our universities surpass those of other industrialized countries in their capacity for first-rate research, the quality of their professional education, the degree of innovation in their educational programs, and their success in opening higher education to . . . the different needs and abilities of a huge student population."[5] According to the most widely accepted rankings, the United States accounts for seven out of ten of the world's top-ranked universities.[6] Seventy-five years ago, fewer than one in twenty Americans had a college degree.[7] Today, academic institutions educate half of all Americans directly, and reach the other half indirectly through research, public education, and community service. Literary critic Elaine Showalter notes that "[m]ore young people than ever before in history want and expect to go to college. . . . Today's undergraduates have better research facilities, educational opportunities, counseling, living arrangements, [and] scholarship aid . . . than ever before."[8] Academic institutions are crucial in creating the informed citizens essential to democratic self-governance and the skilled workforce essential for prosperity in a competitive global economy. American universities are also responsible for most of the nation's scientific research; they produce 60 percent and employ 70 percent of the world's Nobel science laureates.[9]

Such achievements have not escaped public notice. Over 90 percent of surveyed Americans have some, or a great deal of, confidence in four-year colleges and universities, and view them as one of the nation's most valuable resources. Only the military inspires a higher level of trust.[10] In other popular opinion polls measuring the prestige of some 730 occupations, college presidents and professors of math and physics rank in the top ten.[11] At least three-quarters of college graduates report being satisfied, or very satisfied, with their undergraduate experience.[12] Faculty, for their part, are also relatively content with their worklives. In the most comprehensive recent surveys, satisfaction levels have ranged between 75 and 90 percent, and over four-fifths would choose an academic career again.[13] One reason, explored more fully in the discussion to follow, is that the working conditions of most American faculty stack up well next to their European counterparts and to other similarly qualified individuals in terms of compensation, job security, and autonomy.[14] As one law school dean aptly reminded his whining colleagues, they were having a "virtual spa experience" compared with the day-to-day life of a practitioner.[15]

Yet these comparisons—with other professions, other nations, other eras—are not the most relevant concern. The key issue is how well the academy is performing relative to the needs of its multiple constituencies: students, faculty, staff, donors, community, and society in general. Measured by that standard, American higher education falls short. Both the public and the profession express strong concerns about some aspects of higher education, although their members generally have quite different views about the nature of the problem and the most appropriate responses. From the public's perspective, the overwhelming concern is cost. American universities may be the best in the world, but they are also the most expensive, and most individuals believe that the price is too high. Over two-thirds agree that academic institutions could maintain quality standards while cutting costs, and over four-fifths think that students are incurring too much debt to finance their education.[16] By contrast, faculty see the opposite problem, at least at their own universities. About three-quarters think that tuition and fees are not too high at their institutions, only a tenth "strongly agree" that campus resources are sufficient to meet faculty needs, and less than a seventh are very satisfied with their own salary and benefits or with the funds available for research.[17] Leaders of American higher education hold similar views, and an increasing portion of their job consists of trying to cajole increased financial support from government, alumni, and other funders.

Both the public's and the profession's concerns have a strong factual basis. As subsequent discussion makes clear, the financing structure for higher education is problematic on multiple levels. Too many students lack access to universities at a price that they can afford, and too many faculty lack sufficient time and resources for the level of scholarship that they face increasing pressure to produce. Much of the reason for both difficulties lies in the escalating competition in higher education and the spiraling cost of the pursuit of status as well as the pursuit of knowledge.

THE PURSUIT OF KNOWLEDGE

At the abstract level, the goals of American universities are not in dispute. Their fundamental objectives, endlessly affirmed in mission statements and ceremonial pronouncements, are to advance and transmit knowledge. In Cardinal Newman's classic nineteenth-century formulation, *The Idea of a University*, higher education "cultivates the intellect and expands the capacity to reason"; it is an "end in itself," independent of practical consequences.[18] However, as recent history amply demonstrates, the academy's commitment to free inquiry does in fact have such consequences. It advances individuals' capacity to understand and shape their environment, to reason and write effectively, to comprehend and value their history, to extend the frontiers of science and culture, and to exercise the rights and privileges of self-government. University research and teaching have been essential to progress in health, technology, and the protection of natural resources. Higher education is, in short, critical to our social welfare and social progress. In more prosaic terms, it is also the way station to occupations with the greatest status, income, and power.[19]

Yet although there is wide agreement about the academic mission, there is equally wide disagreement about how best to advance it and how to reconcile competing demands. Beyond a vague commitment to "excellence," university faculty share no consensus about purpose, priorities, and accountability. "Excellence" is what we agree on because it has no real content and fudges the difficult choices.[20] How should academic institutions measure performance? How should they balance affordability and quality, research and teaching, applied and basic knowledge, service and scholarship? In the absence of consensus on those issues, or on widely shared and easily implemented standards for measuring quality, universities are left with less satisfying proxies for achievement such as growth or reputation in national rankings. Yet the effect of such measures is to link the pursuit of knowledge with the pursuit of status, which has unappealing by-products.

THE PURSUIT OF STATUS

Recognition and Rankings

Desires for recognition shape much human behavior, but they are particularly pronounced in American academic settings. The nation's competitive culture reinforces a preoccupation with rankings. And higher education attracts individuals with especially strong needs for achievement. Those who end up in faculty and administrative leadership positions are individuals who, by definition, have done well in competitive educational settings and who value the form of recognition that academic reward structures provide. By the same token, once these high achievers become academics, their status is in part derivative; their standing depends to some extent on the prestige of their employers. Almost nine out of ten surveyed faculty report that the reputation of their institution or department is "important" or "very important to them personally."[21] There are tangible as well as psychological reasons for that concern; faculty salaries are higher and teaching loads are lower in prestigious institutions.[22] The vast majority of academics are understandably invested in their schools' rankings, however imperfectly measured.

The same is true for other constituencies of higher education. Students, parents, alumni, donors, and funders are all concerned with how well their institutions measure up in comparison with rivals, and they exert powerful pressure on academic priorities. As Thorstein Veblen observed almost a century ago, the "felt need for prestige has a major share in shaping the work and bearing of the university. Whatever will not serve the end of prestige has no secure footing."[23] Since that observation, the escalation of competitive pressures has amplified the importance of reputation. Today's universities may "strive for quality but they trade on reputation."[24]

Yet in the absence of reliable comparative information about quality, reputation hinges on highly imperfect proxies. The most influential are rankings such as those by *U.S. News and World Report*. Ours is a culture that cannot resist ratings, no matter how tenuous their factual basis. An estimated six-and-a-half million copies of campus rankings and guides that reflect them are sold annually, and an even greater number are distributed free.[25] Yet the foundations for these academic scorecards are problematic in multiple respects. They typically place heavy reliance on reputation, measured by the subjective perceptions of top administrators. As these individuals freely acknowledge, they rarely possess enough systematic knowledge about other institutions to make accurate comparative judgments.[26] Those surveyed often depend on word-of-mouth reputations and prior rankings, which yields a kind of echo chamber with self-perpetuating dynamics. Past recognition creates a "halo effect," which perpetuates high scores even when the evaluator knows nothing about current performance. This explains why MIT's law school and Princeton's professional schools do so well, even though they do not exist.[27] Rankings also affect the size of applicant pools and alumni giving, which are again part of what the rankings measure, and which add to their self-reinforcing effects.[28]

The more objective factors that influence ratings are problematic for other reasons. Almost all of these factors measure inputs, such as the test scores of the entering class, alumni contributions, and library books per student. These factors receive arbitrary weights and bear no necessary relationship to the quality of the learning experience.[29] The main measure of output is graduation rate, which, as Chapter 3 notes, has more to do with the preparation and capabilities of incoming students than with the education that they receive. Moreover, even minor changes in the way that data are collected or assessed can cause significant fluctuations in rankings, which affect admissions, morale, and alumni relations out of all proportion to what the changes signify about the institutional environment.[30]

Worse still, the undue importance of these rankings among students, faculty, employers, and alumni donors has led to various unwelcome behaviors. Some institutions have fudged the facts.[31] Others have engaged in strategic behavior, such as giving unjustly low evaluations to close competitors in reputational surveys; denying admission to qualified minorities with low test scores or placing them in part-time programs that do not count in ratings; and rejecting applicants with outstanding credentials who are likely to choose another school and depress the institution's yield rate.[32] Legal educators, schooled in the arts of exploiting technicalities, have pioneered particularly creative accounting strategies. Examples include manipulating academic leaves and titles to improve student-faculty ratios, recalculating the fair market value of discounted library services to inflate per-student expenditures, or hiring their own graduates on a short-term basis to improve job placement records.[33]

Clara Lovett, president of the American Association for Higher Education, underscores the socially counterproductive consequences of this pursuit of prestige: "Instead of investing in learning environments that help students of varied backgrounds and preparation succeed, too many institutions now spend their resources aggressively recruiting students with high SAT or ACT scores," which boost the school's selectivity ratings.[34] Lavish student services, athletic programs, and merit scholarships do more to improve *U.S. News* rankings than do labor-intensive teaching approaches and other factors that enrich the classroom experience.[35] For example, law school rankings exclude many factors that materially enhance educational quality, such as access to clinical courses, well-designed public service programs, and a diverse faculty and student body. Instead, the premium placed on reputation encourages glitzy and expensive public relations campaigns that do nothing to improve the learning environment.[36] Similar problems plague ratings of other professional and undergraduate programs, and surveys that include measures such as commitment to public service or socioeconomic diversity produce vastly different results than those from *U.S. News.*[37]

That is not to imply that all comparative ratings are counterproductive. Some relevant characteristics can be objectively assessed, and schools should be held accountable for their performance. Ratings can supply a counterweight to complacency and a check on puffing. In their absence, applicants would undoubtedly encounter an educational Lake Wobegon, where all institutions were above average. But the problem with rankings such as those in *U.S. News* is that they assign a single score based on arbitrary weightings of a partial list of characteristics, many of which bear little relation to the quality of education. This pecking order then implies a false precision that assumes undue influence, and skews decision making by applicants, donors, and the institutions themselves. Even one of the principal architects of the *U.S. News* system is "shocked and startled" at how important it has become, although he appears to believe that schools should be "mad at themselves."[38]

Growth

Another flawed proxy for institutional achievement is growth. The "goodness of growth" is a fundamental principle of academic administration; it confers "at least the illusion of increased power" and serves as a tangible symbol of success.[39] Expansion of buildings, budgets, libraries, laboratories, and even the campaigns that finance them seems evidence of accomplishment. Yet this empire building can become an end in itself. The result can be unnecessary duplication across institutions and diversion of resources from more vital but less visible ends. Veblen once criticized many institutions' costly neo-Gothic "architecture of notoriety" as ill-suited to any functional purpose "beyond whatever prestige attaches to ornate and opulent display." In his view, universities also were squandering scarce resources on other forms of "tawdry pageantry," "showy magnitude," and "sentimental rivalry" among schools, particularly in athletics.[40] The problem has, if anything, intensified over the past century, along with the increasing scale and aspirations of higher education. Administrators and donors often want to leave a tangible legacy, and even tight-fisted legislators can sometimes be goaded into gaudy building plans and oversized athletic budgets that will do their flagship university proud.

The Price of Prestige

This scramble for status is partly attributable to what scholars variously term "upward drift" or "mission creep"; the tendency of institutions lower on the prestige pecking order to imitate rather than innovate and to replicate the priorities of more prestigious universities rather than to develop distinctive strengths.[41] In two classic articles, sociologists Paul DiMaggio and Walter Powell describe this "iron cage" of conformity, and John Meyer notes the pressure on institutions to achieve such legitimacy, which they can then confer on students.[42] One obvious consequence of this status-seeking behavior has been the escalating pressure to promote activities such as scholarship and athletics, which have visible reputational value, at the expense of teaching and service, which carry little weight outside the school.

The pursuit of prestige has adverse consequences for individuals as well as for institutions. Students are often less concerned with educational content than with credentials, and make decisions about schools, majors, and courses accordingly. This is not, of course, a new development. Henry Ward Beecher noted two centuries ago that Americans viewed higher education as a pedigree, valuable more for the status than the learning it might signify: "If a man has been to college, he has a title. . . . It saves the pride and ministers pleasure to the vanity, long after it has in every other respect become utterly useless."[43] The more prestigious the institution, the more valuable that title becomes. No other country attaches so much significance to academic affiliations for such a broad segment of the public; only in America are these affiliations considered worthy of display in car windows.[44]

The problem, however, is that students are often poorly informed about the trade-offs that pursuit of prestige entails. How much will the factors that confer institutional status improve the quality of learning for undergraduates?[45] Those who see their degrees in largely instrumental terms—as tickets to jobs or to graduate and professional schools—are missing an important part of what education should be about. Course selection becomes a strategic exercise, designed less for learning than for transcripts. The result, warned Robert Hutchins, a celebrated president of the University of Chicago, is that "soon everybody in the university will be there for the purpose of being trained for something else."[46] In today's "culture of credentials," interest in the humanities is on the decline. The fields that prosper are those that study money, attract money, or promise money.[47] The fields that dwindle are those that encourage pursuit of knowledge for its own sake and see learning as preparation for life, not simply for careers.

For faculty, the scramble for status can be even more corrosive. As the Gilbert and Sullivan stanza has it: "where everybody's somebody, nobody's anybody." The significance of status generally intensifies in graduate school, where self-esteem becomes ever more intertwined with esteem by others. Seminars become occasions to impress rather than inform; the unnamed but ever present subtext is, as English professor Jane Tompkins describes it: "Am I smart? Am I really smart? Am I the smartest?"[48] Even well-established faculty find it difficult to escape the sometimes toxic effects of intellectual hierarchies. In a world in which financial compensation and opportunities for advancement are highly constrained, smaller emblems of status become increasingly critical. Awards, speaking invitations, titles, publications in prominent journals, and references by scholars and media commentators all become coveted signals of success. They are, in French sociologist Pierre Bourdieu's phrase, the "cultural capital" of campus life.[49]

This pursuit of prestige takes a variety of unbecoming forms described more fully in the chapters that follow. Although the desire for recognition can spur productivity, it also has less welcome offshoots. Among the most obvious are the pretentious style, esoteric subjects, and excessive references common in academic writing. The result, as Chapter 2 notes, is that much contemporary scholarship is arcane, trivial, and "unread or unreadable" by all but a few fellow specialists.[50] Because academic reputation and rewards are increasingly dependent on publication, faculty have incentives to churn out tomes that will advance their careers regardless of whether they will also advance knowledge. Yet as professors focus ever greater attention in professing only for each other, they find less time for other crucial work. Chapter 3 explores the consequences for undergraduate teaching, which is too often off-loaded to adjuncts and graduate assistants who lack adequate time, training, and oversight for the task. A majority of new faculty are now hired in non-tenure-track positions, which carry disproportionate classroom obligations. Research universities have seen the greatest decline in teaching responsibilities.[51]

In many fields, a growing emphasis on narrowly specialized scholarship has also discouraged potentially more useful publications for practitioners and general audiences. As Chapter 5 notes, we have vastly more intellectuals than ever before, but fewer "public intellectuals." That role has often been abdicated to pundits with less expertise and independence. Ironically enough, even as a college education has become more widely accessible, its scholarly output has become less so. In effect, "people outside the academy rarely care, and even more rarely can understand, what academics are talking about."[52]

The pursuit of prestige has other unpalatable by-products. Self-promotion can hijack virtually all forms of collegial interaction, including the conference, panel, and meeting pathologies described in Chapters 4 and 5. John Kenneth Galbraith's satirical novel *A Tenured Professor* captures the essence of many campus dinner parties: "By long convention, social discourse in Cambridge is intended to impress. People talk; it is not expected that anyone will listen."[53] For academics intent on upward mobility, the display of rapt attention is a helpful accomplishment. John Aldridge's *The Party at Cranton* captured the pose: an aspiring acolyte "stared up into [the professor's] face as if it were frescoed on the ceiling of the Sistine Chapel."[54] A naturalist attending any academic conference would be struck by the similarity between participants angling for attention and the courtship rituals of peacocks. Intellectual plumage must be flaunted, not just on panels, but in corridor chitchat. Any academic celebrity attracts a host of fawning suitors. As they compete for recognition, they are also scanning the surroundings to determine whether, in Aldridge's phrase, they are "really spending time in the best company or whether it might not be more politic to crash *that* circle."[55] An observation attributed to Lord Mancroft holds particular force for academic life: "All men may be born equal, but quite a few eventually get over it."

Yet for a large proportion of the profession, this pursuit of status is a setup for frustration. There are, after all, so many ways of falling short. Academics can be at lesser institutions, hold lesser positions, publish in lesser journals, and so forth ad infinitum. Those who live the life of the mind generally have achieved a substantial measure of success up through graduate or professional school. They then encounter a job market that makes replicating such accomplishments increasingly difficult. The major research universities, which produce the vast majority of entry-level academics, have nothing close to the number of tenure-track positions necessary to employ them.[56] As a consequence, most new faculty end up at institutions less prestigious than the one they attended, or in part-time, provisional roles. Because scholarly status is to some extent derivative, it is often difficult for academics at less distinguished campuses to receive appropriate recognition for their achievements. Bourdieu puts the point bluntly. Cultural "capital breeds capital"; success begets more success, and those who begin without it may be unable to move from the margins of the academic establishment.[57]

In effect, a preoccupation with self-promotion will often prove self-defeating. The arms race for relative status has almost no winners and many losers. There is, in fact, no room at the top. Few academics will achieve true eminence as scholars, and even those who do typically find that there is always someone more distinguished. As an English professor in Gerald Warner Brace's novel *The Department* noted, individuals' sense of not having lived up to their "hopes and promises" can exist in any endeavor, but scholars "compete in a very big league. They measure themselves not only against each other but against Aristotle and . . . Kant and all the other immortals. They are in daily touch with philosophical and literary grandeur. . . . Whatever they publish claims room on the same shelf with the classics." In some, this may breed arrogance, but others feel the "powerful backbite of conscience, a guilt, an inner gnawing. They have not done, or been able to do, that which they ought to have done."[58]

Sociologists similarly remind us that achievement in higher education is particularly elusive and ephemeral: "Whatever you did, you could always have done it better, or done more of it. . . . With something as open ended as reputation, productivity, or impact, there is no clear limit."[59] Today's landmark achievement may be quickly supplanted. With appalling speed and regularity, contributions are forgotten, or replicated anew by a generation that fails to notice, much less credit, its predecessors. So too, those who have success early in their careers do not always sustain it. Some, like the embittered Oxford don in C. P. Snow's *The Masters*, continue to jump through the same hoops, but their audience has ceased to pay attention.[60]

A final, and, from the public's standpoint, most corrosive aspect of the pursuit of status is its financial price. As a recent Rand Corporation study noted, institutions' attempts to move up in the pecking order are often costly, high-risk ventures. The major beneficiaries are faculty and administrators, but the major costs are born by others: taxpayers, donors, funders, students, and their families.[61] Of course, some of these constituencies bask in reflected glory if the colleges' efforts are successful. But whether the additional prestige is worth the gamble is another question, and one that has become increasingly important in light of the escalating costs of higher education.

THE PURSUIT OF MONEY

Increasing Costs, Declining Subsidies

The past quarter century has witnessed a substantial growth in higher education costs and enrollments, and a substantial decline in government support.[62] The share of state general funds going to higher education has shrunk by a third.[63] Tuition has doubled; in private institutions, it has been rising twice as fast as inflation, and in public universities, several times that fast.[64] Unsurprisingly, many families and government funders question whether those increases are justified, particularly when millions of students cannot afford four-year institutions or must incur crippling debt burdens.[65] Only a fifth of qualified high school graduates from the bottom income quarter of the population have a chance of getting a four-year college degree, compared with about two-thirds of those in the top quarter.[66]

Such concerns are compounded by the focus of press and politicians on seeming excesses: a growth in salaries, sometimes totaling over $1 million for a president or athletic coach, and lavish perquisites and amenities for students as well as administrators. These expenditures are, of course, partly subsidized by taxpayers and government or nonprofit funders and sometimes result in well-publicized scandals.[67] Examples include a president who flew a private chef to Europe for a fundraising junket, or others who used university aircraft, staff, and credit cards for nonbusiness purposes.[68] One recent exposé of exceptionally generous compensation packages at the University of California coincided with a series of tuition hikes for students, and provoked predictable outrage. In response, a beleaguered president invoked the need to stay competitive, particularly in the health-science field, in which top earners were disproportionately located.[69] His letter ran next to a cartoon showing a pipe-smoking academic with a placard proclaiming "Will Teach for a Small Fortune." Adjacent to the cartoon was another letter to the editor from an irate UC professor. As he noted, "3 of the 10 highest compensated UC employees are coaches. Remind me, this cures cancer how?"[70]

The relatively light teaching loads for faculty at major research universities has also attracted public ire. Legislators who approve state budgets for higher education wonder why professors who spend less than a dozen hours in the classroom per week can command six-figure salaries, full benefits, and summers off.[71] To many observers, including economist Martin Anderson, the academy seems to offer the "best combination of working conditions and pay of any large occupational group."[72] Whether this serves the public interest is a matter of long-standing dispute. For example, Adam Smith, in his eighteenth-century *Wealth of Nations*, maintained that universities were "in general controlled not for the benefit of students but for the interest . . . of the masters."[73] Many American legislators now hold similar views, which are the driving force behind a proposed federal statute requiring institutions that are increasing their tuitions by over twice the rate of inflation to submit a cost-cutting plan to the U.S. Department of Education.[74]

Yet academics have their own complaints about money, which start from different premises. From their vantage, the attitude of public funders seems highly unreasonable. As Katherine C. Lyall, then president of the University of Wisconsin system, put it: "They want high access, low tuition, top quality, and no tax increases to pay for it."[75] Faculty also point out that much of the recent increase in tuition has gone to finance more generous financial aid, and has been offset by expanded tax breaks and subsidies for families with college students.[76] Two-thirds of students at private schools pay less than the "sticker price," and that price covers only about 60 percent of their education; the rest has had to come from the institutions.[77]

Moreover, the recent spikes in tuition have not resulted in a corresponding growth in faculty pay. Over the past quarter century, professors' salaries have increased only between a half and one percent faster than inflation, and most academics feel undercompensated.[78] As they note, classroom hours are a small fraction of their total responsibilities; course preparation, research, student counseling, committees, conferences, and related activities generate workloads comparable to those in other professional settings.[79] Adjuncts, part-time professors, and graduate students, who do much of the undergraduate teaching in research universities, generally receive modest pay and few benefits in exchange for demanding hours.[80] Without greater support for higher education, institutions will face increasing pressures to pursue profit-oriented, funder-driven activities that can compromise academic priorities. Industry's contribution to academic research has increased fourfold since 1980, and as Chapter 2 indicates, many grants come with troubling strings attached.[81]

This contemporary debate over money raises long-standing issues about the academic mission and academic life. American higher education has always confronted competing criticisms: that it is too worldly or not worldly enough; too removed from society's practical needs or too sullied by the pursuit of profit. To put today's concerns in context, some historical perspective is helpful.

Historical Perspectives

Traditionally, the life of the mind was thought to entail a certain obliviousness to material rewards. In the earliest American colleges, many faculty either had independent sources of income or were individuals with religious backgrounds and modest worldly expectations.[82] Those expectations were reinforced by leaders of cash-strapped institutions, who sought to make a virtue of necessity. In his 1869 inaugural address, Harvard president Charles Eliot took this time-honored approach:

> The poverty of scholars is of inestimable worth in this money-getting nation. It maintains the true standards of virtue and honor. . . . The poor scholars and preachers of duty defend the modern community against its own material prosperity. Luxury and learning are ill bed fellows.[83]

Low salaries, a *New Republic* editorial piously intoned, "free professors from the pecuniary criterion of values," and a good thing too.[84]

In commenting on this approach, historian Frederick Rudolph observes that "there are all kinds of psychic income, but it is doubtful whether many college professors thought that salving the conscience of a materialistic society was really a justification for their inadequate salaries."[85] Moreover, during the nineteenth and early twentieth centuries, scholars' much-lauded imperviousness to creature comforts often was pressed to the limits. In the absence of adequate revenues, faculty sometimes were paid with produce from local farmers or compensated through "profit sharing" schemes that turned out to involve mainly deficit sharing. Institutions occasionally closed for a year so professors could be sent out on the road in search of funds and students.[86] "Whoever heard of a college professor that was not poor?," Henry Ward Beecher inquired rhetorically in 1868.[87] "Shabby and underfed" was Willa Cather's description of her professors at the University of Nebraska several decades later.[88] Surveying the national situation in the early twentieth century, Upton Sinclair concluded, "There are few more pitiful proletarians in America than the underpaid, overworked, and contemptuously ignored rank and file college teacher." His evidence included a survey titled "How Professors Live," which compiled instructive survival strategies by young faculty. Among the favored techniques were keeping chickens, using butter substitutes, "postponing dental attention," and avoiding nonessential purchases such as books, journals, newspapers, and "amusements."[89]

Such dire conditions were not, of course, typical of all institutions, and faculty fared substantially better than ministers and secondary school teachers. But neither were most academic appointments a way station to prosperity. What little systematic data are available indicate that average salaries for academics around the turn of the twentieth century were about the same as for skilled industrial workers.[90] One reason for the relatively low pay of academics was the frequently low regard for the "impractical" knowledge that they offered.

A persistent criticism of the "ivory tower" has been that it is just that: an institution too removed from daily concerns. In America, the criticism draws on anti-intellectual biases that have ebbed and flowed with broader socioeconomic trends. In the nineteenth and early twentieth centuries, men of "practical affairs" often indicted the "uselessness" of the traditional liberal arts curriculum and the seeming triviality of scholarly pursuits. A representative 1929 caricature, "Doctors of Dullness," portrayed "monkish groups milling lifelessly over stacks of hastily scribbled library cards, chanting 'Professor Tweetzer and the recognized authorities say . . . .'"[91] Andrew Carnegie doubted that academic institutions were effectively preparing their graduates for the pursuit of profit. "Future captains of industry" needed to be "hotly engaged in the school of experience. . . . College education as it exists is fatal to success in that domain."[92]

Responses to these critiques took two main forms. The initial approach was to defend the traditional liberal arts curriculum, with its heavy emphasis on ancient languages and civilization, as essential to the role of higher education. The goal of early American colleges, affirmed in their mission statements and in presidential addresses, was to develop both the mental and moral capacities of the student body. To that end, instruction in the great books, in their original language, was deemed more important than mere vocational skills. An influential 1828 Yale faculty report rejected calls to drop requirements of Greek and Latin and offered a classic defense of the classics. The purpose of education was to "form the taste and discipline the mind." To abandon the "dead languages" in pursuit of relevance would compromise "the general standard of intellectual and moral worth."[93] Or as one defender of the faith reportedly predicted, if the core curriculum permitted French, "could whittling be far behind?"[94] Just after the turn of the twentieth century, Thorstein Veblen similarly argued that a school of law "belongs in the university no more than a school of fencing or dancing."[95] Woodrow Wilson offered variations on the same theme as president of Princeton; its campus was not "a place where a lad finds a profession but a place where he finds himself."[96]

Yet many who were paying for higher education expected more tangible returns. An exchange between a trustee of the University of Missouri and a member of the State Board of Agriculture typified the dispute. As the trustee put it, "Too much in practical education should not be expected as the main purpose is to develop the social and mental nature of the students." "That is good" responded the board member, "but what are [the faculty] going to do about hog cholera?"[97] When the University of Illinois added classics to its curriculum, critics from the world outside wondered "why not crocheting, embroidery, and lessons on the harp?"[98] When critics from inside the academy questioned the University of California's decision to add a course in cosmetology, defenders claimed that "the profession of beautician is the fastest growing in the state."[99]

Gradually, of course, higher education moved in the direction that pragmatists demanded. Universities reduced or eliminated classics requirements, broadened the curriculum, and established professional schools. But basic tensions have persisted over the mission of higher education and continue to play out on a variety of issues. What curricular offerings, fields, and continuing education programs belong in the academy? What courses and capabilities should be mandated? Many defenders of liberal arts curricula have been disdainful of the practical skills once associated with land grant "cow colleges."[100] By contrast, opponents of the "great books" approach have been equally critical of its parochial biases and inability to prepare students for careers in a technology-driven global economy.[101] As Chapters 2 and 3 note, higher education has been faulted both for failing to ensure basic reading, writing, and quantitative skills and for focusing instead on insular scholarly topics of little relevance for students and the general public.

Yet at the same time, universities have also been criticized for moving in the opposite direction and becoming too "relevant" and too hostage to market demands. Concerns about commercialization take multiple forms, but the most common involve the diversion of attention to funder-driven or for-profit activities, and the infiltration of bottom-line business methods in educational administration.

These are not, however, entirely new developments, and it is important not to romanticize the past. Higher education has always been a cash-strapped and partially cash-driven enterprise. Donors' support has been a consistent priority, and their direct interference with curricula and faculty appointments was much greater in earlier eras. Indeed, as Chapter 5 points out, such intervention inspired the campaign for protections of academic freedom and tenure in the first part of the twentieth century. The founders of my own institution, Leland and Jane Stanford, dictated certain faculty appointments and dismissals.[102] Trustees at the University of Wisconsin purged reading lists with comments in the margin such as "fool professors."[103] So too, overt marketing and profit-oriented activities occurred in even the most well-heeled universities early in the twentieth century. The University of Pennsylvania established a Bureau of Publicity, Columbia ran a correspondence course, MIT hosted a corporate-sponsored laboratory, and any number of institutions, including Harvard, hired football coaches at over twice the salary of full professors.[104]

So too, many trustees and administrators long took the view that the "business of education should be regarded in a business light," and that administrative structures should be adapted accordingly.[105] Growth was good, as were efforts to "corner the intellectual market."[106] Governing boards of private institutions were selected with an eye more to fundraising capacities than educational expertise. Surveying this trend, a Harvard alumnus in 1909 complained that "the men who control Harvard today are very little else than businessmen, running a large department store which dispenses education."[107] Other prominent critics were even more scathing. Thorstein Veblen's *Higher Education in America*, published in 1918, and Upton Sinclair's *The Goose-Step*, released a few years later, both offered extended critiques of commercialization in the academy. Sinclair portrayed elite universities as run by and for "plutocrats," while Veblen offered a more nuanced account of how the pursuit of "creditable notoriety" was distorting academic values.[108]

Commercializing the Campus

While "academic capitalism" is scarcely a new phenomena, its scale and scope are unprecedented. Experts on higher education have extensively documented the "raw power" that money now exerts in academic life.[109] Over the past quarter century, as the commercial value of universities' intellectual property has grown more apparent and the financial needs of higher education have escalated, the boundaries between town and gown have increasingly blurred. Although no one doubts the advances that market competition and revenue-producing activities can make possible, these bottom-line priorities also have come at a cost.

The most obvious adverse effects are the diversion of academic effort and the distortion of academic priorities. With some poetic license, Hutchins once warned: "When an [academic] institution does something in order to get money, it must lose its soul."[110] Of course, by that standard, strictly applied, few souls are left to lament. But the more insistent the pursuit of profit, the greater the risk that it will subvert the goals that it seeks to serve.

In an ideal world, research priorities would be determined by what is most likely to advance the pursuit of knowledge. In the world as we know it, the focus is often on what is most attractive to government, foundation, corporate, or individual funders. And when institutions or their faculty can take a cut of the revenues through patents or partial ownership interests, or when sponsors insist on secrecy or controls over publication to protect their investment, the corrosive possibilities are still greater.[111] Why should so much effort focus on basic research "when all the money is in developing no-snag panty hose?"[112] A more subtle, but similarly compromising temptation involves the creation of centers, programs, chairs, or facilities that serve the interests of donors rather than the priorities of the institution. But in a culture that makes growth a measure of prestige, something is usually better than nothing. So as long as some plausible intellectual purpose is available, sponsors typically get their bang for their buck.

The same forces are at work in lucrative academic sideshows, such as big-ticket athletics, consulting arrangements, or continuing education programs that lack serious academic content. The problems associated with these ventures have been amply documented, long lamented, yet inadequately addressed. For example, a majority of faculty earn income from services provided outside their universities.[113] Yet although almost all institutions have rules that limit consulting by full-time faculty, virtually none make efforts to monitor professors' own self-reports. And not all of those on the honor system find virtue to be sufficient reward. If, as in my own university, academics are limited to one day a week of outside work, many will find that day to be a very "important day among [their] days."[114] Athletic scandals come and go, with much wringing of hands and few meaningful sanctions.[115] About two-thirds of Americans think universities place too much emphasis on sports, a perception widely shared by faculty and widely ignored by central administrations.[116] The conflicts of interest posed by university-corporate business transactions generate endless statements of concern but little significant action. The best that one conference of leading universities could manage was the consensus that there was no consensus on a "right" policy, but that each institution "should address the problem vigorously."[117]

Part of the difficulty is that the benefits of profit-generating ventures are immediate and quantifiable, while the risks are diffuse and cumulative.[118] Ultimately, what is at stake is the academy's reputation for disinterested inquiry. To considerable extent, that reputation is a common good. For any single professor or administrator, the temptation is to assume that his or her own commercial activities pose no great threat. But when everyone makes that assumption, the effect is corrosive. The more aggressively entrepreneurial higher education becomes, the more it jeopardizes its claim to public trust and public funds.

The problem is likely to intensify, as nonprofit institutions face increasing competition from for-profit competitors. These proprietary schools are the fastest-growing segment of higher education; they prosper by offering inexpensive, convenient courses from underpaid faculty with no job security and little, if any, time or support for scholarship.[119] Some estimates suggest that the number of faculty in the for-profit sector now equals those in traditional higher education settings.[120] The University of Phoenix is America's largest academic institution. For-profit institutions generally operate with little if any quality control, and many provide courses with equally little or no academic content, such as massage therapy, auto repair, and medical report writing (with emphasis on "keyboarding skills" and technical terminology).[121]

"Digital diploma mills" that exploit distance learning technology pose still greater concerns.[122] Some institutions operate on the fringes of fraud; they mislead applicants about whether credits will transfer to accredited institutions and make claims about credentials, skills, and job placement that go well beyond puffing.[123] One of the many offers clogging my e-mail inbox promises "Get a University Degree from a reputable school in weeks. Here are some of our features: Degree in 2 weeks, No Study Required, 100% Verifiable Certificates, Many 6-figure . . . high 5-figure salaries." Another promises: "Obtain a prosperous future: money, earning power, and the prestige that comes with the degree you have always dreamed of. Non-accredited university degree based on your present knowledge and experience. If you qualify, no tests, study, books. We have Bachelors, MAs, Doctorates, and Ph.D degrees available in your field. Confidentiality assured." So why bother with accredited universities, with all their irksome requirements and pricey tuitions, when this alternative is available?

In one all too rare effort to hold these schools accountable, a student who spent eleven fruitless years in search of the perfect state of life advertised by Maharishi International University finally sued for fraud. Although the university had represented that the plaintiff would learn to fly, he had only learned to hop with legs folded in the lotus position. And contrary to the university's claims, chanting in the method prescribed did not reverse the aging process or enable him to self-levitate.[124]

Academics respond to creeping commercialism in several ways. The most common is worldly cynicism or resigned indifference. What is the point in lamenting lost ideals? As law school dean Richard Matasar advises, "Get over it. Commercialism is here, now, and it is not going away. . . . We are a business, deal with it."[125] To the extent that there is a problem, academics generally see it as someone else's problem. Only when their own interests are directly threatened, by significant cutbacks in resources or increases in institutional obligations, do professors pay much attention.[126] Even then, as Chapter 6 notes, the response is often simply to rally around the flag of academic freedom and denounce any efforts to curtail tenure or downsize faculty positions and support.[127]

Part of what fuels such attitudes is a sense of relative deprivation. Although few university faculty experience the genteel poverty of earlier eras, their expectations have improved faster than their incomes. Unlike their predecessors, today's academics have extensive educational credentials, often coupled with equally extensive educational debts. They feel entitled to rewards commensurate with those of other similarly credentialed professionals, and are particularly offended by disparities within their own institutions or disciplines. Liberal arts faculty are unhappy about their pay scales compared with those in the professional schools. Yet members of those schools also consider themselves underrewarded: their comparison

group is practitioners. In response to complaints by a professor of literature, one of my law school colleagues acerbically suggested, "if he thinks he
is worth as much as I am, let him go out and practice English."[128] Women
voice other pay equity concerns. Female faculty are overrepresented in
the least-well-rewarded teaching and administrative positions, and underrepresented among the tenured "stars." The highest salaries belong disproportionately to senior male professors, who have fewer family constraints
than their female counterparts and more ability to move, or threaten to
move, in response to better offers.[129] The compensation of part-time faculty members is also of growing significance, particularly in light of their
limited bargaining leverage and increasing numbers.[130]

Ironically enough, the least visible complainants are those with the
strongest grievances: nonunionized clerical and maintenance staff, whose
frequently below-living wages are an embarrassment to the ivory towers
they serve. As social critics such as Barbara Ehrenreich have observed, if
universities have so much to teach about humane values and social equality,
many should look closer at their own labor relations. Ehrenreich proposes
field trips through university presidential dwellings that are equipped with
saunas, wet bars, and exercise rooms, together with side excursions to the
"trailer parks favored by the housekeeping and maintenance staff."[131]

Other stakeholders caught in the crossfire of competing demands feel
beleaguered as well. University leaders are often expected to do more with
less. Most face stable or declining revenues and spiraling costs, particularly
in areas such as technology, scientific facilities, and health care.[132] The consensus among experts is that the situation is unlikely to improve.[133] Legislators are caught in crossfires of their own, and the needs of higher education
often do not appear as urgent as those of national security, law enforcement,
health care, social security, and other entitlement programs. Nor do many
politicians see why generous tuition assistance should be a priority for the
large number of students who are not in significant financial need. Almost
40 percent of children of families with incomes over $200,000 attend pub-
lic universities and receive the benefit of regressive taxpayer subsidies.[134]

Many politicians are even more reluctant to underwrite the bidding wars
for faculty celebrities that the pursuit of institutional prestige entails.[135] These

academics boost reputational rankings, but their actual presence on campus and contribution to its community are frequently minimal.[136] A profession that traditionally styled itself as "other worldly" has become increasingly candid about the pursuit of perks and the prestige they connote. In one of British novelist David Lodge's celebrated portraits, the American academic superstar Morris Zapp unabashedly acknowledges to a young admirer, "Before I retire, I want to be the highest paid English professor in the world."[137] That desire, in somewhat scaled-back form, drives campus star-war negotiations that can involve everything from luxury housing, reduced teaching, and season basketball tickets to full employment for an entire retinue, including colleagues, spouses, and doctoral students. One exasperated administrator finally lost patience when a spiral of escalating demands culminated in requests that the recruit's children receive placements in prestigious private schools: "If our star signed on, would she be calling me at midnight to have French champagne delivered and her Pradas polished?"[138] If these luminaries need lab facilities, the going rate can run to $20 million.[139] Even for more modestly rewarded humanists, the price tag may ultimately prove substantial. Not only will it include compensation for the recruit and retinue, it may also reflect demands for lateral adjustments by the institution's current faculty, who will bear the brunt of their absentee colleague's avoidance of mundane teaching, committee, and related responsibilities.

The competition for talented students has some equally unsettling consequences. At the same time that consumers of higher education decry excessive tuition, they demand more expensive services: greater faculty-student contact and more state-of-the-art facilities and amenities. A recent *New Yorker* cartoon captures the expectations. It pictures a female high school student explaining to her guidance counselor, "My first-choice college should have lots of closet space."[140] In an increasingly competitive marketplace, where rankings depend partly on the selectivity of admissions, universities are vying for the best and brightest applicants by offering everything from gourmet meals to personal trainers. "It's not about pampering," one dean of students attempted to explain with a straight face: "It's about community building."[141]

It is also about money. To attract the top-scoring students, universities are increasingly relying on merit-based scholarships. According to recent estimates, only about fifteen to twenty private institutions give exclusively need-based financial aid, and about a quarter of the aid in public institutions is granted irrespective of economic status.[142] The effect is to diminish assistance for those who need it most, and to reduce access for those at the bottom of the income scale.[143] Over the past decade, the United States has slipped in college participation from first place to thirteenth among developed nations.[144] Educational inequality based on family income is as pronounced now as it was thirty years ago, and the inequity is greatest at selective institutions that could most readily afford to address it.[145]

In the face of inadequate access, escalating financial demands, and stable or declining resources, many universities face unhappy choices. Curtailing expenses is typically the most painful alternative. From the faculty's perspective, salary and hiring freezes are generally strategies of last resort. Selective program cuts can be similarly unpalatable because academic communities seldom agree on what is most expendable, or even on the criteria for making those decisions. Once established, most programs build constituencies that are hard to kill; on many campuses, "sunset is an hour that almost never arrives."[146] The preferred alternative understandably has been to add more revenue sources. But the resulting commercialism comes at a price, and too often undermines the academic values it was intended to serve.

The Pursuit of Meaning

A final challenge for the academic profession lies in reconciling the pressures of money and status with deeper needs for meaning and community. For many faculty members, career satisfaction has less to do with material conditions than with more fundamental issues of common purpose. Surveys of new professors have found that their greatest disappointment is the lack of collegiality, and a majority of more senior faculty have reported similar unhappiness.[147] In short, the academic community is becoming less of a community, and institutions as well as individuals are paying the price. Here again, it is important not to romanticize the past. Some isolation is inherent in the life of the mind. Academic institutions have always attracted a fair share of free spirits who thrive on solitary life or whose need for autonomy makes it inevitable. Yet recent trends in higher education are eroding the sense of shared mission and collective responsibility that sustain a well-functioning professional community.

One such trend involves the growth in scale and specialization of academic life. Most faculty now teach in large institutions, which have difficulty cultivating a strong sense of common identity. Those difficulties are compounded by the increasingly specialized nature of scholarly inquiry. Academics know more and more about less and less. Subfields have proliferated, and discourse has become more technical, jargon-laden, and inaccessible to nonexperts. This balkanization decreases faculty members' ability to provide the informed interchanges that enrich research. It also makes consensus on curricular and appointments issues harder to achieve. Many faculties have no shared vision of what constitutes scholarly excellence, a core education, or the most cost-effective use of institutional resources.[148]

Increasing diversity within the academic profession can further erode a sense of collective identity. Differences across race, gender, ethnicity, and sexual orientation often leave underrepresented groups feeling isolated or marginal. Disparities in status similarly work against a commitment to common purpose. At the top of the pecking order, academic "free agents" can negotiate their way out of teaching and service obligations that would otherwise connect them with their campus communities.[149] At the bottom of the hierarchy are the growing legions of part-time lecturers and adjuncts who have no job security or role in institutional governance, and correspondingly limited allegiance to their provisional workplaces. The problem is compounded in for-profit institutions, which rely heavily on distance education and short-term faculty who have little direct or continuing contact with colleagues.[150]

Academic incentive structures further undermine a sense of community attachments and obligations. As subsequent chapters note, universities pay lip service to the value of teaching and service, but what they principally reward is publication. To advance in the status sweepstakes, academics need national recognition within their disciplines, which can occur only through scholarship and external activities. Many professors' primary allegiance lies outside their university, and their time is allocated accordingly. Mentoring, advising, and administrative tasks fall by the wayside or are left to non-tenure-track faculty and staff. All too often, the most distinguished scholars "no longer behave like good citizens, or even citizens at all. They are more like resident aliens."[151] The "insistent individualism" that prevails in many academic contexts can readily become self- perpetuating.[152] As fewer faculty feel responsibility to sustain an intellectual community, the quality of workplace interaction diminishes. That, in turn, increases faculty's tendency to look outside the institution for stimulation and support.

In his classic essay on the American scholar, Ralph Waldo Emerson asserted that the "true" academic "must relinquish display and immediate fame." He should be "happy enough if he can satisfy himself alone that this day he has seen something truly."[153] It is a noble ideal, but one hopelessly removed from reality. The reward structures of American culture in general and academic institutions in particular push in different directions. Recognition is now a centerpiece of career status and self-worth, and money is a tangible way to keep score. But acknowledgment of that fact need not breed resignation. We are unlikely to transform most academics' deep-seated need for recognition, but we can alter how they achieve it. As the following chapters argue, the university could do more to reward key values that it claims to value, particularly teaching, public service, and administrative contributions.

We are just as unlikely to escape the financial pressures that the pursuit of knowledge and the pursuit of status entail. But these pressures also create opportunities to be clearer about our priorities. What forms of scholarship are most socially valuable and how do they compare with teaching, service, and other public intellectual pursuits? What are the most cost-effective strategies of rewarding accomplishment in these other spheres? Are there ways of minimizing the corrosive effects of status hierarchies and market dynamics? What is the right balance between pursuing institutional prestige and broadening educational access? How can we bring universities closer to their professed ideals: the pursuit of knowledge in the service of individual fulfillment and social progress? These questions are the focus of the chapters that follow.

Chapter Two

Scholarship

George Eliot once characterized "excessive literary production" as a "social offense," and many contemporary commentators view excessive scholarly publication in similar terms. By their account, it is occurring on an unprecedented scale. According to most estimates, over one hundred thousand academic journals are in print worldwide, and over one hundred thousand books are published every year. More information has been published in the past thirty years than in the previous five thousand.[1] The vast majority of scholarship vanishes without apparent influence. Most scientific articles are never cited. In fields that lack an extensive tradition of secondary reference, the rate of noncitation is even higher; 98 percent for arts and humanities and 75 percent for social sciences.[2]

The problem, according to conventional wisdom, is that the pressures to publish have spawned far too much material that is unreadable as well as unread. Like Tolstoy's unhappy families, each discipline is unhappy in its own way, but common pathologies emerge. Too much research is inconsequential and unintelligible, presented in obscure and pompous prose. In many fields in the humanities and social sciences, esoteric theory has displaced more empirically grounded and potentially useful analysis. In other disciplines, the preference for mathematically sophisticated models has diverted focus from real-world problems. Publication pressures have also encouraged too many academics to cut ethical corners: fudging results, misappropriating credit, repackaging identical work in multiple guises, and tailoring scholarly studies to satisfy funders' priorities.

Yet despite the widespread consensus that all is not well in contemporary scholarship, no comparable agreement has emerged about how serious the problem is or what can be done about it. The most sweeping indictments tend to be themselves strikingly unscholarly. Deans, journal editors, and other commentators complain about the amount of wasted effort in their fields; estimates of pointless publications run as high as 90 percent.[3] But how critics reach these conclusions is never disclosed. Nor do these commentators generally address the structural forces driving the paper flow they disparage.

Many academics, for their part, are reluctant to think self-critically about the scholarly enterprise or to risk reinforcing public criticisms that are often overdrawn. Faculty who do enter the debate can invoke a comforting repertoire of rationalizations. Some, following George Ade's advice, decide that if no one today is interested in what they are writing, they will "write for posterity."[4] Others adopt a kind of sociobiological perspective on academic productivity. According to law professor and federal judge Richard Posner, "[s]cholarship, like salmon breeding in the wild, is a high-risk, low-return activity." On average, it takes 6,000 eggs to get two fish capable of living to maturity. "Does this mean that 5,998 eggs are 'wasted'? Only if there is a more efficient method of perpetuating the species." In Posner's view, there is not. A vast amount of "trivial, ephemeral" output seems to him the "unavoidable price of . . . creative scholarship."[5] Legal philosopher David Luban makes a similar claim.

> [G]ood scholarship can only arise out of a culture that values scholarly writing and encourages scholars to set their hand to it. The result will inevitably be lots of bad scholarship, but there is no system that can produce only good scholarship. An academic culture that eliminates the bad scholarship will not provide a seed-bed for the good.[6]

Although these analogies are helpful to a point, they glide past the central issue. While some level of waste is inevitable, can the rate be reduced?

Under the salmon standard, almost any level of inefficiency seems acceptable. This is hardly a test that most academics would apply to performance in other contexts. Why should scholarship get special dispensation? Our unwillingness to think critically about the structure of academic research may result more from inertia and self-interest than from any "unavoidable" feature of the current system.

The discussion that follows evaluates conventional critiques of contemporary scholarship. My own assessment is that the popularized critiques are generally overstated and oversimplified, but do raise legitimate concerns. Too much academic writing is unnecessarily unintelligible and inconsequential, directed at too narrow an audience and too insignificant a set of topics. A more sensible allocation of scholarly efforts will require pushing beyond the customary polemics and platitudes. That, in turn, will demand a deeper understanding of the forces that have made research an increasingly central academic priority and benchmark for academic status.

SCHOLARSHIP AS AN ACADEMIC PRIORITY

The focus on scholarship in higher education is a relatively new development, as is the concept of a "research university." In common usage, which is followed here, the terms *scholarship* and *research* are more or less interchangeable. However, scholars of scholarship often use *research* to refer to work that discovers new information, as distinguished from other academic work that integrates or applies such knowledge.[7] References to research universities emerged in England in the 1870s by reformers who wanted Oxford and Cambridge to emphasize scholarship as well as teaching. A similar campaign began in American higher education in the early twentieth century, inspired by German research institutions. The dramatic growth in government funding for academic research following World War II further pushed leading universities in that direction.[8]

Broader social and economic forces have contributed to this trend. One is the vast expansion in knowledge and the close relationship between education and productivity. Over the past half century, estimates suggest that advances in knowledge have accounted for about one-third of the increase in America's gross national product; most of those advances have resulted from research in colleges and universities.[9] Our national health, security, standard of living, and cultural accomplishments depend in no small measure on the commitment to scholarship in academic institutions.

Unlike many European and Asian nations, which rely heavily on freestanding research institutes, the United States has found it efficient to combine scholarship and teaching missions. As Charles Vest, former president of MIT, has noted, that system enables every dollar to do "double duty"; it supports both the advance of knowledge and the education of those who will continue the process.[10] Faculty who are actively engaged in scholarship are best qualified to guide and inspire students to carry on that tradition. Learning is a lifetime commitment, and professors convey that fact most effectively when they are active contributors to their fields.

Academic institutions have their own interests in emphasizing scholarship. As Chapter 1 indicated, increasing competition in higher education has placed a premium on reputation. And for universities, research is primarily what determines reputation. Unlike teaching, which is difficult to assess and affects only those within a particular institution, research can be evaluated and ranked in multiple ways: number of publications, peer review, frequency of citation by others, and so forth. Of course, all of these methods have limitations, which subsequent discussion explores. But taken together, these assessments provide at least some benchmark of quality. The status they confer also can attract additional financial support, which further reinforces the importance of research as an institutional priority. As a consequence, higher education has experienced a form of "upward drift"; an increasing number of schools have sought to enhance their reputations by supporting research.

Faculty, for their part, have faced similar reward systems and responded in similar ways. More are engaged in scholarship and more are likely to make it a priority. Between the mid-1970s and the 1990s, professors identifying research as their primary focus increased from about a fifth to a third.[11] Over four-fifths reported engaging in scholarship, and three-quarters of those in four-year institutions reported that it was difficult to obtain tenure without publications.[12] Although, as subsequent discussion notes, most academics' primary allegiance is still to teaching, that is not true at research universities. And throughout the American academy, scholarship has become the principle foundation of status. It is increasingly the basis for job offers, promotions, grants, invitations, awards, compensation, and reputation. Studies on motivation among academics find that a desire for recognition is a key influence on individual priorities and self-esteem.[13] The English professor profiled in Margaret Edson's Pulitzer Prize–winning play, *Wit*, puts it bluntly: scholarship is "a way to see how good you really are."[14]

For many academics, research also carries less tangible rewards. One is the sheer satisfaction that comes from pursuing knowledge on subjects that the scholar finds interesting and important. Intellectuals are sometimes described as those who have found something more fascinating than sex. And they can hope, undisturbed by evidence to the contrary, that whatever sense they make of their subject will have some social value, and leave a lasting legacy. As a writer in Tom Stoppard's play *The Real Thing* notes, sometimes "if you get the right words in the right order, you can nudge the world a bit."[15]

Yet although critics of contemporary scholarship acknowledge its contributions, they still claim that too much is unintelligible or unimportant, and that it diverts too much effort from more useful pursuits. A well-known commentator on legal scholarship summed up the conventional view: "There are two things wrong with . . . [academic] writing. One is style. The other is substance."[16]

Critiques of Style

Good writing does not come naturally, even to those who write for a living. It requires practice, perseverance, and self-discipline. Above all, it requires that authors care about style as well as substance, and that they revise until they get it right. Yet what "right" means in a scholarly context is not self-evident. To be sure, academic writing has its share of simple sloppiness—sentences that beg to be put out of their misery by almost any standard. But the critiques of style in contemporary scholarship go deeper, and involve practices that are distinctive to academic writing.

The most common criticism is that such work is "unintelligible to the uninitiated."[17] In some fields, the technical nature of the subject inevitably renders advanced work accessible only to specialists, but that is not typically the case in the humanities, social sciences, and professions such as law and business. In those disciplines, as philosopher Judith Butler has noted, scholars are expected to "clarify how their work informs and illumines everyday life."[18] Their frequent inability or unwillingness to do so has provoked long-standing concerns both within and outside the academy.

These concerns had an unusually public airing in the late 1990s when Butler herself received one of the celebrated "Bad Writing Awards" annually bestowed by the journal *Philosophy and Literature*. Her response ran in the *New York Times* as an op-ed under the title "Bad Writer Bites Back." The controversy then attracted widespread coverage in the press and in an edited collection of essays, *Just Being Difficult*.[19] At stake in this and similar controversies are deeper questions about the objectives and conventions of academic discourse. What exactly makes "bad" writing bad? Is clarity always desirable? If so, for whom? To what extent should scholars seek an audience beyond their peers? When it comes to footnotes, is less ever more? What makes exhaustive references a mark of scholarly distinction rather than superficial showmanship?

Obscurity

*The professor must be an obscurantist or he is nothing. He has
a special unmatchable talent for dullness; his central aim is not
to expose the truth clearly, but to exhibit his profundity—in
brief, to stagger the sophomores and the other professors.*

H. L. Mencken[20]

The "Bad Writing" award goes every year to what editors of *Philosophy and Literature* judge to be the most "stylistically awful prose" in the humanities.[21] The basis for the judgment is not disclosed. Offending passages are simply quoted without context; the apparent assumption is that the genre speaks for itself. What seem to be the criteria are obscure language, unconventional syntax, and run-on or ungrammatical sentences. Whether these *should* be the criteria, and what distinguishes "bad" from "difficult" writing, triggered the controversy over Butler's award. As one of the world's preeminent "queer theorists," Butler is an influential scholar who appears deliberately difficult. As her *New York Times* op-ed illustrates, she is plainly capable of clear, readily accessible writing. But her scholarly style, which draws heavily on the most opaque social theorists of the Frankfurt School, is challenging even to sophisticated readers. One of those readers, Martha Nussbaum, herself a leading philosopher, notes that "if you are not familiar with the Althusserian concept of interpellation, you are lost for chapters."[22] Similar points have been made about other postmodernist scholarship, which is laden with neologisms such as "alterity," "seriality," and "Hybridites." Many prominent feminist and literary theorists have been infamously labeled as "muddy mazemakers of soggy, foggy poststructuralism."[23]

In responding to such critiques, scholars such as Butler maintain that "difficult and demanding language" can "provoke new ways of looking at a familiar world."[24] According to Herbert Marcuse, if what a radical philosopher says "could be said in terms of ordinary language, he probably would have [used it] in the first place."[25] Other literary theorists make a similar point. When the objective is not to transmit a cultural heritage but to challenge what it takes for granted, then "critical prose must call attention to itself as an act that cannot be seen through."[26] Language that is difficult to decipher forces a reader "to think outside of received categories"; its "'indeterminateness' is exactly what prompts critical inquiry."[27] The reader who rises to that challenge may also find a certain satisfaction in the achievement. Novelist Jonathan Franzen, in responding to complaints about his use of "fancy words" such as "diurnality," asserts that the "pleasure that demands hard work . . . the outlasting of lesser readers, is the pleasure most worth having."[28]

Yet even if that is so, is it worth the price of allowing all those lesser souls, otherwise capable of enlightenment, to fall by the wayside? When the text is a complex theoretical analysis, critics such as Nussbaum identify special risks: "[I]f so much effort is necessary to decipher the prose then little energy [may be] . . . left for assessing the truth of the claims." It is "difficult to come to grips with [the author's] ideas because it is difficult to know what they are." When the field is one such as feminist or queer theory, which grew out of concerns about concrete inequalities, there are particular costs in writing at a level of abstraction that loses touch with the "material conditions" and needs of that group. The danger, Nussbaum observes, is that "verbal and symbolic politics" will become a "substitute for real politics."[29]

When academics write in forms accessible only to other specialists in the field, they exclude many potential audiences. That is particularly problematic in disciplines that have relevance for practitioners, policymakers, and other nonacademic readers. My own field, law, is a representative case. The trend in legal scholarship over the past several decades has been to import the style and conceptual frameworks of other disciplines, particularly economics, philosophy, psychology, political science, literary criticism, and feminist theory. Although this interdisciplinary influence has had many positive effects, it has also produced some unappealing offspring. Too many publications are all dressed up with nowhere to go; their borrowed finery, "hermetic jargon," and "puffed up self-indulgent posturing" have no real relevance to the subject at hand.[30] As a result, their audience consists largely of tenure committees. Even scholarship addressed to urgent social problems is often offputting to busy judges, practitioners, and policymakers with influence over solutions. Few of these individuals now consult law reviews with any frequency; many do not look at them at all.[31] There are multiple reasons for that trend, but unintelligibility is surely one of them. A half century ago, C. Wright Mills noted the paradox in professorial prose. "A desire for status is one reason why academics slip so readily into unintelligibility. And that, in turn, is one reason why they do not have the status they desire."[32]

The costs of this increasing insularity might be tolerable if obscurity was, for the most part, essential and effective in serving the transformative objectives that scholars such as Butler embrace. But much of the ungainly prose that now clutters the academic landscape is neither necessary nor successful in that effort. Obscurity is hardly the only or even the best way to challenge conventional cultural understandings. Historically, the most influential political and social theorists generally wrote in language far more accessible than that now common in their fields. Plato, Locke, Rousseau, Bentham, Mills, Marx, Freud, and De Beauvoir are among the obvious examples. To the extent that more opaque contemporary theorists have been influential, it has often been through the efforts of talented intermediaries who make such work available to "lesser" readers.[33] Indeed, broadscale social transformation ultimately depends on such lucidity. As George Orwell noted in "Politics and the English Language," an ability to think and write clearly "is a necessary first step toward political regeneration." Among the many virtues of such clarity is the likelihood that "when you make a stupid remark, its stupidity will be obvious even to yourself."[34]

By contrast, one of the liabilities of an inscrutable style is that it can camouflage work that is unworthy of the efforts required to decipher it. Arcane jargon and a "phony technicality" are the "emperor's clothing of choice" for work that would otherwise appear trivial at best.[35] One of the first lessons of graduate school is the importance of sounding profound, particularly if one has nothing profound to say. "When ideas fail, words come in handy," observed Goethe. And for too many contemporary scholars, pretentious prose is a handy substitute for original insights. Obscure language and allusive references to equally obscure texts can disguise the author as a serious intellectual or even brilliant thinker. W. S. Gilbert captured it well in his light opera *Patience*:

> "If this young man expresses himself in terms too deep for me,
> Why what a singularly deep young man this deep young man must be."[36]

In effect, the reader is bullied into believing that "since one cannot figure out what is going on, there must be something going on."[37] The point is brought home in John Kenneth Galbraith's satirical novel *A Tenured Professor*. There, the main character, an aspiring economist, receives some crucial career advice from a senior colleague in the field. "Never forget, dear boy, that academic distinction in economics is not to be had from giving a clear account of how the world works. . . . Economists value most the colleague whom they most struggle to understand. . . . And anyone who cannot be understood at all will be especially admired. All will want to give the impression that they have penetrated his mystification."[38]

Erudition in Excess

Obscurity is not, of course, the only means of scholarly showmanship. Techniques vary by discipline. In some fields, statistical virtuosity is the strategy of choice. Sophisticated mathematical modeling can transform the most trivial subjects or implausible hypotheses into something approaching academic respectability. Even the smallest unrepresentative samples, or other products of armchair empiricism, can be spun into an impressive array of charts, graphs, tables, and methodological appendices. Another form of academic exhibitionism is the runaway text, aided and abetted by runaway references. Here the objective is to demonstrate an exhaustive and exhausting command of the material, and everything even remotely related to it. Footnotes are the "visible manifestation of research," so the more the merrier.[39] Legal scholarship is among the worst offenders in terms of excessive length and documentation. Over the past century, the average length of articles in leading law reviews has quadrupled, and single footnotes can meander along for over five pages.[40] It is now possible to find an article of some 490 pages and 4,800 footnotes all devoted to a single section of a single securities statute.[41]

Although such ostentatious scholarly displays are often taken as evidence of thorough research, they are in fact a highly imperfect proxy. There is no guarantee that authors have actually read the sources cited. Indeed, with technological advances, they need not even trouble to type them; entire string citations can be electronically lifted from other publications. Nor does it follow that the sources listed establish the proposition for which they are cited. Even when someone checks the notes, it is generally to determine only whether particular authorities support the text, not whether they are reliable or respected among experts. Errors can survive, as long as the author can correctly cite someone who made them first.

In some disciplines, this trend toward excessive documentation has spawned a number of particularly unappealing conventions. In law, where most journals are edited by students rather than knowledgeable peers, the tendency has been to require scholarly adornment for even the most obvious propositions. Authorities must be assembled for the claim that Plato was an "influential philosopher," or that "one of the values of American life is equality."[42] This practice discourages original insights, which by definition cannot be attributed to someone else. If conventional reference material is unavailable for a given statement, the gap can be filled by "fugitive sources" incapable of authentication or usefulness to other scholars: personal conversations or correspondence, unpublished manuscripts, and so forth.[43] Footnotes have also become occasional safe havens for other personal asides, such as dedications and declarations of assorted allegiances: for example, "The author is an open lesbian, in a monogamous and committed relationship. . . . "[44]

A particularly cloying variation on this convention is the use of footnote acknowledgments to curry favor or claim approval from a celebrity in the field. Among these efforts to establish an academic pedigree, the parodies can be difficult to distinguish from their targets: "I would like to thank Laurence Tribe, Sandra Day O'Connor, Richard (I like to call him 'Rick') Posner, Judge Lance Ito and a lot of other legal personalities with good name recognition. They didn't have anything to do with this article, but there's no law that says I can't thank them just for being them in this important space for name dropping."[45] It is not necessary to know suitable luminaries in order to express gratitude for their "insights"; as one critic notes, what law review editor is going to check?[46] A related practice among even established scholars involves mutually incestuous references, the academic equivalent of "love display among peacocks."[47] Some law journal articles include effusive thanks to thirty or forty colleagues.[48] Academics may trade fawning acknowledgments of each others' contributions in the hope, not necessarily conscious, that the compliment will be returned in kind. This, in turn, can help identify them as members of an in-crowd, or at least boost their name recognition and frequency of citation.

CRITIQUES OF SUBSTANCE

Triviality

The stylistic concerns discussed in the previous section often seem like minor irritants when compared with the more substantive indictments of contemporary scholarship. Polemics abound. As chair of the National Endowment for the Humanities, Lynne Cheney denounced the increasing proliferation of publications that serve "no purpose beyond expanding the author's c.v.'s."[49] Academics are endlessly denounced for their attempts to "take an obscure little problem that no one has thought much about, blow it all out of proportion, and solve it, preferably several times, in prestigious [journals]."[50] All too often, in trendy metatheoretical tomes, "the artist and art get lost in the critical shuffle."[51] From critics' vantage, an unacceptably large number of academics meet Emerson's description of Lord Macaulay: "No person ever knew so much that was so little to the purpose."[52]

Such sweeping denunciations are, however, themselves strikingly unscholarly. Critics offer no hard evidence of the frequency of pointless publications or any reason to believe that the problem is growing. Certainly in my own field, we should not long for a return to some hypothesized happier era. In the not so "good old days," even the most prominent law reviews typically focused on less than pathbreaking doctrinal developments in areas such as "The Law of Icy Sidewalks in New York State."[53] So too, other fields have long sponsored a share of patently inconsequential or implausibly ambitious pursuits. Fictional portraits well capture the pathology. Among the most famous is the self-absorbed Casaubon, who broods over George Eliot's *Middlemarch* in his ill-conceived search for the "Key to all Mythologies."[54] Kingsley Amis's *Lucky Jim* profiles an even more miserable British academic who recognizes the "niggling mindlessness" of his article on the "strangely neglected topic" of "The Economic Influence of the Developments of Shipbuilding 1450–1485": its "funereal parade of yawn-enforcing facts . . . [and] the pseudo light it threw on non problems."[55] Such self-awareness is missing among Scottish scholars comically portrayed in Stevie Davies' *Four Dreamers and Emily*, who view their definitive work on the use of the semicolon and dash in Anne Bronte's fiction as "daring and sensational."[56]

In the absence of hard data about the frequency of trivial pursuits, critics rely largely on argument by anecdote. They round up the "usual suspects," which appear identifiable by title. This was the technique that the late Wisconsin Senator William Proxmire popularized in his Golden Fleece awards for pointless federally subsidized research. Contemporary examples, not all of which received government funding, include

- The Evolution of the Potholder: From Technology to Pop Art
- The Dialectic of the Feminine: Melodrama and Commodity in the Ferraro Pepsi Commercial

- Does Foraging Success Determine the Mating Success of the Male Tundra Frog?
- Aspects of Iconicity in some Indiana Hydromys
- Why study Pacific Salmon Law?[57]

A variation on the Proxmire honor is the Ig Nobel Prize, celebrated annually at Harvard for "achievements that cannot or should not be reproduced." Recent winners include

- The First Case of Homosexual Necrophilia in the Mallard [Duck]
- Will Humans Swim Faster or Slower in Syrup?
- A Survey of Frog Odorous Secretions, Their Possible Functions and Phylogenetic Significance [cataloguing the odors of 131 species of frogs under stress][58]

Such potshots make good polemics but poor policy. Titles alone are an inadequate basis for assessing scholarly value. And a small selection of seemingly inconsequential publications is an equally inadequate basis for condemning scholarship in general. In an era of increasing academic specialization, advances in knowledge will often come through narrowly focused and readily parodied research. Significant insights about child development, brain function, sexual drives, and species preservation have emerged through an accumulation of studies like those identified above.

Triviality is often in the eye of the beholder. For those who work on environmental issues, the question "Why Study Pacific Salmon Law?" is anything but rhetorical, at least in the sense the critic intended. The United States is now spending over seven billion dollars annually on efforts to save salmon, and the campaign raises a host of legal and policy issues worthy of analysis.[59]

Even the analyses of popular culture that critics love to ridicule can enrich understanding of the media's influence on values, roles, and expectations. The way Pepsi packaged Ferraro is a window into the way our culture subordinates women in general and powerful women in particular. On average, Americans bump up against some fifteen hundred advertisements daily, which are selling not only products but also ideals and images.[60] A sophisticated analysis of how the media sees women, and women see the media, can deepen our awareness of the relationship between symbolic representations and gender inequalities. As for potholders, they need not be considered "great art" to be studied as illuminating artifacts. Virtually every culture has used common household objects as vehicles for aesthetic expression, and they are a frequent focus in archaeology, anthropology, and cultural studies. If critics have a theory of what makes some but not other textiles worthy of analysis, they have yet to disclose it.

This is not to suggest that criticisms of the triviality of contemporary scholarship are always off the mark. The point, rather, is that there is no basis for sweeping indictments, and that identifying which publications make no significant scholarly contribution requires closer analysis and greater expertise than critics typically offer.

Too Much Theory, Too Little Practice

A more serious criticism involves the frequent mismatch between the research priorities of academics and the needs of practitioners and policymakers. In many fields, particularly in the social sciences and professions, what yields the greatest return for scholars is not what would have the most direct value for society. The best way of building an academic reputation is typically through high theory and sophisticated quantitative analysis, not time-consuming empirical research that could help address practical problems.[61] Nor does the academy have an impressive record in identifying those problems and bringing them to the public's attention. In an influential Carnegie Foundation report, former Harvard president Derek Bok notes, "What Rachel Carson did for risks to the environment, Ralph Nader for consumer protection, Michael Harrington for problems of poverty, Betty Friedan for women's rights, they did as independent critics, not as members of a faculty. Even the seminal work on the plight of blacks in America was written by a Swedish social scientist [Gunnar Myrdal] not a member of an American university." And, Bok adds, once a problem has been documented, academics are unlikely to give it serious attention "unless outside support is available and the subjects involved command prestige in academic circles."[62]

The insufficient attention to social concerns is particularly evident in the disciplines most equipped to address them. For example, a survey of articles published over an eleven-year period in a preeminent economics journal, the *American Economic Review*, found not one overview of major American policy concerns, or of the key European challenge at the time: the transition of former socialist countries to market structures. What the study found instead were highly sophisticated analyses of rather less urgency, such as ski lift pricing, retail fashion marketing practices, and basketball salary structures.[63] While such articles may have made significant scholarly contributions, they did little to assist decision makers grappling with more serious concerns. One high-level national policy adviser during this period could recall no instance during hundreds of meetings on economic issues when anyone mentioned academic research.[64]

Many scholars express similar concerns about what Ian Shapiro labels "The Flight from Reality" in political science.[65] In an effort to "embroider fashionable theories" or demonstrate intellectual "rigor," researchers too often seek to mimic the natural sciences in a search for false certainty.[66] What is lost is a capacity to illumine what is actually going on in the world and to "enhance the capacity of people to practice a richer form of politics."[67] Scholars who focus on theoretical and quantitative refinements that are uninteresting and unintelligible to all but a few fellow travelers may, as Shapiro notes, enjoy "professional success of a sort." But they will be unlikely to "persuade anyone who stands in need of persuasion," and academic recognition will come "at the price of trivializing their discipline and what one hopes is their vocation."[68]

Professional schools have long attracted criticism on similar grounds. M.B.A. graduates and deans frequently complain that too little management research has any relevance for managers. The conceptual frameworks endlessly refined in the leading journals may be statistically sophisticated, but the most relevant question is the one posed by the former dean of Dartmouth's Tuck School of Business: "How many discounted-cash-flow models does the world need?" In his view, "a lot of what passes for research has no value."[69] As other leaders in M.B.A. education acknowledge, the prevailing model of scholarship responds more to the interests of academics than to the constituency they ostensibly serve. It gives "respectability to the research they enjoy doing and eliminates the vocational stigma that business school professors once bore. In short, the model advances the careers and satisfies the egos of the professoriate. And, frankly, it makes things easier. Though scientific research techniques may require considerable skill in statistics or experimental design, they call for little insight into complex social and human factors and minimal time in the field discovering the actual problems facing managers. . . . The problem is not that business schools have embraced scientific rigor but that they have forsaken other forms of knowledge."[70]

The same is true of legal scholarship. It is glutted with theory and starved for facts. Systematic empirical work is relatively uncommon. Many law professors have internalized W. H. Auden's celebrated injunction, "Thou shalt not commit a social science," and with reason. Data are a luxury good. Few legal academics have ready access to financial support on the scale necessary for major empirical research, and raising funds through grants or private donations is a skill that few have shown interest in acquiring. Moreover, money is only one of many obstacles. Rigorous empirical work generally involves a substantial commitment of time, and an equally substantial tolerance for drudgery. Particularly for younger faculty, who face pressure to demonstrate immediate productivity, data collection is an unattractive alternative to doctrinal analysis. Why bother with burdensome empirical research when you can leap instantly into print by reading some prominent legal cases and commentary in the comfort of your office and saying what you think?

The obstacles to such research can be substantial even in disciplines that claim to value it highly. C. Wright Mills, one of America's leading sociologists, famously confessed that "I do not like to do empirical work if I can possibly avoid it. If one has no staff, it is a great deal of trouble. If one does employ a staff, then the staff is even more trouble."[71] Methodological complications can be equally vexing for reasons other researchers note: "Computers crash; data are incomplete, irrelevant, or miscoded; informants refuse to be candid or fail to return [questionnaires and] telephone calls. . . . "[72] Worse still, after considerable time, expense, and effort, the results may not justify the investment. The response rate may be too low or too unrepresentative of the sample as a whole. Alternatively, findings may appear too obvious; they "'merely' confirm what everybody (especially in retrospect) already knows."[73]

Not only do many scholars face substantial obstacles to pursuing empirical research, but they also confront disincentives for less ambitious yet useful work for nonacademic audiences. Trade books, practitioner-oriented publications, or journalistic commentary are often viewed as déclassé. Mere "popularizer" is an epithet to be avoided.[74] Of course, a few celebrity scholars with access to the national media can wear the label as a badge of honor. But for most academics, whose nonscholarly options are far more limited, the taint can be a significant deterrent. It is generally safer to produce some deeply theorized if unread tome in an obscure academic journal than to write something useful in plain English for practitioners or the public.

The overproduction of esoteric theory at the expense of more accessible analysis has been a particularly serious concern in the humanities. A common lament is that in English departments, the "mania for theory . . . tends not so much to explain literature as to replace it."[75] Allen Bloom tapped widely shared frustrations in his best-selling indictment, *The Closing of the American Mind*. Among his principal targets were philosophy and literature departments, whose impenetrable analytic frameworks "repel" students who come with fundamental questions about life and art. In Bloom's view, too many professors "simply would not and could not talk about anything important."[76] A chronic temptation, aptly described by British scientist Kenneth Goulding, is to focus on the relatively unimportant questions that can be answered rather than the important ones that cannot.

An alternative strategy is simply to problematize the question. A case in point occurred at my own university several years ago when a prominent philosopher advertised a lecture titled "What Is Living the Good Life?" The academic community turned out in record numbers, hoping to see a great mind engage with one of the great issues. As it turned out, the focus of the lecture, and of the speaker's forthcoming publication, was why it was possible and desirable to ask the question; no effort was made to give an answer. The event was reminiscent of a scene from David Lodge's novel *Changing Places*. Its main character, an internationally respected literary theorist, expressed his frustration at his colleagues' increasingly "pathetic attempts at profundity largely interrogative in mode." Their tendency was to introduce a work with a statement: "I want to raise some questions about so and so," and assume that they had done their "intellectual duty by merely raising them. One couldn't move in English studies these days without falling over unanswered questions which some damn fool had carelessly left lying about."[77]

The point is not, as some conservative critics maintain, that such scholarship is without value. Indeed, as subsequent discussion notes, even research that does little to advance inquiry in a field may promote the intellectual growth of authors and their students. The process has worth independent of what it produces.[78] But the critical issue is always: compared to what? Critics are surely correct on several points. The first is that a greater part of scholarly effort could be usefully redirected to work that has direct application to societal needs and concerns. A second widely acknowledged point is that more attention should focus on quality rather than quantity. Increasing pressures to publish can push scholars to leap prematurely into print and to slice single projects into ever smaller publishable segments.[79] Those pressures are particularly intense in the natural sciences and academic medicine, which typically demand a large volume of publications as a condition of promotion. In one Carnegie Foundation study, over a third of the faculty believed that at their institution publications were "just counted, not qualitatively measured"; at universities with Ph.D. programs, a majority of professors shared that view.[80]

The tendency is encouraged by the growing specialization of scholarship, which makes it harder for colleagues even in the same discipline to judge the quality of each others' work. In some fields, the difficulty is compounded by a lack of consensus over what counts as quality. When turf warfare among subfields has taken over, the simplest way to achieve consensus on appointments and promotions is to focus on how much a candidate has published, not how good it is. In urging me to produce journal articles early and often, one of my senior colleagues explained, "Whatever you publish, there will be disputes about its significance. If you do not publish, there can be no disputes."

Science in a Buyer's Market

Although a pervasive problem in the professions and social sciences is the lack of social relevance, a serious problem in the natural sciences is just the opposite. A growing share of research funding now comes from private industry, which wants data that will have immediate commercial applications. In an era of declining government support and increasing research expenses, faculty feel ever greater pressure to focus on what corporate sponsors will subsidize. The risk, as leaders in academic science note, is that this short-term commercial agenda will distort scholarly priorities and divert focus from the basic research on which socially productive applications ultimately depend. Nobel laureate Paul Berg offers an apt illustration. His work on splicing DNA laid the groundwork for what is now a billion dollar biotech industry with enormous potential for improving the quality of life. Yet as Berg has pointed out, "the biotech revolution would not have happened had the whole thing been left up to industry." It did not want to fund anything in the area that did not have "obvious commercial or short-term impact . . . [including] the basic research that made biotechnology possible."[81]

Similar distortions of academic research agendas are occurring in other fields in which public funding is in short supply. For example, in areas involving occupational health and environmental safety, scholars are devoting more and more attention to studies that will be useful in litigation. Funds are readily available to demonstrate that a given corporate product or practice was or was not responsible for health problems among workers, consumers, or community residents. Funds are far less available for basic research that would be more socially useful in determining appropriate public policy and preventive measures.[82] The consequences of commercial influence were apparent in a recent Harvard survey of some two thousand life-science faculty. It found that researchers who get over two-thirds of their funds from industry were less likely to be academically productive and to produce articles of influence in their field.[83]

Summarizing these trends, Marcia Angell's widely circulated editorial in the *New England Journal of Medicine* put the question bluntly: "Is Academic Medicine for Sale?"[84] A dispiriting number of responses viewed the question as rhetorical. "These days, everything is for sale," observed one University of California medical professor. The only denial came in the form of a quip: "Is academic medicine for sale? No. The current owner is very happy with it."[85] Moreover, as the subsequent discussion of research ethics makes clear, the problems arising from commercial sponsorship involve not simply distortions of academic priorities but also threats to academic integrity. As that discussion also suggests, we need better ways to manage university-industry collaborations that will preserve the profession's core values and the public's long-term interests.

Research Versus Teaching

Another unwelcome by-product of the increasing emphasis on publication is the devaluation of other academic responsibilities that compete for attention. A common lament is that scholars "are in full flight from teaching."[86] In "pursuit of their own interests, they have left the nation's students in the care of an ill-trained, ill-paid and bitter academic underclass," adjuncts and graduate students.[87] And even when the university's best and brightest do descend on the undergraduate classroom, they reportedly insist on offering specialized courses that suit their research agendas rather than broader curricular needs.[88]

This is not a new complaint. University professors have long been lambasted for shirking teaching obligations. At the turn of the twentieth century, the president of Vassar felt "obliged to suspect that the student comes to be regarded as a disquieting element in what, without him, might be a fairly pleasant life."[89] What is, however, more recent is the reduction in classroom hours at research universities. According to a report by the National Endowment for the Humanities, the overall course loads at some of these institutions have declined by as much as half since the 1920s.[90] Faculty on campuses with doctoral programs teach about a third less than faculty at other universities.[91] Only a third of full-time faculty at research universities consider teaching their primary interest.[92]

Public concern over these priorities has also increased, partly due to widely publicized cases of academic stars who negotiate reduced teaching loads and academic shirkers who accomplish the same end through more indirect means. A typical exposé involved a senior professor who taught only two graduate seminars on Friday afternoons, a time slot designed to minimize enrollment. When his department chair suggested shifting one course to the beginning of the week, he responded with incredulity: "If you don't have Mondays off, what do you have?"[93]

Yet such cases are far from typical. The vast majority of professors do not work in the leading research universities, and most of those who do assume significant classroom responsibilities. The median time spent teaching or preparing to do so has not changed since the 1950s. The course load at nearly three-quarters of colleges and universities is four or more courses per semester.[94] Moreover, the relevant issue is not simply the quantity of time that professors spend in the classroom, but the quality of education that they provide. Whether involvement in research enhances or competes with teaching is a far more complicated question than either critics or defenders generally acknowledge.

Most critical commentary assumes that the more importance that academics and academic institutions attach to research, the less effort they will invest in basic undergraduate teaching. A related assumption is that not all gifted teachers are gifted scholars, and when scholarship dominates hiring and promotion decisions, students will pay the price.[95] Defenders of the research mission challenge both assumptions. In their view, the quality of teaching and the quality of scholarship are inextricably linked; professors' understanding of their discipline is best tested through dialogue with other experts, made possible through publication. Excellence in the classroom reportedly depends on a thorough understanding of the field, and a capacity to create as well as communicate knowledge.[96] The common view among university leaders is, as one president put it: "A professor's account of original cutting-edge research has an unsurpassed capacity to . . . inspire as well as to illuminate."[97] In theory, it is possible to convey deep knowledge without attempting to advance it. But in practice, Nobel laureate economist George Stigler maintains, it is "improbable psychologically; it asks a man to have the energy to read widely and the intellectual power to think freshly, and yet to . . . [keep his contributions] secret. Only the man who has tried to improve the ideas will know their strengths and weaknesses. Scholarship is not a spectator sport."[98]

Neither critics nor defenders of the research orientation generally provide factual support for what are, in essence, factual claims. And efforts to test the relationship between involvement in scholarship and effectiveness in teaching have yielded no clear answers. Part of the problem lies in the difficulty of assessing quality or even determining the appropriate framework for analysis. Is the relevant comparison between the overall educational experience at institutions that are research oriented and those that are not, or between the classroom performance of academics who are producing a significant body of scholarship and those who are not? How should we measure the quality of teaching at either the institutional or individual level? As Chapter 3 indicates, student evaluations, while relevant, are by no means an adequate gauge. Their assessments reflect without resolving important trade-offs. For example, in one study comparing professors who were involved in research and those who were not, students indicated that the researchers used more up-to-date material but also were less available and more likely to structure the curriculum around their own interests.[99]

Other studies of the teaching-research relationship yield similarly mixed results. Although it is clear that professors at research universities have lower course loads than faculty at other institutions, it is less clear how involvement in scholarship affects educational quality. The results are inconsistent, but they suggest that both critics' and defenders' claims are overstated. Much depends on the intensity of professors' research demands and their commitment to effective teaching techniques. Many academics at research universities manage to accommodate both teaching and scholarship by working longer hours.[100] Some, but not all, evidence indicates that involvement in scholarship has no adverse effect on class preparation, contact with students outside of class, and availability for undergraduate teaching.[101] Of thirty studies over three decades, about a third found a small positive correlation between professors' research and teaching; only one found a negative relationship, and close to two-thirds found no relationship.[102]

Of course, studies finding a positive correlation do not establish that engaging in research *causes* better teaching, or that if it does, the modest improvement is worth the price. Even if faculty members' scholarship improves their individual classroom performance, students' overall educational experience may not benefit if scholars teach significantly less and if the institution compensates for their reduced load by greater reliance on large lectures or classes taught by adjuncts and graduate students. Qualitative assessments of higher education here and abroad suggest that excellent undergraduate teaching can occur at institutions that are not research oriented.[103] And some evidence suggests that the overall quality of teaching suffers at universities that most heavily emphasize research.[104]

In short, the relationship between teaching and scholarship is more complicated than conventional wisdom acknowledges. There is no single "right" balance. Academics have different interests and talents, students have different needs and preferences, and institutions have different missions and constraints. Trade-offs are inevitable and long-standing. One of the earliest examples dates from 1610. When Galileo moved from the University of Padua to the University of Pisa, he negotiated a release from classroom obligations.[105] The research resulting from that arrangement became the foundation for modern physics. Yet we should also consider how often scholarship makes such contributions, how much release time it necessarily requires, and how it compares to the value of educating the next generation of scholars.

This is not to imply, as critics often do, that the decisions of individual professors are what determine universities' growing emphasis on research and what account for any inadequacies in undergraduate teaching. Academics' priorities are a function not simply of their own preferences but also of their institution's concerns and reward structures. Moreover, as Chapter 3 indicates, the quality of students' educational experience is shaped not simply by the time that individual professors spend on teaching but also by educational structures that reflect broader social forces. For example, the rise in large classes and increasing reliance on non-tenure-track faculty are primarily due to the unwillingness or inability of legislatures, donors, and students themselves to subsidize more expensive alternatives. The balance that academic institutions strike between teaching and research depends heavily on the values of these external constituencies and their ability to hold academic institutions accountable. If the current trade-offs between teaching and research are poorly serving societal goals, the answer is not just to lambast faculty for selfish careerism and status concerns. Rather, it is necessary to realign the structural forces that are driving academic priorities.

Research Ethics

A final set of concerns about contemporary scholarship involves ethics, and here too, the emphasis should be not just on faculty conduct but also on the forces that underlie it. Part of the problem is that we lack any systematic information on the frequency of ethical abuse, and the strategies that might best address it. Indeed, acknowledgment that there *is* a serious problem is a relatively recent development. Only in the past quarter century has the academy begun to focus on research-related misconduct. In earlier eras, the situation in most disciplines was similar to that reported in a 1980 study by the American Association for the Advancement of Science (AAAS). Its survey of affiliated organizations reported that "little attention and only minimal resources have been devoted to professional ethics."[106] The American Association of University Professors (AAUP), the only organization that cuts across the disciplines, has an ethical code that speaks in only the most general terms to research ethics. For example,

> Professors' primary responsibility to their subject is to seek and to state the truth; . . .
>
> A faculty member should: practice intellectual honesty; exercise critical self-discipline in using, extending, and transmitting knowledge; acknowledge significant academic or scholarly assistance from students; and acknowledge academic debt. The responsibility of clarifying and enforcing such obligations, however, remains with individual academic institutions and professional organizations.[107]

Despite increasing efforts, that responsibility has not been adequately met. At the government level, both the National Institute of Health and the National Science Foundation have adopted policies on scientific misconduct and expanded efforts to detect it. Academics' own professional organizations have taken similar measures. Yet according to an AAAS survey of 126 of these organizations, although three-quarters had ethical statements of some sort, only a minority spoke to research-related issues such as authorship credit (30 percent), plagiarism (26 percent), reporting misconduct (26 percent), and timely, complete reporting of data (17 percent). Only a minority had ethics committees (37 percent), annual programs (40 percent), publications (30 percent), or resource materials (15 percent).[108] No systematic data are available about how often ethics codes are enforced, and professional associations generally lack resources for enforcement.[109]

The Frequency and Causes of Misconduct

We also have no comprehensive evidence on the frequency of research-related misconduct. Nor do we even have consensus about how to define the term. Many codes of ethics use definitions similar to that of the National Science Foundation: "fabrication, falsification, plagiarism, or other serious deviation from accepted practices in proposing, carrying out, or reporting results. . . . "[110] But insufficient guidance is available on what constitutes "accepted practice" or "serious deviation."[111] Some codes use more narrow definitions and exclude references to accepted practice. Other codes define misconduct still more broadly, and include issues such as authorship credit, whistleblowing, conflicts of interest, and bias in peer review.

Moreover, many academics lack knowledge about rules governing these issues. One Acadia Institute study of some four thousand professors and graduate students in chemistry, civil engineering, microbiology, and sociology found that only about half reported familiarity with the research misconduct policies of their institution and discipline. Only a third of graduate students recalled receiving significant instruction on research ethics from someone in their department.[112] Another survey by the Pew Charitable Trust of graduate students in eleven disciplines from twenty-seven universities found that only a minority had clear understandings of ethical issues such as determining authorship credit (26 percent), refereeing papers fairly (22 percent), and avoiding conflicts of interest (12 percent).[113] Faculty and student understandings of disclosure policies may be equally lacking. Although many academic journals require authors to indicate any financial support that might create conflicts of interest, fewer than 1 percent of some sixty-two thousand surveyed articles included such disclosures.[114]

In one of the few comprehensive efforts to estimate the frequency of ethical abuses, the Acadia Institute survey asked faculty and students whether
they had observed or had "other direct evidence" of specified misconduct
in their department over the past five years. Six percent of faculty and nine
percent of students reported falsification or plagiarism of research by a faculty member. Almost a third of faculty were aware of inappropriate assignment of authorship or student plagiarism.[115] Although over three-quarters
of surveyed faculty believed that they should exercise collective responsibility for the ethical conduct of their graduate students, only a quarter believed that they actually did so; about half thought that they should assume
similar collective responsibility for their colleagues' conduct, but only 13
percent believed that they in fact did so. Part of the reason may be concerns
about reprisals. About half of the students and a quarter of the faculty believed that reporting faculty misconduct would result in retaliation.[116]

The other most comprehensive recent survey involved some thirty-two
hundred scientists who had received grants from the National Institute of
Health (NIH).[117] It asked whether they had engaged in ten behaviors that
university ethics compliance officers considered serious and likely to be
sanctionable. A third of those responding admitted at least one of those
behaviors. The self-reported incidence of some offenses was low: fewer
than 2 percent acknowledged falsifying data, failing to disclose financial
conflicts of interest, or ignoring significant human subjects requirements.
However, other ethical violations were more common: failing to present
data that contradicted one's own previous research (6 percent); circum-
venting minor human-subject requirements (8 percent); overlooking
others' use of flawed data (13 percent); and changing the design, methodology, or results of a study in response to pressure from a funding source
(16 percent).[118]

Such reports are, of course, a highly imperfect measure of misconduct.
Although both the Acadia and NIH surveys had reasonable response rates,
those who replied may not have been representative of the academic profession as a whole, and their reports of misconduct do not establish the
actual frequency of abuse. Yet the fact that a significant number observe or
acknowledge ethical violations, together with similar findings from other,

smaller-scale studies and case histories, raises serious concerns.[119] The problem is exacerbated by academics' conceded unwillingness to exercise collective responsibility for ethical conduct and the limitations of other, external oversight strategies.[120] The resulting abuses erode confidence in the research process, frustrate the search for knowledge, inappropriately socialize students, and waste resources that are required to respond to dishonesty and to redo flawed studies. Falsification of medical or scientific data may also endanger the health and safety of those who rely on inaccurate results. Academic institutions clearly have a strong interest in developing more effective responses to research-related misconduct and the forces that underlie it.

Studies of ethical abuses in academic and similar professional contexts identify various contributing factors: pressures to succeed, opportunities for misconduct, low risks of detection, inadequate disciplinary sanctions, and corrosive cultural norms.[121] The temptations to cut ethical corners are obviously greatest when individuals feel a strong personal or professional need to publish too much or too quickly, or to reach a certain result. The temptations escalate when oversight and mentoring are lax and where supervisors, peers, and funders have little capacity to detect misconduct. Factors that inhibit individuals from reporting misconduct include fear of alienating colleagues, inviting retaliation, jeopardizing grants, or compromising the reputation of their department or institution.[122]

As the Acadia Institute survey also makes clear, the frequency of perceived misconduct and the norms and opportunity structures that drive it vary considerably across disciplines. These variations undercut the common assumption that misconduct is primarily attributable to the character defects of a few "bad apples." To devise effective responses, we need to know more about what accounts for variations across the disciplines. Why are faculty reports of plagiarism and data falsification by colleagues higher in civil engineering than in other fields? Why do professors of chemistry feel more collective responsibility than counterparts in other disciplines, and why do professors of sociology feel less?[123] We also need far more information about the effectiveness of particular strategies in dealing with different forms of misconduct. For example, what are the costs and benefits of random audits, stricter oversight of research procedures, or external review boards that respond to possible academic misconduct? Do more stringent prohibitions on conflicts of interest reduce the incidence of bias and related ethical violations? What organizational structures are most likely to encourage adequate supervision and whistleblowing?[124] More research on research ethics and policies should be a high priority.

Allocating Credit: Plagiarism and Authorship

In a profession in which publication is a primary source of status, credit for authorship has obvious importance. The etymology of *plagiarism* conveys as much; the term comes from the Latin, *plagiarius*, referring to someone who abducts the child or slave of another. In principle, the rules are clear: ideas, or the expression of ideas, should not be appropriated without credit.[125] But in practice, matters become murkier, given conflicting cultural norms and disciplinary conventions. American society is tolerant of some forms of "borrowing," and higher education is no exception. Prominent academics often have escaped sanctions. One widely publicized case involved an Ivy League president whose plagiarized commencement address ran in the *New York Times* along with the original, in a column titled "Funny Coincidence." Another well-known example is the scientist who became the director of the National Science Foundation despite having quoted work without attribution in a scholarly article.[126] Some 40 percent of college students admit to plagiarizing material from the Internet, although many do not consider it plagiarism; a common view is that anything "out there" on the Net is meant for "public consumption."[127]

Norms are also fuzzy about the need to attribute material that is slightly modified from the original, or that borrows conceptual schemes without full credit, or that cites from primary source materials without identifying the author who did the original research.[128] Ralph Waldo Emerson, who stressed the importance of radical originality in scholarship, nonetheless conceded that "all my best ideas were borrowed from the ancients."[129] Many contemporary academics lack a clear sense about when such borrowing should be identified. Plagiarism that results from sloppy research practices or other unintentional appropriation has also been problematic.[130]

In a culture whose leaders are used to claiming credit for speeches, memoirs, and columns ghostwritten by others, analogous practices by academics may seem less deviant.[131] Criteria for attributing credit are often ill-defined, and the potential for abuse lies at both ends of the spectrum: too much recognition may serve to curry favor with senior authors who do not deserve it, and too little credit may go to junior authors and students who do.[132] In some scientific disciplines, the pressure to multiply publications has led to corresponding pressure to multiply authors regardless of the significance of their contribution. The practice has sometimes gone to such ludicrous lengths that it is impossible to determine who is truly responsible for the research. One six-page article in a physics journal devoted a third of its space to listing the names and institutional affiliations of 437 authors; another article in the same journal weighed in with 403.[133] Abuses persist because subordinates who do the real work often fear retaliation if they protest, or because they benefit from the association with, or references from, a prominent "honorary" coauthor. Such practices can foster a corrosive cynicism, which encourages vulnerable graduate students and postdocs to engage in misconduct that has a low risk of detection, such as borrowing from foreign language sources.[134]

Even when institutions receive a report of misappropriation or plagiarism, they are sometimes reluctant to incur the costs of documenting abuse, as well as the risks of retaliation and the reputational damage of imposing public sanctions. Such reluctance is not without foundation. Examples abound of academics accused of misconduct who sue, or threaten to sue, for libel, slander, intentional infliction of emotional distress, and related injuries.[135] Although such litigation is seldom successful, it can be extremely expensive.[136] Concerns about costs, together with limitations on remedies, have also deterred professional associations from responding to ethics-related claims. Some organizations, such as the Association of American Law Schools, have never created complaint channels; others, such as the American Historical Association, have decided to stop evaluating grievances.[137] Academic publishers have been similarly disinclined to investigate abuse; their role is generally limited to printing a correction when they receive well-documented evidence of false, plagiarized, or misappropriated material.[138] Moreover, many publishers both of books and journals lack clear and consistent standards regarding authorship credit, which makes enforcement of appropriate norms still more difficult.

The solution is again straightforward in principle but difficult to achieve in practice. Prominent reports on research integrity have long recommended that academic institutions, professional associations, ethics compliance bodies, and scholarly journals develop clearer, uniform policies regarding authorship. Models for best practice standards are readily available, such as those adopted by the International Committee of Medical Journal Editors.[139] Requiring multiple authors to disclose their respective contributions and explicitly endorse major conclusions could foster greater accountability and oversight.[140] More stringent sanctions and more resources for enforcement are also necessary.[141] But establishing better policies and oversight structures is not enough. Enforcement is likely to occur only if someone reports misconduct. Individual professors must assume a greater collective responsibility for scholarly integrity and a greater willingness to call their colleagues on conduct that fails to measure up.

Bias and Conflicts of Interest

Efforts to minimize bias in the research and peer review process have bumped up against similar obstacles. Total objectivity is, of course, an unattainable ideal. Academics have personal, professional, and ideological commitments that inevitably shape their scholarly activities. Yet although it may be impossible to eliminate all forms of bias, it is reasonable to expect authors to recognize and disclose obvious conflicts of interest, and to expect academic institutions, associations, and journals to design appropriate responses.

Unethical peer review can take several forms. Reviewers can be tempted to appropriate ideas or methods before they are published, or to use delay and negative evaluations in order to disadvantage a competitor. Personal friendships or animosities, and desires to curry favor, can also compromise independent judgment.[142] The prestige of the authors or their institutions may similarly skew evaluations. In one telling study, researchers took twelve articles that had been published in the preceding two-and-a-half years and resubmitted them with minor changes to the same journals in which they had appeared; the authors' names were changed, they were given less prestigious institutional affiliations, and the opening paragraphs were slightly revised. Only three of the articles were recognized as resubmissions. The other nine previously published manuscripts went through the full review process, and eight were rejected, most of them for "serious methodological flaws."[143]

Financial conflicts of interest pose a related threat to research integrity. Sensitivity to this issue has increased dramatically over the past two decades, partly because business is supplying a growing share of academic research funding. Faculty have correspondingly greater opportunities to obtain not only research-related support but also equity shares in the results, as well as lucrative consulting arrangements. More well-publicized abuses have occurred as a result.[144] Academic institutions now generally have policies requiring disclosure or avoidance of specified conflicts of interest. Some government funders prohibit their grantees from entering into private consulting or investment relationships posing risks of bias.[145] Increasing numbers of academic journals have policies like that of *Science*, which requires every manuscript to include "any information about the authors' professional and financial affiliation that may be perceived to have biased the presentation."[146]

Yet current policies too often fall short. Many are overly general, underinclusive, and underenforced. Seldom do institutions prohibit researchers from holding economic interests that would be affected by their results, a strategy that ethics experts generally recommend.[147] Nor do a majority have adequate provisions guaranteeing noninterference with the content of publications and timely release of data.[148] Rarely are efforts made to audit compliance. Academic journals and institutions rely largely on the honor system. What limited evidence is available suggests that honor is in insufficient supply. A case in point is the extremely low incidence of conflict of interest disclosures in surveyed journals noted earlier: under 1 percent. Another indication of the problem is the acknowledgment by the *New England Journal of Medicine* that nearly half of its reviews of drugs over a recent three-year period were written by researchers with a financial interest in the companies that make the drugs, in violation of the *Journal*'s own policy.[149]

These economic ties raise well-documented concerns. Studies consistently find that researchers paid by private industry are more likely to report results favorable to their corporate sponsors than are researchers without such funding.[150] For example, one review of articles on cancer drugs found that only 5 percent of those with unfavorable conclusions about the drug's cost-effectiveness had industry support, compared with 38 percent of articles with nonprofit funding.[151] Other studies find similarly skewed results, which suggests obvious grounds for concern in a nation where 70 to 80 percent of the funds for clinical drug trials come from industry.[152] Data adverse to sponsors' interests may remain unpublished because researchers do not want to jeopardize relationships that will produce future financial support and access to industry-controlled information.[153] Even more troubling are cases in which scholars have knowingly failed to adjust their findings to take account of new data that bear on products' health or safety risks.[154] Faculty with high levels of industry sponsorship also are much less likely to publish findings promptly or to share data with other colleagues, often because they are subject to confidentiality restrictions in funding agreements.[155]

Moreover, in fields other than medicine and science, many journals and professional societies lack disclosure requirements entirely, or do not mandate sufficiently specific information to gauge the likelihood of bias.[156] The consequences of such inadequacies are well illustrated by Exxon's funding of research critical of punitive damage awards while a $5 billion dollar award against the company was on appeal. Experts estimate that Exxon spent over $1 million dollars to support scholarly studies that have been cited by at least ten courts, including one that overturned the initial Exxon verdict as excessive. The company has been known to cut off funding for research that came to unwelcome conclusions. Many of the briefs and opinions citing these subsidized articles made no mention of their funding. Nor did most of the articles themselves give any indication of the extent of Exxon's support or the conditions that it had imposed.[157]

How to restructure the research relationship between the industry and academy raises a host of complex economic as well as ethical issues. The details are beyond the scope of this overview, but the general direction of reforms is clear. We need a framework that ensures greater ethical safeguards but that also recognizes the enormous value of industry-university partnerships, and that avoids creating overly restrictive rules that risk redirecting funds into for-profit institutions with fewer protections. That risk is already apparent. During the 1990s, industry support for university drug trials dropped by about half; subsidies went instead to contract research organizations.[158] Neither the profession nor the public can afford a race to the bottom, in which funding goes to those with the fewest ethical constraints.

To avoid that result, universities, journals, professional associations, and government agencies need to work together to institutionalize common standards.[159] At a minimum, these standards should prohibit researchers from holding any financial interest that would be affected by their results.[160] Safeguards should also be in place to protect academic independence on matters such as control over research design, timely publication of findings, and sharing of data.[161] These requirements should be enforced by academic institutions, journals, and government funders. More stringent disclosure standards and enforcement strategies are equally necessary, as are more collaborative funding structures.[162] By pooling resources from multiple public and private funders, institutions can support research that might not serve the short-term interest of single sponsors. For example, the Environmental Protection Agency and a consortium of auto manufacturers provide five-year commitments of funding to the Health Effects Institute, which subsidizes air pollution research meeting high ethical standards.[163]

Finally, the academic profession needs to focus more attention on ethics-related education and scholarship. It is shameful that so few graduate students report a clear understanding of ethical issues such as authorship credit and conflicts of interest. The problem is not only the absence of sustained treatment of these issues in the graduate curricula but also the lack of quality control for much of the education that does occur. Although funders such as the National Institute of Health require ethics training for students working on its sponsored projects, some institutions view a single workshop or online self-study as sufficient.[164] More research concerning the effectiveness of ethics instruction, policies, and enforcement structures should become a central academic priority.

ACADEMIC ACCOUNTABILITY

In the final analysis, the greatest problem in contemporary scholarship is convincing academics that there *is* a problem, and that they have some collective responsibility to address it. A central paradox is that academic freedom and academic competition are the sources of both the strength of American scholarship and its limitations. The ability to pursue and express ideas unconstrained by prevailing orthodoxies is what ultimately advances knowledge. And the competitive pressure for recognition among peers is what drives many academics to produce their best work. Yet the relative freedom from public accountability carries a cost, as does the scramble for status within an insular academic community. A joint report by the federal Office for Research Integrity and the American Association for the Advancement of Science put the point succinctly: educational institutions with too much autonomy, "despite the best of intentions, fail in representing the public interest."[165] Society has a substantial stake in ensuring that the reward structure of the university reflects societal concerns outside it. What ultimately preserves academic freedom is the public's confidence that it is exercised responsibly. When unconstrained autonomy permits self-serving priorities, the entire governance structure is at risk.

Here again, the objectives of reform seem clear. Knowledgeable commentators agree that we must focus more on the quality and less on the quantity of scholarship; provide greater support for empirical and policy-oriented empirical research; make academic writing more accessible; strike a better balance between scholarly and teaching priorities; and respond more effectively to ethical misconduct. Ideally, the impetus for such reforms would come from within the academy, but that is most likely to occur when external constituencies demand it. Part of our task as scholars is to educate a wider constituency both in and outside the academy about the challenges we face and the strategies necessary to address them. It matters whether we "get the right words in the right order," and we need to be accountable when our efforts fall short.

Chapter Three

TEACHING

Former Harvard president Charles Eliot once reportedly quipped that the university was a "storehouse of knowledge because the freshmen bring so much in and the graduates take so little out." Contemporary commentators often agree about the departing seniors and find plenty of blame to go around. Faculty members are faulted for spending too much time on their own research at the expense of undergraduate teaching, for failing to master effective classroom techniques, and for inadequately supervising graduate students who pick up the teaching responsibilities that professors have abdicated. Universities are faulted for letting this happen and for placing too little emphasis on the quality of education that they provide.

Critiques are often sweeping and unstinting. As one put it, "The academic culture is not merely indifferent to teaching, it is actively hostile to it. In the modern university, no act of good teaching goes unpunished."[1] Professors who spend too much time on classroom rather than scholarly activities pay the price in missed promotions and other rewards. Although the nation's leading institutions generally claim to value teaching as much as research, that commitment is "honored in the breach."[2] A "secret shame" is the "contempt for teaching among teachers" and the overreliance on untrained graduate students, which amounts to "children teaching children."[3]

To the average university undergraduate, the senior faculty is assertedly un-approachable and unintelligible.[4] And the curriculum is an incoherent grab bag, assembled by professors who "want to teach what they want to teach," which is not necessarily what students need to learn.[5]

These critiques, however overstated and oversimplified, do raise important concerns that more thoughtful experts share. As former Harvard president Derek Bok notes, "Few knowledgeable observers would deny that research universities rarely insist on the best possible teaching or make a substantial and systematic effort to improve the quality of their educational programs."[6] Other experts agree, and do not view the problem as limited to research universities. Yet underneath this broad consensus are deeper, more contested issues about the scope of the problem and how to address it. What exactly does, and should, the academy seek to teach? How should we evaluate its effectiveness? If many institutions are failing to deliver quality education, what are the primary causes of that failure and what are the most promising responses?

THE EDUCATIONAL MISSION

"The aim of education should be to teach us
rather how to think than what to think."
James Beatty[7]

Most experts on higher education agree that its central objective should be to develop capabilities for critical thinking.[8] The goal should be to create habits of mind that will enable individuals to recognize the limits of their own knowledge and to assimilate, assess, and apply new information. Faculty need to teach not simply facts, which are readily forgotten or supplanted, but how to deal with facts.[9] Learning requires a lifetime commitment. The best that higher education can do is to equip students with the basic skills needed to function effectively in a diverse, democratic, and rapidly changing society.

What skills are most critical is the point at which consensus begins to unravel, although most experts agree on certain key abilities. A review of the literature on universities' teaching mission and their role in giving students "workplace competencies" suggests a representative list:

- "personal competencies," such as self-motivation; moral reasoning; and analytic, cognitive, quantitative, and problem-solving abilities
- "communication competencies," such as writing, listening, public speaking, and information technology skills
- "organizational competencies," such as leadership, management, and interpersonal skills
- "cultural competencies," such as a knowledge of other cultures; an ability to work effectively with those of different backgrounds; and the capabilities and commitment to be active, informed participants in democratic self-governance
- "substantive competencies," such as an understanding of the basic concepts of the natural sciences, the social sciences, the humanities, and the arts, as well as skills relevant to particular fields[10]

That is not a modest agenda, and many of the desired capabilities are not easily measured. In a world of scarce resources, academic institutions need to establish priorities and assess performance. Yet both processes can raise widespread controversies and concerns. In recent years, much of the dispute has centered on the core curriculum: What courses should be mandatory and what should they include? These conflicts have subsided, less because the underlying disagreements have been resolved than because the process has been exhausting, and pragmatic compromise seems preferable to endless wrangling. Yet the focus on what faculty should teach has too often diverted attention from how well students are actually learning.

EVALUATING EDUCATIONAL EFFECTIVENESS

Quality

Given the enormous sums that students and their families invest in higher education, it is striking how little information is available on what they receive. We know that a college degree increases earnings, but we lack reliable data on the effectiveness of teaching within and across institutions.[11] Moreover, much of the information that we do have suggests grounds for concern. For example, in a Rand Corporation survey, over half of a national sample of college juniors and seniors could not complete basic cognitive tasks at a high school level.[12] A National Adult Literacy Survey similarly found that only about half of the graduates of four-year colleges could demonstrate intermediate competence in reading and interpreting written materials such as newspaper articles; in working with documents such as charts and bus schedules; and in using elementary math to solve problems such as the cost of a restaurant meal. A majority of individuals with college degrees were unable consistently and accurately to perform tasks such as calculating the change from $3 after buying a $.60 bowl of soup and a $1.95 sandwich.[13] Comparable deficiencies have surfaced in other studies. In one survey by the National Endowment for the Humanities, a majority of seniors were unable to link major works by Plato, Shakespeare, and Milton with their authors.[14] A project of the National Conference of State Legislatures found that two-thirds of students knew the name of the latest American Idol winner but only 10 percent knew the speaker of the United States House of Representatives.[15] In a Global Geographic Literacy Survey, students from the United States came in second to last among the nine nations tested; only 12 percent could locate Afghanistan, and less than a fifth knew four countries with nuclear weapons.[16]

Another way of evaluating educational effectiveness is to focus not on graduates' capabilities but on their gains over the course of their college experience. The limited data available give a mixed picture, but indicate that higher education falls short in certain key objectives. More than 90 percent of surveyed professors claim that improving critical thinking is the most important goal of undergraduate education. Yet most do not evaluate students for that capacity, and most graduating students do not report improvement.[17] National studies document the gap between institutional aspirations and achievements. According to Educational Testing Service data, over three-quarters of students are "not proficient" in critical thinking.[18] Nor do most improve in quantitative skills unless they are majoring in math or using it frequently in other courses. The greatest improvements are in substantive knowledge, appreciation of literature, and tolerance for other views and culture.[19]

Information comparing the quality of instruction at particular schools is highly limited. College ranking surveys provide some data, but no direct measures of teaching effectiveness. For example, the most influential survey, published annually by *U.S. News and World Report*, offers only a few comparisons that might bear on student learning, such as the ratio of students to full-time faculty, the student instructional budget, and the percentage of full-time faculty with doctorates. From time to time, *U.S. News* also publishes separate rankings based on reputational surveys; it asks college and university presidents, officers, and deans of admissions to rate other institutions' commitment to undergraduate teaching.[20]

The limitations of all these measures are self-evident. Academic administrators rarely have reliable information on the relative effectiveness of teaching. One university president summarized widespread views: "Having filled out many of these ratings . . . I can testify that college presidents know next to nothing about the quality of education students receive at colleges other than their own."[21] As Chapter 1 notes, an institution's ratings typically reflect its relative prestige, which is in turn affected by its *U.S. News* ranking, thus creating a somewhat circular process. The ratio of full-time faculty to students and the percentage of these faculty with Ph.D.s is misleading without information about the proportion of undergraduate teaching that they provide. Relative budgets are an equally imperfect indicator; they are largely driven by the size of faculty salaries, which bear no demonstrated relationship to the quality of teaching.

In fact, *U.S. News* rankings are not correlated with the use of methods that have proven most effective in promoting student learning, such as small participatory classes, multiple written assignments, and frequent interaction with faculty.[22] Information that *U.S. News* and other publications provide about the percentages of students who graduate, gain entrance to professional or advanced degree programs, or pass qualifying exams is not a good measure of instructional quality; those achievements may be more reflective of entering students' abilities than the "value added" by their educational experience. A study by Alexander Astin, former director of the UCLA Higher Education Research Institute, suggests as much. His sophisticated statistical analysis estimated that about two-thirds of the variation among schools' graduation rates is attributable to differences in the characteristics of entering students.[23]

It is, however, possible to develop more accurate performance evaluations by comparing institutions' actual graduation rates with predicted rates, based on the qualifications of the incoming class. The danger, though, is that overemphasis of this measure will encourage institutions and their faculties to relax standards or "teach to tests" that will qualify students for a degree but not ensure core competencies.[24] One way around this problem is the Collegiate Learning Assessment. This test, developed under the auspices of the Rand Corporation's Council for Aid to Education, is used on some 240 campuses and measures students' capacities for critical analysis.[25] By comparing the performance both of freshmen and of seniors at a particular school, and of seniors at different schools who entered with similar SAT scores, it is possible to obtain a rough gauge of increases in learning capacity, relative to peer institutions with comparable student bodies. Other surveys use longitudinal measures and control groups to help determine whether particular educational initiatives significantly enhance learning and capabilities such as leadership and cultural sensitivity.[26] But until such evaluation strategies are widely adopted, and the results are publicly available, schools may feel insufficient pressure to improve educational quality. That pressure has not been forthcoming, even for public insitutions. Most states do not set measurable goals for student class participation, retention, or graduation rates.[27]

Not only do we lack adequate comparative data about institutions' teaching effectiveness, we often lack adequate measures of individual professors' performance. The problem is widely acknowledged; almost three-quarters of faculty in one national survey agreed that their institution needed better ways to evaluate teaching.[28] Multiple responsibilities are involved: good teaching requires developing students' analytic ability and technical skills, inspiring original insights, conveying crucial information, and serving as an adviser, mentor, and role model. Not all of these are readily assessed. Evaluation of teaching is more difficult than evaluation of scholarship, for which a variety of accepted criteria is available: publication record, frequency of citation, grants and awards, external peer review, and so forth.

Assessment of teaching, by contrast, relies almost exclusively on student ratings, occasionally supplemented by peer reports. Both measures are useful to a degree, but both have significant limitations.

Student responses on well-designed course evaluation forms are moderately correlated with objective measures of learning and with experts' assessments.[29] But not all evaluation processes are well designed, and the results can be skewed by factors that bear no relation to substantive content, such as a professor's enthusiastic style and physical appearance.[30] Nor do undergraduates typically know enough to judge the adequacy of content, and their evaluations do not necessarily reflect how much they have actually learned.[31] The role of snap judgments based on nonsubstantive factors is also of concern. One study found that students' ratings of three, five-second silent videotapes of a teacher were essentially the same as ratings after a full semester of classes.[32] Moreover, some courses are harder to teach than others; large required science courses for nonmajors receive systematically lower ratings than those of seminars in the humanities, and courses with controversial content can provoke backlash unrelated to factors within a teacher's control.[33]

A well-designed system of peer review can supplement student ratings, but it too has limitations.[34] Often reviewers observe only one or two classes and have personal relationships with the instructor that can bias assessments. Many systems rely on peers with no expertise in how individuals learn.[35] Such reviews can provide some useful information: was the teacher intelligible and responsive, was the content up-to-date and adequate in breadth and depth, and did the students seem to be awake and engaged, at least on the day of observation? But these assessments do not measure how much students are actually learning. Nor do many institutions provide peer evaluation for faculty once they receive tenure, or use such evaluation in promotion and compensation decisions.

Although student ratings continue after tenure, they are unlikely to have much impact on the instructors who are most in need of improvement. Ninety percent of surveyed professors consider their teaching above average; only 40 percent report using student evaluations in planning or revising their courses.[36] The philosophy professor in John Gardner's darkly comic novel *Mickelsson's Ghosts* illustrates the problem. At the close of one spectacularly unsuccessful introductory course on Plato, Mickelsson envisions his likely student evaluations:

Knowledge of subject matter: Fair.
Presentation of subject matter: Poor.
Interest in students: Stinko.

He resolves therefore to "do the sensible thing: forget to hand out the forms."[37]

Ethics

As the fictional example from Gardner suggests, some teaching behaviors rise to such a level of irresponsibility that they constitute breaches of academic ethics. Here again, we confront a disquieting absence of attention and information. We know little about how frequently misconduct occurs or what happens when it does. The ethical codes of academic associations seldom stray beyond unhelpful generalities. The American Association of University Professors' "Statement on Professional Ethics" limits itself to the assurance that "as members of an academic institution, professors seek above all to be effective teachers and scholars." The Association of American Law Schools includes somewhat more detail, stressing the need to "prepare conscientiously for class," and the American Sociological Association adds that its members should have "appropriate [classroom] skills and knowledge" or be "receiving appropriate training."[38] Ethical abuses in teaching, like those in research, receive relatively little focus in professional associations' programs or publications.[39] And although universities generally have detailed rules on a few issues such as sexual harassment, many problematic teaching behaviors go largely unregulated.

The frequency of misconduct in teaching is impossible to estimate with any accuracy. Virtually no systematic national data are available. Nor is there a substantial body of smaller-scale empirical research or even case histories. Part of the problem lies in defining the conduct that is sufficiently serious to be considered an ethical violation. The most comprehensive study assessed attitudes of some nine hundred faculty members in four disciplines toward a wide range of inappropriate teaching behaviors. The survey found substantial consensus across institutions and disciplines on certain "inviolable norms," such as those involving overly authoritarian classrooms, ideological bias in course coverage and grading processes, or acts of moral turpitude such as sexual relationships with students and teaching while intoxicated. By contrast, attitudes varied toward other deficiencies, such as inadequate or overly narrow course designs, avoidance of advising responsibilities, and condescending attitudes toward students. On the whole, faculty in research universities were more tolerant of such conduct than were faculty in liberal arts and community colleges.[40] What we do not know is how often those behaviors occur, how often anyone complains, and what happens when someone does.

The few recent efforts to obtain information from students report some disquieting results. In a study commissioned by the American Council of Trustees and Alumni, the University of Connecticut's Center for Survey Research and Analysis polled undergraduates at colleges and universities as ranked in the top fifty by *U.S. News and World Report.* According to about half of the students surveyed, professors frequently injected political comments into their courses even if they had nothing to do with the subject, and presentations on political issues seemed completely one-sided. Almost a third said they felt they had to agree with their professor's political view to get a good grade.[41] The disconnect between students' and faculty's perceptions of conscientious teaching behaviors also emerged starkly in a recent National Survey on Student Engagement. Although over 90 percent of instructors reported that they "very often" or "often" gave students prompt feedback, only 58 percent of students reported receiving it.[42]

The Causes and Consequences of Neglect

Why does a profession committed to the search for knowledge know so little about the effectiveness of teaching, which it claims as one of its primary missions? Several explanations are common. The first involves the increasingly competitive nature of higher education and the lack of market incentives to make teaching a priority. Education is one of the few contexts in which consumers often view less as more. Many students would like to graduate with the least possible amount of work, and they reward institutions and instructors for easing standards. One result has been a reduction in curricular requirements and assignments and an inflation in grades. Almost half of higher educational institutions impose no literature requirement, and about 40 percent of students graduate without taking any such courses. Forty percent of colleges and universities do not require math, and about a third of their graduates take advantage of that omission.[43] Although about two-thirds of students believe that it is essential or very important for college to help them develop personal values, the vast majority get little if any curricular assistance in doing so.[44] Only 11 percent of full-time students report spending more than twenty-five hours a week preparing for class, the minimum that faculty believe is necessary. Forty percent of students spend ten hours or less. Yet 40 percent also report getting mostly grades of A and another 40 percent, mostly Bs.[45]

Other by-products have been the dumbing down and jazzing up of curricular options. A professor who finds Plato a tough sell can boost enrollment by offering the "Philosophy of Pornography and Sex," which combines the classics with snippets of Harlequin romances and racy videos.[46] One parody of courses offered at "Non Campus Mentis" captured the genre:

> Urban Planning: According to Edgar Twinewell, nationally known consultant on city housing, who conducts this seminar: "There are no prerequisites, no reading lists and no tests. The kids and I will sit around and bat the breeze, in the hope that by the symbiosis of minds some solution to our urban problems will be achieved. If not, well, what the hell?"
>
> Religion and Contemporary Society: Guided by the Reverend Doctor Fielmaus, author of *Making the Scene Godwise and Other Sermons*, this course will deal with such problems as "Just how dead is God?"; "Is relevance relevant?"; "Can modern man live a moral life while not giving a damn?"[47]

There are, of course, some checks on the decline in rigor: employer pressures, parental influence, accreditation standards, and the admission requirements of graduate and professional schools. Still, too many institutions see too little to gain from preventing the knowledge gaps noted earlier.

The same is true concerning the quality of teaching. As Derek Bok notes, because students and their families lack reliable information about "how much they are really learning, let alone how much they can expect to learn, they do not make enlightened choices." And because the "results of research are more credibly and more frequently evaluated and compared" than the results of teaching, academic institutions and their faculty often adjust their priorities accordingly. "Given that teaching quality does not significantly affect student enrollment decisions, ranking of academic institutions, or an individual professor's standing," there is insufficient pressure to focus on student learning.[48] Even nonresearch-oriented institutions that are most interested in attracting additional students and responding to their needs tend to compete in more readily measurable dimensions than teaching, such as cost, student services, and convenience in course scheduling and locations.[49]

Moreover, as experts on higher education also note, many faculty are skeptical of the reliability of teaching assessments or find the process threatening.[50] Such assessments may call into question the quality of instruction that they have long provided, and may suggest the need for time-consuming improvements. Particularly for tenured professors, the right to do what they want in their classrooms, as long as they avoid clear misconduct, seems an essential part of academic freedom; any serious efforts at quality control arouse suspicion and resentment. Efforts that might reduce time available for scholarship are especially unwelcome.

The Teaching-Research Relationship Revisited

A story often encountered in academic folklore involves a university president testifying before a legislative appropriations committee. Its chair, who is skeptical of the need for additional taxpayer support, puts the potentially embarrassing question: "How many hours do your faculty teach?" The president performs some quick mental calculations of weekly classroom obligations and office advising, resolves doubts in expedient directions, and estimates "Twelve hours." "Long day," acknowledges the chair. "Fortunately, it's light work."[51]

The dialogue may be apocryphal, but the anecdote captures the genuine difficulty that those in higher education confront when accounting for their time to the world outside it. In fact, teaching is not light work when done responsibly, and classroom hours capture only a small part of the academic workload. Yet this fact is hard to convey, particularly for academics at re-search universities, who face perennial charges that they have abdicated classroom responsibilities in pursuit of their own scholarly interests.

Of course, as the preceding chapter noted, research and teaching are not competitors in a simple zero sum game. Indeed, it is an article of faith among most university leaders that scholarly and classroom activities are mutually supportive. Teaching encourages a clarity in understanding and expression that enhances professors' own intellectual development, as well as their students'.[52] A telling example appeared in a recent *Chronicle of Higher Education* essay on introductory courses titled "Teaching the 101." There, an instructor recounted his unsuccessful efforts to explain a complicated concept to un-comprehending freshmen and sophomores. The glazed expressions of his captive audience finally made clear that he might as well have been speaking Hittite. "My inclination was to blame them for not understanding me," he recalled, "but the more I thought about it, I didn't understand me" either.[53]

Just as teaching can enhance skills essential for research, research can enrich teaching. As one commentator candidly notes, the "plain fact is that after many years, some aspects of teaching tend to wear you out, mostly the repetition, the ageless youth of the student mind . . . and the reading and la-borious editing of student exams and papers."[54] Involvement in scholarship, which provides variety and intellectual challenge, encourages a freshness and enthusiasm in the classroom that might otherwise be hard to sustain. Moreover, as discussion in Chapter 2 indicated, the best way for teachers to demonstrate how knowledge is advanced is through their own participa-tion in the process.[55]

Yet an obvious but often overlooked irony is that the same university lead-ers who insist that teachers should also be scholars preside over structures that make this combination impossible for many undergraduate courses. To provide full-time faculty with time for research, an increasing amount of basic instruction must be delegated to low-cost adjuncts and graduate students who lack research experience.[56] Unsurprisingly, the amount of un-dergraduate contact with faculty is inversely correlated with the amount of faculty publications, and discontent with the quality of teaching tends to be highest at elite research institutions.[57] Only a third of professors at four-year public universities believe that effective teaching is important for promotion.[58] Students at these institutions easily can end up almost exclusively in large lecture courses. Enrollments can range from hundreds to over a thousand, and an increasing percentage are taught largely online, by videotape, or by foreign teaching assistants who may have inadequate English language skills or who "don't know squat about how to teach."[59]

Full-time faculty with substantial scholarly commitments often feel that they cannot afford the time-intensive classroom techniques that are most likely to enhance student learning, such as written evaluations, interactive exercises, collaborative projects, and supervised clinical or community service learning.[60] Rather, the lecture is the prudent choice. Its main advantage is explained by a prominent professor in John Kenneth Galbraith's satire of Harvard life: "Lectures . . . are our flexible art form. Any idea, however slight, can be expanded to fill fifty-five minutes; any idea, however great, can be condensed to that time. And if no ideas are available, there can always be discussion. Discussion is the vacuum that fills a vacuum."[61]

TEACHING THE TEACHERS

Another irony of American academic life is how little we do to educate educators. An early twentieth-century parody of British universities noted that they generally chose someone to teach solely "on the ground that he was once able to learn."[62] Yet as American philosopher William James rhetorically inquired in his polemic against the "Ph.D. octopus," "Will anyone pretend for a moment that a [doctorate] degree is a guarantee that its possessor will be successful as a teacher?"[63] In fact, many institutions still do pretend. In my first year as a law professor, I was let loose on students without any prior teaching experience or instruction, and my experience remains common. Experts on higher education often put the point bluntly: "Research universities have failed miserably in teaching the art of teaching."[64]

Although this may be something of an overstatement, national studies have found ample grounds for concern, which are not limited to research institutions.[65] Many faculty are not equipped to take advantage of new teaching technologies, and few students find that they have significantly improved classroom instruction.[66] In a survey by the Pew Charitable

Trust, only about a third of surveyed graduate students felt that they were prepared by their program to teach a lecture course; fewer than half felt qualified to teach a lab course; and only about a quarter felt able to teach a specialized graduate course. Only half reported that they had been encouraged to use a teaching development center, and a majority had no teaching assistant training course that was at least a term long.[67] Many failed to take advantage of the resources that were available, perhaps in part because they had picked up cues from faculty about where they should concentrate their efforts. Emily Toth, who writes the "Ms. Mentor" column for the *Chronicle of Higher Education*, notes that professors who are abrupt or even rude may seem to be modeling "correct professional priorities . . . ; [undergraduate] students are swarmy things to be swatted away in the interests of Pursuing Knowledge. . . ."[68]

Student Ethics and Incivility

Most institutions also do far too little to assist both new and established faculty in developing crucial teaching skills, particularly coping with inappropriate student conduct. Campus incivility is a challenge widely acknowledged but seldom addressed in any systematic fashion. We lack data on either its frequency or the effectiveness of faculty responses. What information is available, however, suggests that professors' coping strategies are often inadequate.[69] When confronted by apathetic, unprepared, discourteous, or disruptive students, many faculty members respond with ill-disguised hostility or resigned cynicism. Chiming cell phones, late arrivals, snoozing sophomores, and snotty responses are commonly dismissed as unavoidable by-products of broader cultural pathologies.

Yet although professors' understandable tendency is to blame the students, students' understandable response is to blame the professor. Part of what this generation expects for its tuition is teachers who can control a classroom and avoid the problems that provoke disrespect, such as habitual lateness, unrealistic assignments, boring lectures, and condescending comments.[70] Steven Carter's novel *The Emperor of Ocean Park* offers an uncomfortably realistic portrait of reciprocal incivility at work. The main character, an African-American Yale Law School professor, responds to what he perceives as sullen insolence, or "perhaps unsubtle racism," by humiliating the white student responsible. After grilling the student on the extent of his ignorance, the professor discovers, too late, that while class members do not much like their arrogant classmate, they like their arrogant teacher even less.[71]

Technology has expanded the range of inappropriate student conduct by increasing access to victims, providing anonymity for perpetrators, and reducing time for reflection. "Cyberbullies" harass faculty as well as classmates; electronic messages range from the absurdly demanding to the shockingly hostile. At one end of the spectrum are the annoyingly trivial but cumulatively burdensome questions such as what kind of notebooks students should buy, whether they missed anything in class, and if so, could they borrow the teacher's lecture notes.[72] At the other extreme are chatroom "bashboards" and "flame-mail" that serve to harass and humiliate, often through racist, misogynist, or homophobic comments.[73]

Many faculty fail to respond effectively. Some wish to avoid publicizing hurtful slurs or worry that exposing the problem will raise questions about their teaching ability. Others are concerned that any public report will invite retaliation, ignite controversy, and make a bad situation worse.[74] Few academic institutions have given professors effective techniques for addressing such behavior, such as how to set boundaries for e-mail inquiries, how to respond to abusive comments, and how to educate students to become ethically responsible citizens of online communities.[75] Programs targeted at students do not always focus on the most serious civility problems. For example, the University of Kansas hosts a "Spring Etiquette Dinner" that offers instruction in the do's and don'ts of formal dining: how to fold a napkin, eat angel hair pasta, and avoid inappropriate conversation topics such as asking whether salad will solve a constipation problem.[76]

So too, many institutions fail to provide faculty with adequate assistance in dealing with student dishonesty. Cheating and plagiarism are widespread. Most studies find that a majority of undergraduates report that they have engaged in such misconduct, and the availability of material on the Internet exacerbates the temptations.[77] Yet fewer than half of surveyed professors report any training on how to respond to student dishonesty, and only a third of surveyed colleges and universities have offices charged with coordinating efforts concerning these ethical violations.[78] Such institutional neglect may help account for faculty members' reluctance to report misconduct. At schools that require reports, between 70 and 80 percent of academics indicate that they have ignored the reporting requirement, and a significant number have failed to take any action in response to suspected cheating.[79]

The Mismatch Between Student and Faculty Concerns

A further problem is the mismatch between professors' expectations and students' needs, abilities, and concerns. The vast majority of academics end up teaching at institutions unlike the large research universities where they earned their Ph.D.s. Many do not quickly or entirely recover from the culture shock of students who are uninterested in the cutting-edge theory that academic graduate programs have stressed. Even experienced teachers may find it frustrating to encounter a class with priorities at odds with their own. The mutual frustrations that can arise from this misalliance are well captured in poet laureate Billy Collin's portrait, "Introduction to Poetry":

> I ask them to take a poem
> and hold it up to the light like a color slide. . . .
>
> But all they want to do
> is tie the poem to a chair with rope
> and torture a confession out of it.
>
> They begin beating it with a hose
> to find out what it really means.[80]

What perpetuates the problem in teaching priorities is the inability of many academics to perceive it as *their* problem, or as something that they could at least reduce, if not entirely prevent. As research in cognitive psychology demonstrates, a common tendency is for individuals to overestimate their abilities and understate their responsibilities for adverse results.[81] Academics are no exception, and their fallibilities are compounded by their skepticism toward experts who might help. A common slur is that "those who can do, do, those who can't, teach, and those who can't do or teach, teach teachers." Yet if learning about learning were a priority, many academics would discover a wealth of research that calls into question their most common teaching strategies.

TEACHING TECHNIQUES

My own discipline, law, is a case study in ineffective teaching strategies, and its deficiencies are typical of problems in other fields. Legal education's most common classroom approach is a combination of lecture and Socratic discussion. These formats are also the dominant strategies in higher education more generally.[82] Their appeal rests primarily on their adaptability for large classes (and corresponding cost-savings), their perceived ability to sharpen verbal and analytic skills, and their platform for professors to display erudition and exercise control. Yet these approaches also have major limitations, which even the most casual survey of learning theory makes evident. At its worst, Socratic dialogue becomes a shell game in which the teacher first invites the student to "guess what I'm thinking," and then finds the response inevitably lacking. The result is a climate in which "never is heard an encouraging word," and "thoughts remain cloudy all day."[83] This approach also can foster a highly competitive atmosphere in which the search for knowledge becomes a scramble for status and participants vie with each other more to impress than inform. A wide array of studies makes clear that such an atmosphere increases stress, erodes self-esteem, and disproportionately silences women and minority students.[84] Both lectures and Socratic dialogues can promote passivity among those who are not directly participating in the discussion. These strategies are demonstrably less effective than more active, experiential forms of learning that subsequent discussion describes.

CURRICULAR GAPS: INTERPERSONAL SKILLS, ETHICAL RESPONSIBILITIES, CIVIC ENGAGEMENT

Other deficiencies common to many disciplines are inattention to the practical, interpersonal, and ethical dimensions of the subjects at issue. For example, a substantial majority of lawyers report that law schools neglect the skills that they have found most critical in practice, such as counseling, negotiating, and problem solving.[85] Although legal education prides itself on teaching students to "think like a lawyer," what it teaches best is how to think like a law professor. The practical and interpersonal dimensions of lawyering are left to clinical courses, which occupy second-class status and generally lack sufficient resources to meet student demand. So too, although ethical issues arise in all areas of legal practice, they are missing or marginal in most legal curricula. The vast majority of law schools largely relegate the subject to a single required course.[86] Yet when faculty treat issues of professional responsibility as someone else's responsibility, they encourage future practitioners to do the same. Students pick up messages from subtexts as well as texts, and silence is a powerful, however inadvertent, teaching tool.

These curricular gaps are by no means unique to law schools. Few academic institutions require courses in ethics and fewer still make any systematic attempts to integrate ethical instruction throughout the curriculum.[87] As is clear from a recent study sponsored by the Carnegie Foundation for the Advancement of Teaching, explicit attention to moral concerns and civic responsibilities are highly limited and occur primarily in extracurricular programs.[88]

The formulation of career goals and the interpersonal aspects of learning are similarly relegated to nonacademic activities and student support services. English professor Jane Tompkins's thoughtful critique *A Life in School* points out the price of this neglect. Universities urge students to follow Socrates' mandate, "Know thyself," but provide scant resources for them to do so. Although students occasionally have opportunities to respond to assigned topics from their own experience, this approach is widely regarded as "soft," "unrigorous," or "touchy-feely." Rather, Tompkins notes, "As far as the university is concerned, the core of the human being, his or her emotional and spiritual life, is dealt with . . . on the sidelines, and the less heard about it the better."[89]

One reason for the neglect of these issues is the assumption that it is neither effective nor appropriate for academics to use their podiums as bully pulpits. In a survey by the Higher Education Research Institute, fewer than a third of faculty attached high importance to developing students' capacity for responsible citizenship and commitment to community service; only a

quarter attached high importance to developing students' moral character, self-understanding, and sense of meaning and purpose in life.[90] Many
professors assume that ethical responsibility and civic engagement are
primarily a matter of moral character, and students either "have it or they
don't" by the time they reach college. A few classroom hours of instruction
are unlikely to affect values acquired over many years from more powerful
socializing agents such as parents, peers, media, and churches. Yet while
the role of higher education should not be overstated, neither should it be
undervalued. Research on ethics education finds that moral views change
significantly during early adulthood, and that well-designed courses can
increase capacities for ethical reasoning and conduct.[91]

So too, clinics and service learning, which integrate public service with
academic instruction, are particularly effective ways of enhancing crucial
skills: well-documented improvements occur in ethical analysis, problem
solving, leadership, and responsiveness to social needs.[92] These approaches
can enable students to understand "complex issues where competing values are at stake" and "develop judgments . . . in respectful dialogue with
others," including those from diverse racial, ethnic, and class backgrounds.[93]
Courses that expose the direct human consequences of social injustice can
encourage deeper understanding of policy choices and continuing commitments to public service among both faculty and students.[94] When individuals working with low-income communities begin to see "their problems"
as "our problems," the foundations for civic engagement grow stronger.[95]
Providing opportunities for guided reflection about projects on which students are actively involved is one of the most successful teaching strategies.
As one expert puts it, we learn best "neither by thinking or by doing" but
rather "by thinking about what we are doing."[96]

Contrary to skeptics' views, service-learning courses do not pose distinctive threats of partisan proselytizing. Professors who teach such classes
generally share an explicit goal of respecting diverse views and building students' own capacities for independent judgment.[97] The greatest obstacle to
expanding clinical and service learning opportunities is not lack of evidence
about their effectiveness but lack of institutional support. Such approaches
require a substantial investment in faculty time, and too few incentives have

been available to support such involvement. Developing service opportunities, ensuring appropriate supervision, and providing skills instruction and prompt feedback on student work can add significantly to normal teaching responsibilities. Unless faculty members receive sufficient rewards and course credit, such offerings are likely to remain on the margins of academic landscapes.

Learning Environments

In short, too few classrooms offer the "learner-centered environments" that research on teaching finds most effective.[98] These environments require faculty to know enough about students' diverse knowledge, skills, experiences, motivations, and attitudes to help them master and apply new subject matter. Professors also need to avoid replicating the neglect or discourtesy that they want students to avoid. Students, for their part, must have opportunities for continuing feedback, out-of-class interaction with faculty, and active participation in the learning process.[99] A shift from teaching to learning environments will demand strategies that move beyond the conventional "talk-and-chalk" lecture approach of most undergraduate classrooms. Commonly cited best practices include role simulations, collaborative and team projects, and problem solving through case histories and structured assignments, as well as the clinical and community service opportunities noted earlier.[100]

The National Survey of Student Engagement, sponsored by the Carnegie Foundation and the Pew Charitable Trusts, provides a useful index of learning environments. For example, the survey asks students how often during the current school year they have participated in activities such as

- Asking questions in class or contributing to discussions
- Working with classmates outside of class to prepare assignments
- Offering assistance in a community-based project as part of a regular course
- Discussing ideas from readings or classes with faculty outside of class
- Receiving prompt feedback from faculty on academic performance

Students also report how much time they spend preparing for class and how much written work they complete.[101] Yet most institutions do not collect this information, and fewer than 10 percent of those that do have made any of the responses public or available for comparisons in national rankings such as those in *U.S. News and World Report*.[102] It is also unclear how often the results of this survey or the others described earlier have prompted reform efforts on particular campuses. Such information must be broadly accessible, and additional forms of accountability must be in place to ensure reform at institutions where it is long overdue.

EDUCATIONAL EXCELLENCE AS AN INSTITUTIONAL PRIORITY

Few issues in higher education evoke greater consensus than the need for universities to take the quality of teaching more seriously, and to treat it as an institutional as well as individual responsibility. In the words of former Stanford president Donald Kennedy, we must "reaffirm teaching . . . as our primary task and provide more respect and rewards for those who do it well."[103] That will, in turn, require more adequate measures of performance at both the institutional and individual level.

Evaluation

A threshold challenge is to develop better assessments of faculty teaching. Although many professors are deeply skeptical of such efforts, it is hard to maintain that adequate techniques are available to evaluate students but not themselves. One strategy is to improve the course evaluation process. Students can be asked not simply to fill out forms at the end of the semester but also to provide periodic assessments while the course is still in progress and to suggest ways of improving both the class and the evaluation system.[104] Surveys should request more information about conduct that may raise issues of ethics as well as effectiveness, and both faculty and senior administrators should pay more attention to the responses.[105]

Academic departments can supplement these measures by ensuring better training and supervision of graduate students and by improving the hiring and peer review process of faculty. Universities can require graduate teaching assistants to take at least one course in pedagogy, and to work with learning resource centers to obtain evaluation of their own classroom performance. Teaching portfolios can be required as part of faculty hiring, promotion, retention, and award processes. These portfolios can include descriptions of teaching techniques, course syllabi, active learning exercises, and videos of classroom performance. Job candidates also can be expected to teach a class or give a lecture for students. Adding such requirements would not only provide useful information in comparing applicants' skills but also send a message about the importance of teaching and the need for graduate programs to provide appropriate classroom training. A related strategy is to give faculty members more education about how to evaluate and improve their own teaching. Professors can form interdisciplinary teams or invite outside experts to observe classes and provide ideas for improvement.[106] Peer review would work more effectively if there were more reviews of the reviewers.

Institutions, for their part, can do more to monitor and compare their own educational performance. They can conduct studies involving the College Learning Assessment, the National Survey of Student Engagement, and related initiatives, such as those identified by the federal Commission on the Future of Higher Education.[107] The results of those surveys can be made public and used as benchmarks to assess the effectiveness of teaching-related initiatives. Institutions can also collect systematic data on inappropriate classroom-related conduct by students and faculty, as well as the adequacy of the responses. If more schools were willing to share information about strategies that proved most cost-effective, the benefits could be considerable. Yet additional incentives and pressure may be necessary to promote change among those whose priorities now lie elsewhere.

Rewards, Recognition, and Support

Not only do universities need better ways to identify effective teaching, they must also act on what they find. One obvious strategy is to create more rewards for teaching excellence. High-visibility awards and distinguished teaching professorships are helpful in principle, but they can be divisive in practice if the selection process is perceived as unreliable. For example, delegating the decision to students can unduly reward professors with especially entertaining styles and penalize those who do not teach large classes. By contrast, if a selection committee reviews nominations and teaching portfolios, it may reward those who are most skillful in packaging their materials, not those who are most gifted in educating a class. The problems are compounded in large institutions with a small number of awards, where the process almost invariably reflects factors irrelevant to the merits: who is on the selection committee, what they think about the candidates and their references, which departments have recently been represented among award winners, and so forth.[108] Designing a relatively credible selection process is itself a challenge, and institutions need feedback on the perceived fairness of whatever system is in place.

Universities also need to create other forms of recognition for the many faculty who provide consistently excellent teaching but who will not receive one of the few awards available. External organizations such as foundations, government agencies, and professional associations can play a role by providing funds to reward teaching, to improve evaluation techniques, and to educate educators. For example, the National Endowment for the Humanities has given matching grants to institutions that establish Distinguished Teaching Professorships, the Mellon Foundation has supported innovative uses of technology in teaching, the National Science Foundation has subsidized projects aimed at improving undergraduate education in the sciences, and the Association of American Law Schools sponsors awards, teaching workshops, and annual meeting programs.[109]

Universities also can provide more resources for faculty to develop courses and classroom techniques that enhance student learning. Examples include adequately funded teaching centers, financial incentives, release time, and appropriate course credit for collaborative teaching, service learning, and other innovative projects. Support should also be available to develop curricular and extracurricular offerings in crucial areas that are inadequately addressed in most institutions, such as moral reasoning and civic engagement.

Some institutions have made progress in recasting the teaching-research trade-off by supporting courses that involve undergraduates in their teachers' own research projects.[110] Other universities encourage collaborative ventures that do not necessarily involve the expense of multiple faculty members in every class session. For example, courses that share some overlap can meet together on selected occasions to discuss varying approaches to shared texts or themes.[111] Faculty from different disciplines can visit each others' classes to present a common issue or a case history involving multiple fields. Many ethical and policy questions cut across departmental boundaries in fields such as law, business, engineering, and the environment. Collaborative teaching offers economies of scale in course preparation, gives participants new interdisciplinary perspectives, and provides informal opportunities for peer review of teaching techniques. But to make such collaborative approaches attractive, institutions may also need to change the way they schedule courses, allocate space, and assess faculty workloads.[112]

Accountability

Three-quarters of recently surveyed college and university presidents believe that higher education should be held more accountable for educational outcomes.[113] However, few presidents have made "serious sustained efforts" to address problems of student learning.[114] Other claims on their time and resources often seem more urgent, particularly given the risks of exposing institutional inadequacies or alienating faculty with irksome new requirements. More pressure from external bodies is necessary to make the quality of student learning a priority.

Obvious sources of pressures include publications that rank educational institutions and accrediting and state governing boards that oversee institutional quality. All of these bodies can attach greater significance to educational outcomes and insist on more disclosure of information concerning student learning, such as contact with full-time faculty, opportunities for small classes, and availability of clinical or community service placements. Accrediting and governing bodies could also establish standards that focus more on learning and on graduates' preparation for employment and advanced degree programs.[115] As Chapter 6 notes, a wide range of strategies have been developed here and abroad that could make universities more accountable for educational performance.[116] The federal

Commission on the Future of Higher Education has emphasized the need for such strategies, and if academic institutions do not voluntarily assume greater responsibility for learning outcomes, others may well impose those responsibilities.[117]

On individual campuses, administrators must do more to motivate their faculties to take advantage of the resources and incentives available. Common strategies include disclosing student course ratings and requiring professors with poor performance evaluations to seek expert assistance and devise appropriate responses. Teaching colloquia can also become standard parts of departmental programming in order to showcase effective classroom strategies. Greater attention should center on improving both faculty and institutional responses to student dishonesty and incivility. Better training, programming, and enforcement should be priorities. More research is also necessary to determine the most successful approaches. Too few long-term studies are available on outcomes and on the cost-effectiveness of various learning initiatives.[118]

In short, we need more systematic attention to teaching responsibilities, which often have little effect on academics' own career advancement. Jane Tompkins offers an example that cuts uncomfortably close to home. A colleague caught up in his own scholarship came to view teaching and student-related activities as a diversion from seemingly more important professional pursuits. But as his career progressed and he charted up what he had done that really mattered, his perspective changed. "You know, my whole life I have been complaining that my work was constantly interrupted until I discovered that my interruptions were my work."[119]

Chapter Four

Administration and Service

The University of Chicago's president Robert Hutchins once famously observed that academic institutions are a "collection of departments held together by a common heating system."[1] They are also linked by a burgeoning administrative structure. This structure began to emerge in the post–Civil War era, largely in response to the rise in importance of financial and public relations issues.[2] However, until the turn of the twentieth century, administrative staffs were generally small and faculty involvement in institutional governance was minimal. Presidents, backed by boards of trustees, tended toward autocratic decision making.[3] That changed significantly over the next half century, as principles of academic freedom and faculty control over curricular and appointment matters became well established.

Yet after World War II, the increase in size and complexity of most institutions also created an increasing role for central administrations. Since the 1970s, nonteaching positions and budgets have grown dramatically, and power has shifted back to presidents and top administrators.[4] Particularly in large universities, decision-making structures look more like those of corporations.[5] Issues only indirectly related to core academic missions now occupy a growing amount of faculty time, both in committee work and in part-time administrative positions. Attention increasingly centers on matters such as fundraising, facilities, personnel, financial management, information technology, regulatory compliance, and student services. Managing a research university often involves running a host of satellite enterprises: restaurants, hospitals, libraries, athletic events, recreational facilities, law offices, police departments, even shopping centers and cemeteries.[6]

The administrative challenges that most directly affect faculty are the focus of the discussion that follows. What problems arise in shared governance, and how well are they managed by presidents and trustees? How do these problems shape the lives of academics when they serve in administrative positions or interact with university decision makers and external regulatory bodies? What are the limitations of conventional faculty and committee meetings in addressing academic needs? What reforms might be effective? This focus should not, however, be taken to imply any wholesale indictment of academic administration. The petty politics and managerial bumblings that are such popular targets in press and fictional accounts offer a misleading portrait. Compared with other complex administrative systems, or with academic institutions in other nations, American higher education has coped remarkably well with competing demands from multiple constituencies. But our relative success should not blind us to the challenges that remain and that are likely to intensify in an increasingly competitive and financially constrained academic universe.

SHARED GOVERNANCE

Higher education subscribes to the principle of shared governance. As interpreted by the American Association of University Professors and the Association of Governing Boards of Universities and Colleges, this principle allocates authority among the faculty, president, and oversight board.[7] In general, the faculty has primary authority over curricular, appointment, and promotion issues, as well as its own research agenda. The president is responsible for the day-to-day management of the institution. In consultation with faculty and trustees, the president attempts to forge a shared vision of goals and policies, and to develop resources to support them. Governing boards have fiduciary responsibility for the institution. They choose the president and have a major role in fundraising. Authority is also shared with external regulatory bodies, including state governing boards and accrediting institutions. This allocation of responsibility seems reasonable enough in theory, but in practice each branch faces significant challenges in performing its designated role.

Governing Boards

After ten years of research and dozens of engagements as consultants to nonprofit boards, we have reached a rather stark conclusion: effective governance by a board of trustees is a relatively rare and unnatural act.

Richard P. Chait, Thomas P. Holland, and Barbara E. Taylor,
Improving the Performance of Governing Boards[8]

One of the most distinctive, and at times dysfunctional, characteristics of American higher education is its reliance on governing boards whose members generally lack educational expertise. The selection process for these boards differs in public and private institutions, but in neither case does it generally produce membership with much academic experience or diversity in background. According to the most recent data, the vast majority of trustees are business executives and lawyers; about 90 percent are white, three-quarters are male, and less than 5 percent are faculty or academic administrators.[9] In public institutions, most board members are appointed by governors and ratified by legislatures; a minority are elected by the general public. Virtually all experts oppose elections, because few voters are sufficiently informed to choose the most qualified candidates, and campaigns politicize issues that should be decided on more disinterested grounds.[10] But the appointments process has its own difficulties; political patronage, personal friendship, and loyalty to governors rather than to institutions are often the dominant criteria for selection.[11] The system in private colleges and universities is typically better, but has limitations as well. Most of their trustees are chosen by the board itself; a minority are elected by the alumni. Here the dominant consideration is often wealth, or ability to tap it, and many boards run short on diversity and academic expertise.[12]

To be sure, the vast majority of trustees are accomplished individuals with a genuine commitment to public service and to the institutions that they serve. Many work extremely hard and bring insightful external perspectives to bear on academic issues. But as experts note, there is a fundamental mismatch between the orientations of board members and their institutions. Trustees have typically succeeded in workplaces oriented toward short-term, bottom-line results and hierarchical managerial styles. By contrast, higher education values less quantifiable goals, more consensual decision-making processes, and principles of academic freedom.[13]

The clash among these perspectives is apparent both in the agendas of some candidates for elected trustee positions and in occasional public rows between boards and university faculty or administrations. There have been candidates who say that they are seeking office in order to fire the football coach, close a controversial department, prevent "obscene" or radical content in courses and conferences, eliminate tenure, or require professors to be in their offices or classrooms between 8 A.M. and 5 P.M. (with an hour off for lunch).[14] Conflicts between appointed trustees and faculty have sometimes turned on similar issues, as well as matters such as diversity, budgets, free speech, and faculty exclusion from presidential selection processes. In one notorious Virginia case, a board rejected a proposal for a new major in African-American studies that had been extensively reviewed and approved by the relevant disciplines.[15] Another, more far-reaching example involved the decision of the California Board of Regents to end affirmative action in university admissions, hiring, and contracts. That decision, which was overwhelmingly opposed by faculty and administrators, appeared to be related more to the governor's political ambitions than to any well-informed assessment of the performance of affirmative action policies.[16] Many of the academic freedom controversies discussed in Chapter 5 have involved efforts to curb faculty speech that trustees find objectionable on ideological grounds.

In some cases, the problem is not trustees' overly intrusive or politicized intervention in academic affairs but their unduly passive roles in institutional oversight. A lack of time, expertise, and independent sources of information can keep board members from engaging with difficult issues. In other cases, administrators are reluctant to bring those issues to trustees because it would complicate the decision-making process. Boards dominated by alumni are sometimes too steeped in tradition to see the need for reforms, and members' friendships with presidents, or even each other, can compromise independent judgment. A lack of clear policies and an unwillingness to hold unprepared or renegade colleagues accountable can compound the problems.[17] Particularly in private institutions, trustees may be selected and socialized to assume the role of golden geese; they are expected to raise money and help manage finances, not to ask hard questions and meddle in internal governance.[18] The result, as board members often testify, is a substantial waste of energy on largely pointless show-and-tell sessions, in which they rubber-stamp decisions made elsewhere or get gussied-up accounts of programs that are exemplary in all respects except for a shameful shortage of resources. As a former member of the governing board of Yale, I passed many hours on the building and grounds committee, reviewing the state of university plumbing and golf course embellishments. I would be hard pressed to identify a single useful contribution that I made on those issues. Such a misallocation of time creates a self-perpetuating cycle of inadequate oversight. When a governing board is not invited to assume a role in significant institutional decisions, its members do not invest the effort that would be required to play that role effectively.

This is a lost opportunity. Trustees can supply useful pressure on issues such as the quality of teaching, which too often get insufficient attention from faculty and top administrators.[19] Although boards are rightly cautioned about not interfering with day-to-day decisions, they can help ensure that those decisions take greater account of core values. The challenge is to create more constructive channels for trustees' time and talents.

Presidents

President Robbins was so well adjusted to his environment that sometimes you could not tell which was the environment and which was President Robbins. . . . President Robbins crooned his speeches. His voice not only took you into his confidence, it laid a fire for you and put out your slippers by it and then went into the other room to get into something more comfortable. . . . [T]hat voice did not sell itself to the highest bidder, it just gave itself away to everyone.

Randall Jarrell, *Pictures from an Institution*[20]

The role of university president has changed dramatically over the past two centuries. Prior to the Civil War, over 90 percent of college presidents were clergy, and their primary responsibility was to set the right moral tone.[21] As American society became more secular, and institutions of higher learning became larger and more complex, the job description evolved accordingly. Presidents needed to bridge the worlds of action and academy; they needed the confidence not only of faculty, parents, and students but also of donors and funders. The role did not entirely lose its moral dimensions. The letters of nineteenth- and early twentieth-century university presidents of Brown and Michigan reveal representative concerns: students were keeping "spirituous liquors" in the dorms and engaging in "libertine" activities that caused the "ruin" of female classmates.[22] However, presidents were also increasingly responsible for the practical minutiae of institutional operations. In the absence of adequate administrative support, the job included much of what Princeton president Woodrow Wilson referred to as the "trifles" that "made or marred" their tenure.[23] Wilson personally ordered lab supplies; Brown's president gave advice on Venetian blinds and classroom chairs; Chicago's law school dean polished floors.[24]

As institutions grew in size and aspirations these functions fell to staff, and presidents increasingly focused on financial management and development. The tendency of successful leaders to take some poetic license when courting donors did not go unchallenged. Upton Sinclair was particularly scathing; his 1920s critique of higher education portrayed the university president as the "most variegated prevaricator that has yet appeared in the civilized world."[25] The general public was more charitable, perhaps in part because prominent presidents often used their platform not only to embellish their own institutions but also to speak responsibly on important social issues.[26] According to a 1966 opinion poll, slightly over 60 percent of Americans reported a great deal of confidence in academic administrators.[27]

Over the next several decades, further increases in the scale, complexity, and competitiveness of academic institutions brought further challenges for their presidents. As Derek Bok has noted, one central irony is that these leaders are typically drawn from the faculty, but have "less and less time to give to the intellectual agenda they were chosen to pursue."[28] About 85 percent of presidents come from inside academia.[29] Yet in a telling survey by the American Council on Education, academic projects ranked last on a list of six activities that consumed most presidential time, lagging well behind work related to fundraising, planning, budgets, and personnel.[30] So too, in a 2005 poll, financial issues were at the top of twenty-nine concerns, and fundraising was the most common daily activity.[31]

The view from the top of academic hierarchies is less exalted than many imagine. Control over key academic decisions lies elsewhere, which may leave the university's leader often feeling like "the man with the pail and broom."[32] Although many presidents complain about how much of their day is taken up with trivial or ceremonial tasks, this allocation of effort may reflect a deeper problem with their role. According to one of the most in-depth studies of American college presidents, their schedules are often filled with minor functions because at least these involve something that can be accomplished rather than bold academic initiatives that cannot.[33]

The financial challenges of the job have also intensified, leaving leaders with less time even to speak out on educational reforms, let alone achieve them.[34] A recent erosion in governmental support and rapid escalation of costs have increased the importance of fundraising. As a former president of Yale, A. Bartlett Giamatti, put it, a president spends much of his day as a "song-and-dance man slipping brightly through the paces of beggars' pantomime."[35] Efforts to manage fiscal difficulties through sharp tuition hikes, program cuts, and related strategies can be highly unpopular, and many presidents lack the power base to secure necessary but painful adjustments.[36] The results have taken a toll in public confidence. Recent surveys find that only about a third of Americans report high confidence in college and university leaders.[37]

The job has other challenges as well. Many presidents find themselves serving as "juggler in chief," constantly struggling to accommodate diverse groups with an ever expanding collection of competing interests.[38] Faculty, students, staff, alumni, donors, and politicians all have agendas that may push in different directions. Except at the most general level, there may be no consensus about objectives or priorities, and the key participants in decision making are a changing group. This can be a setup for "organized anarchy" and policy paralysis.[39] Moreover, many of the forces that most directly affect performance, such as reputation and resources, are ones that presidents often can affect only at the margins. Many leaders lack experience or expertise in key aspects of the job: only a minority of surveyed presidents feel very well prepared for the position.[40] Ironically enough, heads of research universities, who face the most complex challenges, are the least likely to receive formal training.[41] According to the president of the American Association of Governing Boards of Universities and Colleges, a major weakness of higher education is its "failure to grow . . . potential leadership from within. . . . We do a terrible job of preparing presidents to be president."[42]

Despite these challenges, managing complex educational institutions holds many rewards, both financial and psychological. The job continues to attract highly talented and dedicated individuals, and almost all report that they would take it again if given the choice.[43] A dramatic rise in perks and pay scales also provides some compensation for the increased challenges and constraints. At some universities, the annual packages have topped $1 million, and the rate of growth for presidential salaries has far outpaced the rate for faculty.[44] But with this escalating compensation come escalating expectations, and the constraints of the job are often poorly understood by many campus constituencies. Their expectation, as former Georgetown president Father Timothy Healy reportedly described it, is that presidents' accomplishments should match those of "God on a good day."

Faculty

The inmates are running the institution.
Donald Kennedy[45]

The faculty's role in governance has also changed substantially over the past century. The evolution of the tenure system, together with principles of academic freedom, has given senior professors a substantial measure of power and the job security to exercise it. On most issues of curricula, research, appointments, and promotions, tenured faculty are in control. But quips suggesting that they run the institution take considerable poetic license. To the contrary, most academics lack the interest, expertise, or opportunity to control crucial dimensions of educational policy.

The first problem is faculty disengagement. "Administrativia" is precisely what many academics choose the ivory tower to avoid. By taste and temperament, they prefer the life of the mind, and the less time spent on its worldly underpinnings the better. Other professors, while interested in broad questions of educational policy, lack the inclination, time, and background to master the details that drive responsible decision making. Many faculty members who care deeply about resource priorities that affect their own work lives also want to avoid the byzantine budgetary underbrush of financial planning. Even when well informed, some academics are more inclined to wallow in the complexities of an issue than to accept imperfect but necessary compromises.[46]

A related problem is that faculty governance structures are not well designed to provide a representative, informed view on most administrative issues. Particularly in large research universities, the faculty's collective voice is a senate, but the vast majority of professors neither participate in its elections nor attend its meetings.[47] Even in smaller institutions, professors tend to be far more insistent on the right to participate in decision-making processes than on actually exercising that right.[48] One reason is that these senates seldom have power over the issues that most concern the faculty, such as salaries, workload, space, staff support, and selection of presidents and top officials.

So too, the balkanized structure of departmental decision making often makes it difficult to obtain consensus on competing institutional priorities. On these matters, academics are understandably territorial and inevitably self-interested. Whatever their shared concern for the university's welfare, it is often trumped by their more direct stake in the status of their own department, discipline, or school.[49] By contrast, on matters where professors *are* disinterested, they may also be incompetent. Researchers from the Independent Institute describe one "classic example of faculty democracy run amok": reliance on centralized committees to distribute supplemental research funds. "Economists and historians sit in judgment on the relative merits of proposals from faculty in pediatric nursing [and] chemistry," and no members of the committee may have expertise on the subjects it is assessing.[50]

That is not to discount the important role that faculty decision-making bodies sometimes play, even on issues over which they have no direct control. In extreme circumstances, a "no confidence" vote by faculty can pave the way to presidential resignation. The highly publicized revolt by Harvard professors against Larry Summers is a case in point.[51] In more common situations, the faculty can play a significant function in holding administrators publicly accountable for their performance, and requiring credible justifications for particular decisions. For example, faculty senates have helped make progress on diversity and gender equity issues by institutionalizing annual reporting requirements; many central administrations are expected to provide data on matters such as hiring, promotion, retention, and pay equity. The concerns triggered by these reports have in turn prompted further initiatives on issues such as search processes and work-family policies, and the result has been substantial improvements for women and minorities.[52] Yet this oversight function also has obvious limitations; it cannot of itself alter educational policy. If faculty members want influence over more of the decisions that shape their professional lives, they need to invest greater effort through administrative positions, committee work, and related service responsibilities.

ACADEMICS AS ADMINISTRATORS

The Rationale for Combining Roles

To understand the role of academics as administrators, it is necessary first to understand why institutions and individuals choose to combine these roles. Why does higher education rely so heavily for managerial work on faculty members who are not trained for that task? And why do teachers and scholars who prize the intellectual life take jobs that allow so little scope for its pursuit?

Universities' reasons are similar to those that explain their selection of academics as presidents. Most individuals prefer the devil they know, and faculty members who do the central work of the institution want leaders who share their background and concerns. Other status and pragmatic considerations may also be at work. Neither advanced degrees in educational administration nor leadership training programs have carried much cachet in the academy.[53] Deans, departmental chairs, program directors, and other top administrators frequently come to their positions with little formal preparation or managerial experience. Surveys of over two thousand academic leaders find that fewer than 10 percent have leadership development programs in their institutions.[54] Much of the training that is available focuses on campus policies and procedures, not core competencies. Universities do little to provide the kind of preparation in managerial skills that has been effective in other employment contexts.[55] Yet the qualities most conducive to academic success, such as intellectual independence and subject matter expertise, are not the ones essential for administrative effectiveness, such as collaboration, conflict resolution, self-awareness, and interpersonal sensitivity.

Faculty who take on significant administrative responsibility generally assume that they can pick up whatever skills they need on the job. That assumption may reflect unwarranted optimism. My own experience is all too typical. When I took my first half-time administrative position as the director of a small research institute, I had no prior managerial experience or training, and no sense that this might be a major problem. The system persists because most academics, myself included, seem to muddle through without inflicting major damage. But few experts believe that this managerial model makes sense. Modest investments in educating administrators might yield at least modest gains for universities.

A further reason that higher education relies so heavily on faculty for administrative positions is practical. It offers a face-saving alternative for academics who have at least temporarily, and sometimes permanently, exhausted their scholarly and teaching interests.[56] In some instances, these are individuals who have failed to meet tenure standards or who are in fields without tenure openings. In other cases, they are scholars who have run out of research ideas or classroom enthusiasm and are looking for new challenges. Whatever the situation, administration has obvious advantages. It can spare the institution an unpleasant tenure battle, the loss of a valued colleague, or the waste of a faculty position on someone who is no longer productively engaged in teaching or scholarship.

Individual faculty, for their part, sometimes choose administration for the same reasons, but there are many other motivations as well. One of the most obvious, although least publicly acceptable, is the desire for status and influence. At least in the outside world, administrative titles carry more prestige than do faculty positions. Of course, as Randall Jarrell noted in *Pictures from an Institution*, this honor is in some sense paradoxical: "Each member of the [English] Department did something that seemed to the world impractical at best, idiotic at worst; to be in charge of the whole idiocy and impracticality seemed impractical and idiotic to no one."[57] So too, administration can be a way of moving out as well as up. For some professors, serving a few years as a dean or department head at better universities than would have hired them as scholars is a way of eventually sidling into that once elusive faculty position.[58]

For other academics, a leadership position is its own reward. That point emerges in C. P. Snow's fictional account of the bitter struggle among candidates for Master of a Cambridge college. Jago, one of the contenders, is observed by his colleagues prematurely enjoying his expected victory: "He trod on the grass as though he were feeling: '*my* grass'. He trod on the path, and then strayed, for the love of it, on the cobbles; '*my* path, *my* cobbles'. He stood for a long moment in the middle of the court and gazed round him in exaltation: '*my* college'."[59] Administrative positions offer challenge, change, and at least the illusion of influence.[60] Hazard Adams recalls that he "ascended the academic ladder, each time charmed with the prospect of at last getting *something* done."[61] Compared with teaching and scholarship, administration offers the satisfaction of more immediate, tangible accomplishments. Instead of just writing about the world, academics can affect at least a small corner of it, and hope to leave the institution slightly stronger than they found it. Many want to build or breath new life into a department, program, center, or other scholarly community. Administration offers them a chance to leave a legacy and contribute to their profession and their institution.

The structure and interpersonal dimensions of such efforts may also hold appeal. Most academic work is done in isolation and has no clear boundaries. Research, writing, and preparing for class are largely individual pursuits, and more time could always be spent on any of them. For some faculty, the solitary confinement and infinitely expansive workdays become tedious. Administration can provide a welcome diversion, a chance for teamwork and collegial interaction around finite, shared goals. Less benign forms of satisfaction can come from the simple exercise of power. Academic novelists delight in parodying this seamy underside of academic administrative life; their campuses are littered with petty tyrants, mired in minutiae, who stand ever ready to expand their fiefdoms, avenge some slight, or move up the pecking order. Robert Grudin's *Book: A Novel* portrays the quintessential academic despot, bent on retribution against colleagues who had once spurned his advances, ridiculed a pet proposal, and outmaneuvered him on an appointments issue.[62] John Gardiner's *Mickelsson's Ghosts* offers a more pathetic portrait of a professor who, after thirty years of peddling poetry to uninterested undergraduates, saved his true passion for "parking regulations and the careless policing of the faculty cafeteria."[63]

In the real world, of course, there is more camouflage for this aspect of administrative life. Few academics want to admit a desire for status and influence. Some are reluctant to acknowledge even wanting an administrative position. Their "jockeying must be done discreetly, so that . . . greatness may be thrust upon them."[64] Others genuinely do feel drafted; nearly twice as many department chairs report serving because they are conscripted by deans or colleagues than because they affirmatively want the position.[65] For many part-time or intermittent administrators, peer pressure, coupled with additional income or release time, is the primary motivating factor.[66] But any candid campus profile will reveal at least a sprinkling of those with long-closeted ambitions; faculty members who never managed to become student council president finally get their chance to run something.

In some cases, the stint in administration lives up to expectations for both the individual and the institution. Many of these academics cycle in and out of leadership positions for the remainder of their careers, to everyone's benefit. Others have a less happy experience, and "retreat into faculty ranks at the first graceful opportunity, with vows never to let *that* happen again."[67] The problem is that some of those who leave have precisely the qualities that institutions need in administrative roles: vision, integrity, competence, and interpersonal skills.[68] And some of those who stay are short on those qualities, but lack good alternative career options. Neither aspect of the problem is readily solved, but at least some administrative roles could be restructured to become more appealing to talented professors and more effective for their institutions.

The Administrative Role

One unfortunate irony is that the very features of administration that appeal to academics in principle turn out to have substantial downsides in practice. The satisfaction of accomplishing something tangible is clouded by the frequent lack of control over what exactly that something is and the tedium of actually achieving it. So too, the interpersonal rewards of administration can be compromised by the kinds of interaction required. Administrators often learn more about their colleagues than they would like to know.

"It's Lowly at the Top," proclaimed the title of a widely circulated *Washington Post* column on academic administration.[69] There are endless papers to be pushed, formalities to be satisfied, and mind-numbing meetings to be endured. Compared with faculty positions, administrative jobs offer far less flexibility in schedules: face time in the office is generally required.[70] Many who take these jobs with ambitious agendas of institutional reform find themselves instead mired in the mundane; coping with storage, secretarial, and scheduling woes, or filling out accreditation and appointment forms.[71] As one president put it, those who run large universities spend "most of [their] time with small problems."[72]

Of course, a similar point could be made about many managerial positions. But academia also presents some particular pathologies that reflect its distinctive character: diffusion of authority, chronic resource shortages, attachment to tradition, insistence on consultation, and tolerance for inefficiency and inertia. Because academic institutions seldom face the dire consequences that can follow from poor management in the for-profit sector, efficiency may not assume a high enough priority.[73]

The problem is compounded by the petty or parochial interests that some constituencies bring to the table. Clark Kerr, former University of

California chancellor, famously observed that the faculty's preoccupation was always parking.[74] Other administrators have similarly found that an issue such as a poorly performing athletic team, the denial of admission to a powerful donor's child, or even a building design with all-male gargoyles can easily occupy time out of all proportion to its institutional importance. This misallocation of effort can prove especially frustrating to academics who have been accustomed to controlling their own schedules and focusing on matters that they find intellectually challenging and important. Hostage to a less elevated agenda, the academic leader can readily become, in Kerr's phrase, "a galley slave on his own ship."[75]

Not only do administrators lack control over much of their working day, they are often blamed for problems not of their own making. Particularly during times of revenue shortfall, academic leaders are the bearers of unhappy tidings, and a time-honored response is to shoot the messenger. Although virtually no institution can afford preeminence in all fields, a candid acknowledgment of that fact and a rational plan for selective excellence are seldom well received.[76] The greater their financial responsibility, the more likely administrators are to make some constituency unhappy no matter what they decide or how much process they throw at the decision. Those who take a strong stand are often accused of "usurping faculty power"; those who fail to do so are labeled "indecisive or unprincipled."[77]

Administration also requires dealing with the unbecoming side of human nature that it exposes. In *The University: An Owner's Manual*, Henry Rosovsky described a typical day in his life as Harvard's former dean of arts and sciences, much of it dominated by whiny or self-seeking colleagues.[78] The morning began with a professor miffed by his seemingly paltry annual raise, which he had miscalculated due to ignorance about his previous salary. Next came a department chair who hijacked the meeting's agenda to air "perpetual grievances: inadequate office space, too few secretaries, not enough concern for his discipline."[79] Rosovsky, for his part, responded with a similarly perpetual stoicism, a state in which "MEGO, mine eyes glaze over." His next encounter offered a less conventional variation on an equally self-interested theme: a senior colleague wished to be relieved of all teaching obligations because he found students "inauthentic." Then came a "frank exchange of views" with students aggrieved by a scheduling issue. Their unreasonable intransigence prompted Rosovsky's observations that undergraduates, however impressive in other contexts, "as politicians . . . grow up much too fast: verbose, self-righteous, self-important."[80]

These traits were, however, also on display by faculty in two final meetings of the day, one with the academic senate and another with a professor who was being wooed from another institution. The target of the courtship ritual revealed a particularly unflattering mix of arrogance and avarice. In a dean's role, Rosovsky wryly concluded, it was "hard to see faculty or students at their best since nearly everybody wants something."[81] Dealing with unpleasant colleagues and unreasonable demands is part of the job description.

If administrators do not generally view faculty in their finest hour, the feeling may be mutual, and over time, both trust and friendship can be casualties. Professors talk about colleagues who have "gone over to the dark side"; the phrase captures an undercurrent of frustration that may be felt by occupants of both roles.[82] Faculty members often feel thwarted by bureaucratic inertia or threatened by proposals that affect their status, resources, and control.[83] Administrators feel stymied by their former colleagues' resistance to reform and their unwillingness to rise above self-interest on matters of broad institutional concern. Studies of campus governance find that each group sees the other as the primary obstacle to necessary change.[84] Mistrust can be exacerbated by the difficulties of maintaining close relationships between "us" and "them." Faculty do not want to be seen as toadying or currying favor with emigres from their former ranks. Nor do administrators want to be seen as playing favorites. As a consequence, both sides can lose touch with each others' concerns, which makes effective shared governance more difficult.

An obvious response to this problem is to develop adequate informal channels of communication and effective formal structures for joint decision making. Inviting small groups of faculty to meet with senior university officials and trustees is one approach; another is to rely on recommendations from committees and faculty meetings.

Committees

Committee: A group of people who individually can do nothing but together can decide that nothing can be done.

Alternative: A group of the unfit, appointed by the unwilling, to do the unnecessary.[85]

Higher education's reflexive response to potentially divisive issues is to drown them in deliberation. Academia is awash in committees, subcommittees, commissions, consortia, cabinets, panels, advisory boards, task forces, working groups, and various next of kin. The principle underlying this delegation of authority is sensible, but the process can be anything but.

In theory, the committee structure is an efficient way of enabling the faculty's informed participation in the decisions that shape its institutional identity. And for many academics, at least some committee assignments may offer the same rewards as administrative positions without the same demands: a change of pace; a chance for collegial interaction; and an opportunity to gain recognition, exercise power, and leave an institutional imprint.[86] University policies generally acknowledge the value of faculty service and give it equal billing with teaching and scholarship. In practice, however, committee work is often regarded as unimportant drudgery. Rarely do surveyed professors mention service as one of the primary rewards or motivations for an academic career. And rarely do institutions view it as significant in the decisions that matter most: appointments, promotion, tenure, and compensation.[87]

There are, to be sure, some sanctions for egregious shirking, at least for untenured professors or for those who may eventually want an administrative position. Time is usually academics' most precious commodity, and they resent colleagues who noticeably duck their fair share of service. But as with other forms of "good citizenship," peer pressure usually matters less than internal motivations. Professors who want to preserve their workdays for more personally rewarding and rewarded pursuits can develop ample avoidance strategies. The most common is learned incompetence. Academics who acquire reputations as unavailable, undependable, unprepared, or uncivil rarely get assignments that require any heavy lifting. Untenured faculty are often advised against squandering time on demanding committees that others have sufficient seniority to shirk, especially on sensitive topics. An assignment to "explore the role of athletes in admissions" or to "look into" faculty compensation should be avoided at all costs; far better to jockey for a position on the committee that oversees campus landscaping or replaces an archivist.[88]

The result is generally that a small proportion of faculty members perform the vast majority of service. Women and minorities are disproportionate among them.[89] For commendable reasons, institutions want diversity of backgrounds on any important decision-making body. But in many fields, a shortage of diversity among those eligible to serve leaves women and minorities deluged with service obligations. These groups find it particularly difficult to evade the draft because they lack ready replacements and are sympathetic to the argument that decision-making bodies should not be all-white or all-male. But no good deed goes unpunished, as suggested by the recent experience of two African-American female professors, who each landed on eighteen committees at their respective universities.[90] When such burdens are coupled with the disproportionate advising and mentoring obligations that fall to underrepresented groups, the price is often paid in scholarly productivity. Yet academic institutions seldom adjust teaching and research expectations for those who provide exceptional service.

Of course, not all administrative burdens are created equal. One widespread pattern is a small cadre of "good citizens" tend to land on burdensome standing committees with frequent meetings and elastic agendas, which expand to fill the time available.[91] Particularly irritating are committee assignments that are largely exercises in symbolic politics. Some are intended as such by the administration; they serve as window dressing to diffuse responsibility, to legitimate decisions that will ultimately be made elsewhere, or to placate an important constituency that wants Something To Be Done. But the something will be predictably pointless if the committee's membership is stacked, or it lacks sufficient information, staff support, or leverage. The more time-consuming the charade, the more intense the irritation. Faculty who invest long hours on curricular and strategic planning, or on advisory search committees, are likely to feel especially frustrated if their recommendations carry no real weight.[92] Yet as former University of Illinois provost Stanley Fish has noted, many planning exercises seem structured to ensure their irrelevance; they project so far into the future that they are almost certain to be "derailed by contingencies no one foresaw."[93]

In other cases, however, the fault lies not with the administrative assignment but with faculty members who divert its agenda and treat it as a bully pulpit for other ends. The larger the group, the greater the opportunities for posturing or paralysis. A common quip is that committees are most effective when they have three members, two of whom are absent. Gerald Warner Brace's novel *The Department* offers an all too realistic parody of a dysfunctional academic committee. It has a relatively minor assignment: recommending whether all department majors should be required to take a course in bibliographic methods.[94] Members insufficiently inspired by that question quickly manage to transform it into a broader debate about the scope and meaning of intellectual freedom. That, in turn, invites wandering but spirited disputes punctuated by references to Socrates, Rousseau, Whitehead, Castro, Soviet Russia, and Attila the Hun. Having exhausted their time on this broader issue, committee members are finally forced to make some hasty, ill-considered judgment on the matter at hand. The committee's recommendation would then go before the full department, "where, of course, the entire debate will be repeated, with suitable references to . . . Whitehead, Rousseau, Socrates, and probably others."[95] As that example suggests, these pathologies are by no means unique to committees. They can arise in any faculty meeting, and can involve a form of political infighting that is legendary for its vacuity.

FACULTY MEETINGS

In *Claw Your Way to the Top*, columnist Dave Barry divided meetings into two categories: those for which there is some alleged purpose, and those for which there is not. The second category is more common in higher education than is openly admitted. A partial explanation is the one that Barry offers for the vast majority of workplace meetings. They are held for "basically the same reason Arbor Day is observed, namely tradition."[96] John Kenneth Galbraith, a veteran of Harvard academic politics, identifies another reason: meetings are indispensable when you don't want to do anything else.[97] In either case, these gatherings often operate on a principle similar to "show and tell" in nursery school; the main difference, according to Barry, is that "in nursery school the kids actually have something new to say."[98]

Among adults, such rituals often serve to let participants feel involved and informed without the risk that they will have any significant consequences. Meetings of faculty or governing boards that focus on program review sometimes take this form. A common pattern is for featured speakers to follow the basic script that Barry describes: they explain that they and their department are working on whatever it is that they are supposed to be working on. When, as is often the case, other participants have no interest in the subject and no obvious need to acquire one, this can be a mindless misallocation of time. After all, as Barry points out, people generally are doing what they are supposed to be doing, or if they aren't, they *claim* that they are.

Technologies such as PowerPoint, which in theory are designed to make these presentations more bearable, can in practice have the converse effect. Not only do they open opportunities for mechanical meltdowns, they frequently encourage embellishments well beyond what the occasion requires. Fish offers a representative example:

> Someone from a corner of the university you scarcely knew existed arrives armed with overheads, transparencies, and (now) PowerPoints and proceeds . . . [in] agonizing slow motion [detail] to explain how the telephone system works (or is supposed to work) or how purchases are to be transacted and reported. . . . [This is followed by] formulaic expressions of thanks and gratitude; everyone declares an intention to visit the office of the presenter in order to learn more while vowing silently never to think about these matters again.[99]

Speakers who have invested the time in preparing such presentations are typically determined to get through them, even if the time available is too short and the audience is verging on mutiny.

In higher education, however, the vast majority of meetings do have some official purpose beyond show and tell, although it may sometimes be eclipsed by what participants would like the purpose to be. Whatever their stated function, many faculty gatherings have an unstated function analogous to the animal kingdom's plumage display. Those who choose an academic career tend to consider themselves exceptionally intelligent, and, like one of the characters in Edith Wharton's *Hudson River Bracketed*, many "can't rest until the milkman knows it."[100] Any occasion with a captive audience can become an irresistible forum for faculty members to remind each other just how smart they really are. Even appointments and promotion meetings can have this self-serving subtext; the candidate's work may become a launching pad for professors to showcase their own expertise or the importance of their own field. With a little ingenuity, many other topics can serve a similar purpose, and faculty meetings are famous for veering off into unrelated self-promotion and pontification, leaving the official agenda stranded by the wayside. These occasions fit the description that writer Mignon McLaughlin offered for meetings generally: "No one really listens to anyone else, and if you try it for a while, you see why."[101]

POLITICS

The challenges of academic administration are compounded by the faculty's well-documented tendency to turn minor issues of policy into major issues of principle. In addition to the familiar standbys of academic freedom, intellectual integrity, and tradition, there is a range of versatile possibilities famously satirized by F. M. Cornfield in his 1908 *Microcosmographia Academica*. They include the "*Principle of the Dangerous Precedent*," the "*Principle of Unripe Time*," and, in a pinch, the "*Principle of Punctuation and Precision*"; improper syntax can set "the whole pack . . . off, full cry, especially if they had a literary training."[102] As Cornfield noted, these and related principles can be invoked at such length that sooner or later their advocates will prevail, simply so that other colleagues can avoid listening another minute.

As a consequence, faculty meetings can drag on out of all proportion to the importance of the topic. A well-known adage usually ascribed to the late William Sayre of Columbia is that "academic politics are so bitter because so little is at stake."[103] Participants can become deeply invested in minor decisions that they can control as stand-ins for the truly significant issues that they cannot. Issues such as appointments and curriculum can also implicate status and identity; if contributions to their field are devalued, professors often feel that their own achievements are in question.

Moreover, as those who have experienced both academic and national politics point out, some of the civilizing constraints of democratic processes are missing in the ivory tower. The former head of the Federal Food and Drug Agency and Stanford president Donald Kennedy has observed that "[i]n government, people know how to disagree gracefully, and you never scorch the earth because you know that today's opponent is someone with whom you may have to make common agreement tomorrow."[104] In academia, some faculty members feel less pressure to get along to go along; they can nurse grudges in perpetuity with few professional repercussions. The protections of tenure and traditions of academic freedom make it difficult to sanction uncivil behavior unless it reaches egregious levels.[105] And some professors seem to relish the opportunity for confrontation, in what Emily Toth's Ms. Mentor views "zoologically as ground-pawing, antler-crashing, grown-up versions of 'Whose is Bigger.'"[106]

These squabbles carry a cost that extends beyond the individuals most directly involved. Not only do they divert attention from the substantive matters at issue, they also model inappropriate conduct to junior faculty and students and create divisive working conditions.[107] The more colleagues who are drawn into the fray, the more dysfunctional the atmosphere becomes. That in turn poses difficulties in recruitment and retention, and increases the risks of politicizing curricular, promotion, and hiring decisions.

STRATEGIES FOR CHANGE

Many of the administrative challenges facing higher education are deeply embedded in academic culture, traditions, and governance structures. Few are likely to be addressed by the simplistic prescriptions that abound in publications on academic leadership. Suggestions that boards should "pick presidents willing to make substantial changes and back them" or that top administrators should "grab hold of the system and shake it hard" leave all the important questions unaddressed.[108] What sorts of changes are required? What happens when the system shakes back? How do we enable trustees to play a more informed but not intrusive role? These questions are not readily resolved in the abstract, and research on governance structures is surprisingly thin and frequently inconclusive.[109] However, the studies available suggest at least some directions for reform.

Governance Boards

One cluster of initiatives should focus on improving the selection, education, and function of governing boards. Public institutions need merit appointments, not politicized elections or patronage selections. Several states have processes worthy of export. They rely on nonpartisan commissions to develop lists of qualified candidates from which final choices are made. So too, both private and public institutions need more trustees with diverse backgrounds and expertise in higher education, and academic associations should do more to prod colleges and universities to move in that direction. However selected, members of governing boards need more extensive orientation and explicit policies concerning their roles. They also should know more about the challenges facing higher education in general and their institution in particular.[110] That will require sources of information independent of the central administration.

If trustees can be more carefully chosen and trained, they can assume a more productive role in institutional governance. Their goal should be to provide thoughtful stewardship of long-term interests. To that end, their job should include fewer rubber-stamping functions and should build more effectively on their professional expertise. Tapping members' particular talents would better serve both the individuals and institutions involved.

Administrators

Related strategies should aim to increase the capabilities and reformulate the role of academic administrators. The most obvious need is a better system for selecting and preparing those with managerial responsibilities. Demonstrated administrative ability should be essential for more positions. Academics who lack managerial experience should receive more extensive training in core competencies. Preparation for leadership positions needs to focus less on bureaucratic policies and procedures and more on financial planning, development, conflict resolution, and related interpersonal skills.[111] Programs that use case histories, role simulations, external coaching, and formal mentoring should supplement a well-designed system of performance review; administrators need feedback from subordinates and peers as well as from supervisors.[112] Senior positions should be restructured to attract and retain those with the talent as well as taste for administration. That, in turn, may require greater rewards, recognition, staff support, and leadership development initiatives.

In many institutions, the president's position is in particular need of reform. The imbalance between formal responsibility and actual authority has often led to governance gridlock.[113] If, as most experts agree, the pace of change and financial challenges of higher education are likely to increase dramatically over the next half century, leaders must be in a better position to respond. Less of their time should be consumed by minor symbolic functions; more time must be available for proactive strategic initiatives. Broad consultation with stakeholders is essential, but self-interested constituencies should have fewer opportunities to block reform.

To build consensus for change, it may be helpful to engage in benchmarking. In essence, that entails identifying other institutions that have achieved desired goals, analyzing the processes that enabled their success, and adapting those processes to the local campus culture.[114] Universities, both individually and collectively, could also do more to facilitate information sharing and to develop leadership capabilities. Additional training, mentoring, and support programs within and across institutions could help presidents and senior administrators meet challenges for which many now feel ill-equipped.[115]

Faculty Governance

A final set of strategies should focus on improving faculty participation in academic governance. One possibility is to replace or supplement faculty senates. For example, universities could create faculty councils consisting of small but representative groups of respected professors who receive sufficient release time to play an informed role in administrative decision making. Members could be nominated by deans or department chairs, and elected by the faculty for staggered terms of several years. That body could make recommendations and decisions on academic affairs, and meet regularly with senior administrators and governing boards. Unlike the faculty senate in most institutions, council members could acquire the expertise necessary to address complex governance issues.[116]

Faculty committees and meetings may also need restructuring. Appropriate strategies will, of course, vary in light of particular institutional needs. But as a general matter, less would be more. Less faculty time should be squandered on informational, pro forma, or symbolic matters; it should be reserved for issues that would significantly benefit from collective deliberation.[117] Running meetings effectively is an acquired skill, and it should not be assumed that all academics have it. Faculty who play leadership roles also need more training in how to deal with difficult colleagues and divisive issues.

Service should also become a more rewarded as well as rewarding part of academic life. Those who make exceptional contributions should receive appropriate recognition: adequate release time, salary supplements, service awards, and related perquisites. That will require more systematic information on who actually does what. Reports by individual faculty, committee chairs, and senior administrators that detail service contributions would help to provide greater accountability.[118] Every faculty has its share of artful dodgers and worker bees, and performance reviews should take that into account.

More systematic research into governance strategies is equally necessary. Every unhappy institution may be unhappy in its own way, but some remedies are better than others and we know too little about their comparative effectiveness. To borrow Wallace Stevens's metaphor from "The Spanish Guitar": if we "cannot make the world quite round" we can at least "patch it as [we] can."

Chapter Five

THE PUBLIC INTELLECTUAL

Five centuries ago, at the University of Wittenburg, Martin Luther staked out a public intellectual role that has been both shunned and embraced by the generations of scholars who succeeded him. Higher education has always had some faculty who sought a voice in the world outside it, and others who worried about the corrosive effects of that involvement. The discussion that follows examines how best to enable academics to play a constructive role in public affairs and public policy. Attention also centers on the presentation of self in public settings, such as conferences, panels, and media events. These are not always occasions that bring out the best in professors. Although the pathologies are a frequent subject of parody, they also deserve more serious analysis. How the public sees our profession, and how we treat each other in public forums, should be matters of academic concern as well as caricature.

THE EVOLVING ROLE OF PUBLIC INTELLECTUALS

Traditionally, relatively few academics have met the conventional definition of a "public intellectual": someone who writes knowledgeably about ideas for a popular audience on matters of public concern.[1] Throughout the eighteenth, nineteenth, and early twentieth centuries, the most influential individuals who fit that definition generally did not hold university positions. Arnold, Bentham, Emerson, Freud, Huxley, Marx, Mencken, Mill, Orwell, Rousseau, Thoreau, Tocqueville, Shaw, Wollstonecraft, and Wilson are among the best-known examples. A number of factors accounted for most early academics' lack of public engagement. One was the classical orientation of the traditional liberal arts curriculum, and its infrequent attention to broad societal concerns.[2] Another obstacle was the exclusionary character of faculty appointments. Discrimination on the basis of sex, race, ethnicity, class, and religion made it difficult for many individuals who sought a public voice to do so from university positions.[3] Before principles of academic freedom were firmly established in the twentieth century, the intellectuals who did obtain such positions frequently feared for their job security if they spoke out on controversial issues. As subsequent discussion notes, well-publicized purges made clear the price of principle for those with unconventional views.[4] Until the increases in higher education and mass communication in the early twentieth century, faculty also lacked ready access to a substantial audience interested in cultural or social criticism.

So too, academic culture and reward structures traditionally offered insufficient support for the public intellectual role. Most professors saw little to be gained from writing for general audiences. As Chapter 2 noted, with increasing knowledge came increasing specialization, and corresponding tendencies toward more esoteric subjects, technical approaches, and arcane styles. Because scholarly reputation and advancement depended on peer review, professors wrote mainly for each other in forms and forums inaccessible to lay readers. Seldom did academics seek, and rarely did they find, a mass audience.[5] As Russell Jacoby observed in *The Last Intellectuals*, those who obtained faculty appointments generally "had no need to write in a public prose"; therefore "they did not, and finally they could not."[6]

But there were always exceptions. Although some, such as Thorstein Veblen, left a campus atmosphere that they found stifling, others traded on their positions to speak out on public issues.[7] During the latter half of the twentieth century, a variety of forces converged to encourage more academics to play a public role. One involved the expansion of higher education in the post–World War II era. Not only did this growth create new opportunities for faculty appointments, it also encouraged greater reliance on part-time and adjunct professors who kept a toehold outside the campus. The rise in progressive social movements during the 1960s and 1970s encouraged more academic engagement with social issues. It also brought new pressures for diversity in faculty hiring. The resulting influx of groups with personal experiences of injustice similarly fostered greater academic involvement with social concerns, both on campus and in the world outside it. The growth of independent policy institutes provided another berth for scholars who wanted direct influence on public opinion and public policy.[8] Media outlets for public intellectuals also expanded, in response both to the growing numbers of college-educated Americans and to the technological advances that launched cable news coverage and electronic communications. Rising costs and competition pushed more university presses to seek crossover books that would appeal to general audiences.

Moreover, as scholarship became increasingly specialized, the demand grew for experts who could translate academic publications into accessible prose. In earlier eras, intellectuals without advanced degrees could write insightfully on a broad range of subjects. For example, George Orwell published highly influential literary, political, and economic criticism without ever having attended a university.[9] A survey of leading American public intellectuals in the mid-1970s found that only about 40 percent were professors; the rest were editors, journalists, and freelance authors.[10] Today, commentators often categorize such "nonacademic intellectuals" as an "endangered species."[11] This, to be sure, is something of an exaggeration. America still produces a large group of influential social critics without scholarly credentials. Yet few individuals are able to sustain full-time careers as independent public intellectuals, while more academics have part-time opportunities to freelance in that role. Richard Posner, one of America's leading legal commentators, notes an unintended irony: "the market for public intellectuals is becoming dominated by academics at the same time that the growth of academic specialization has made it increasingly difficult for academics to fill the public-intellectual role."[12]

Public Needs and Academic Roles

The demand for knowledgeable, disinterested commentary on social issues has never been greater, but the efforts of professors to provide it bump up against a variety of structural constraints. Any democratic society depends on an informed public but faces obvious challenges in securing one. Americans depend primarily on the media for coverage of social issues, but this coverage is frequently spotty or skewed. Limitations of time, resources, and expertise, together with journalistic conventions of "balance," often work against adequate analysis.[13] In some instances, what passes for fairness is commentary by two extreme partisans on opposite poles of debate. Academics with more complicated, nuanced positions fall by the wayside.[14] A related problem is that equal representation of competing views does not necessarily yield equal insight. Much depends on the capacities and biases of the public intellectuals involved, as well as the ability of journalists to fill in the gaps or supply necessary correctives. Well-financed special interests can distort understanding through sophisticated public relations campaigns with misleading editorials, position papers, and advertisements.[15] Yet many reporters remain wedded to a stance of apparent balance in uncritically presenting such unbalanced views. The result, media experts note, is that public debate can be biased "not in spite of, but precisely because of, the professional journalism standards intended to prevent bias."[16]

A further obstacle to informed coverage is the need for publishers and the media to compete with a widening range of livelier rivals: talk radio, tabloid trash, docudramas, court TV, and polemical roundtables. As Dan Rather once observed, news programs were "putting more and more fuzz and wuzz on the air . . . so as to compete not with other news programs but with entertainment programs, including those posing as news programs."[17] This increasingly competitive media market has encouraged "lowest common denominator information"; anecdotes displace analysis, and factual content is frequently dumbed down and spruced up in ways that preempt informed debate.[18] The public intellectuals who are most successful in this market are not necessarily those with the most expertise, insight, or academically respectable standards. The media wants "snappy certitude," not complex, carefully qualified analysis.[19] Advice for aspiring pundits is that "vitriol sells."[20] "'J'accuse' should be your tone" is the kind of strategy agents offer to academics.[21] The press would rather cover quarrels than resolve them, and barbed harangues are more likely to get coverage than is nuanced discourse.

These journalistic preferences both deter and distort academic participation in public debate. Serious scholars frequently lack the time and taste for self-promotion that success in the media demands. Educating reporters can be a tedious and thankless enterprise. They call at inconvenient moments, need time-consuming explanations, garble quotes, or leave them on the cutting-room floor. Peddling op-eds can be equally frustrating. Few get published in major news outlets, and even those that are can have unappealing by-products. The perspectives that are most needed in the mainstream media are also those most likely to be vilified. Public intellectuals who convey "difficult truths" and challenge received dogmas usually discover that the public doesn't like it much, and that surprising numbers will take time out of their busy days to say so.[22] Scholars writing for public audiences on Islam or Arab concerns have found that it is now, in the "post-9/11 world, a full-contact sport."[23] One historian who recently managed to place an anti-Bush op-ed in the *Los Angeles Times* came to regret his good fortune after a torrent of blistering hate mail and phone calls. Many readers who found him an "arrogant, pompous, conceited turd" were not shy about letting him know it.[24] Those who were sympathetic generally didn't bother.

My own experience with *New York Times* op-eds has been similar. One involved my criticism of a "lawless exercise of law-enforcement prerogatives" under Attorney General John Ashcroft, which permitted surveillance without judicial authorization of confidential communications between accused terrorists and their lawyers.[25] To the readers who choked my inbox, this view aligned me with "scum of the earth," including the "vermin" in the legal profession who defended them.[26] This, it seemed was "exactly what one would expect from a leftist bleeding heart liberal tree hugger from California . . . the land of the fruits and nuts."[27] Another op-ed on a lighter topic was frustrating in other ways. After spending a conference with high-powered professional women hobbled by unnavigable stylish stilettos, I shot off a short polemic about shoe design as the last refuge of closet misogynists.[28] This contemporary analogue to Chinese footbinding was, I suggested, one of the small indignities that kept women back, in this case literally as well as figuratively. Once again my mailbox was flooded, although this time the correspondence included a lifetime supply of sensible shoe catalogues and helpful hints from podiatrists. What rankled were the self-righteous readers, who, after noting all the important issues facing women, chided me for wasting this editorial opportunity on such a trivial matter. These criticisms were all the more irritating in light of the *Times'* refusal to run my original version; editors had deleted my acknowledgment that in a society in which an estimated four million women annually are victims of domestic violence, and about twenty million live in poverty, the height of heels is not at the top of the feminist agenda. Moreover, my prior efforts to publish on those topics had not caught the *Times's* fancy; sexist stilettos were as close as I could get.

These examples are not meant to overstate the frustrations of fleeting notoriety. Most academics, myself included, appear more than willing to share those hardships. But when the odds of getting an op-ed placed in the national press are extremely remote, and the response is not all one might have wished, the effort begins to look less appealing.[29] The same is true for other forms of media exposure. Television is a particularly risky venture for amateurs. If my own limited experience is any guide, academics who are not seasoned performers can seldom count on looking good and sounding good on the same occasion. And even if they manage, there is still the risk of ending up on cutting-room floors. A typical opportunity arises at the last minute on a bad-hair day with no time to prepare. Then, despite a mad scramble to become presentable, the aspiring pundit gets one question on the order of "And so professor, in the fifteen seconds remaining, what does this case tell us about the meaning of justice?"[30]

The reward structure of higher education makes these appearances unattractive in other ways. Writing for a general audience does little to advance a scholarly reputation, and in some ways works against it. National news coverage arouses envy, and publication in less distinguished sources is regarded as faintly declasse. "Mere popularizer" is the epithet of choice. Faculty who remain above the fray often chide colleagues for "hogging the media" or oversimplifying complex ideas.[31] This common view came through with uncommon candor at a widely attended University of Chicago symposium on the public intellectual in the late 1990s. A member of the audience put an obvious question: If scholars would like more public attention, why were they writing in styles that prevented it? Why didn't they make clearer the "gist" of their views for nonexperts? The speaker who responded put it bluntly: "We are not in the 'gist' business."[32]

There are pragmatic as well as intellectual reasons why not. Popular writing will not build a tenure file or influence a field. And it takes time away from more pressing research, teaching, and administrative demands. Richard Posner's recent study of prominent academics found some empirical evidence for the trade-off. The frequency of references to these individuals in scholarly literature was negatively correlated to the frequency of references in the popular media.[33] Others have noted the same pattern. As sociologist Aaron Wildavsky observed, "the more [the public intellectual] talks, however, the less he has to say. He has been using up his intellectual capital, and if he does not watch out, his services will become more and more in demand as his thoughts are less and less worth having."[34]

The problem is compounded by the temptations for academic celebrities to pick topics on which they can pontificate without any serious scholarly effort. Bertrand Russell exemplified an extreme version of this tendency. A partial bibliography lists sixty-eight books and far more articles on themes ranging from "The Use of Lipstick" and "Choosing Cigars" to "The Manners of Tourists." If he was not much interested in a subject, Russell allowed others to publish over his name; his wife ghost-wrote an article for him in *Glamour* called "What to Do If You Fall in Love with a Married Man."[35] For contemporary intellectuals seeking the most exposure for the least effort, television is the medium of choice. As *New York Times* columnist David Brooks notes, it offers "all of the attention and buzz of intellectual activity with none of the actual work."[36]

Of course, opportunities in the leading mass media are readily available only to a small group of celebrities in the most newsworthy disciplines. For those lower on the academic pecking order, attracting popular attention is a difficult and often distasteful enterprise. It is also one for which scholars generally have no training. Most public intellectuals, Brooks notes, "learn career strategies the way fourth graders used to hear about sex—from the bad kids in the bathroom."[37] These strategies have everything to do with marketing and little to do with scholarship. With only slight irony, Brooks summarizes the conventional wisdom about launching a book that will reach a wide general audience. Of "obvious paramount" importance is not the quality or originality of the author's research but who will provide the jacket blurbs. Next among the important considerations are "the publishing house, the title, and the one phrase people will remember. . . ." Francis Fukuyama rode to fame on an essay titled "The End of History" in part because vast legions of commentators could easily shoot off reviews "pointing out that history had not ended."[38]

Yet the more that an aspiring scholar follows market-driven advice, the less of a scholar he or she is likely to become. French cultural critic Pierre Bourdieu describes the style that popular commentary encourages: "swiftly packaged products which intrepidly approach the biggest problems, hitting any moving target and refusing to bother with references, notes, bibliographies, and indexes."[39] As these scholarly conventions fall by the wayside, so too do the standards of accuracy and attribution that the conventions promote. Academics writing in nonacademic forums escape the accountability of peer review that their profession imposes in other contexts. Indeed, as Posner points out, professors' popular publications are not even subject to the correctives that journalism provides.[40] Mainstream media have a strong stake in maintaining a reputation for accurate and unbiased reporting, and they have multiple strategies to promote it, including retractions, letters to the editor, fact checkers, and ombudsmen. Those oversight mechanisms are often missing in the market for public intellectuals. In much popular writing, academics can take an intellectual holiday; they can indulge in armchair empiricism, undocumented claims, and ludicrously impractical policy proposals.[41] In commenting on the irresponsible punditry of British colleagues during World War II, George Orwell concluded that "only an intellectual could be so stupid."[42] Rarely are celebrity scholars called to account for their nonscholarly statements. And as subsequent discussion notes, even in those cases, the safeguards of academic freedom generally prevent serious professional consequences.

Jean Bethke Elshtain puts the problem bluntly: public intellectuals tend to "get more and more public and less and less intellectual."[43] The result is not only to devalue their own commentary but also to compromise the institutional reputation on which they are trading. As an international consortium on academic ethics observed, professors who assume a public voice "almost always allow the presumption that they speak with the authority of scientific and scholarly study. . . . This gives special force to the duty of the university teacher to respect the obligations which are entailed in the custodianship [of such] . . . knowledge."[44] Yet this is not a responsibility widely acknowledged, let alone consistently respected.

Nor do many academic commentators on social problems feel obligated to offer plausible responses. In the most comprehensive survey of motivations for public commentary, the objective that leading public intellectuals most often cited was to "create works which answer to the critical standards of intellectuals and colleagues whom [they valued] most"; fewer than a third cited a desire to provide solutions for social problems.[45] Even when academics do propose a remedy, they do not always believe it necessary to ground their recommendation in the realm of political possibility. According to Henry Kissinger, the role of public intellectuals is "putting forth their perception of what is right. Then let the politicians worry about what is possible."[46] Yet as other experts note, this is an "invitation to irrelevance." Such "Sunday sermons" are ones that "politicians, like everyone, are free to ignore."[47] In his critique of the American intellectual left, Columbia journalism professor Tod Gitlin noted that its purely oppositional stance has preempted development of a constructive response to the social injustices that left critics deplore. Although "resistance has its rewards," it often has led to a "self-righteous purity" and a self-indulgent "flight to theory" that undermines any hope to political influence.[48]

Yet other commentators are worried about the opposite problem: that "tenured radicals" are not radical enough. Traditionally, a distinctive feature of the public intellectual role has been an outsider's "detached attachment."[49] The most influential social commentators have been critical observers of, not participants in, conventional structures of wealth, status, and power. This stance can be difficult to maintain from secure university positions. America's academic celebrities are, as they themselves have some-times acknowledged, "insiders pretending to be outsiders."[50] According to some commentators, this tenured left has been coopted by its cozy relation-ship with the establishment, which has prevented fundamental critiques and alliances with subordinate groups.[51]

Of course, as subsequent discussion notes, the protections of academic freedom also foster one of the greatest contributions of public intellectuals: their ability to challenge conventional assumptions and entrenched power. Yet this role can be problematic in other ways. One value to which academ-ics aspire is disinterested objectivity: a willingness to pursue uncomfortable truths wherever they lead. The difficulty arises when they lead in directions inconsistent with the academic's own ideological commitments. The most effective public intellectuals tend to be forceful advocates. This, however, is not a role readily squared with scholarly standards. Judge Learned Hand summarized the dilemma: "No one can keep a mind always open to new evidence, always ready to change its conclusions, who has other allegiances or commitments. Upon the failure of this necessary detachment right judg-ment is most often wrecked; . . . it is the last habit to be acquired and the first to be lost. . . . You may not carry a sword beneath a scholar's gown. . . . You cannot raise the standard against oppression, or lead into the breach to relieve injustice, and still keep an open mind to every disconcerting fact or an open ear to the cold voice of doubt."[52]

Most contemporary public intellectuals would doubtless disagree. In a postmodern era steeped in skepticism about objective knowledge, the boundaries between academic and advocate look increasingly blurred. Ide-ological commitments inevitably influence the way that researchers frame questions and evaluate evidence. Yet the roles of public critic and disin-terested scholar do sometimes tug in different directions. The complexity and qualification that academic standards demand are beyond the atten-tion spans of most lay audiences. That does not, however, excuse professors who serve in public intellectual roles from all academic norms. As subse-quent discussion notes, those who speak with the credibility of scholars have a responsibility to exercise their public speech responsibly. Clearly, the academy could do more to promote accountability for nonacademic work. Posner proposes collecting it in electronic archives and encouraging critical responses; others have advocated peer-reviewed journals that would publish and critique such work.[53] At a minimum, the academy needs ways of making public intellectuals more self-critical about their role and more willing to hold each other accountable.

The Use and Abuse of Book Reviews

Another way of increasing accountability for public intellectual work is through book reviews in the popular press. Such reviews by academics are a recent phenomena, in part because the concept of independent commentaries is itself relatively recent. When book reviews first became common in the mid-nineteenth century, publishers generally paid for them directly or indirectly, either through covert salaries for reviewers or advertising revenue for the publication that ran their work. That system broke down after a celebrated incident of retaliation for an anonymous critic's assessment of Longfellow's *Hiawatha*. The reviewer labeled it "childish nonsense," and the publisher wrote an outraged letter withdrawing its advertising from the offending newspaper. The paper then printed the letter under the title "Attempt to Coerce the Press."[54] The scandal exposed and ultimately helped to deter the worst abuses, but it by no means eliminated bias. During the early twentieth century, not only publishers but sometimes even the most celebrated authors still attempted to coax favorable reviews from friends and editors; Thomas Mann, Marcel Proust, and the Bloomsbury group were well-known examples.[55]

Partly to avoid such influence, and partly to ensure a reliable supply of material at modest cost, many publications decided to hire their own stable of reviewers. These were often writers of no particular distinction or expertise in the subject matter that they were discussing. In his famous essay "Confessions of a Book Reviewer," George Orwell acerbically portrayed a typical member of this profession. Alternating between malnutrition and hangovers, the reviewer took on at least a hundred books a year, about which he had to "invent reactions." Most of these books dealt "with subjects of which he is so ignorant that he will have to read at least 50 pages if he is to avoid making some howler which will betray him not merely to author . . . , but even to the general reader." This "prolonged indiscriminate reviewing" produced largely "humbug." The author was "pouring his immortal soul down the drain, a pint at a time."[56]

In recent decades, greater reliance on academics has seemed a welcome alternative. In theory, everyone benefits from the involvement of independent experts who can afford to be selective in the publications they review. Readers get informed advice about what is worth reading and how to evaluate its contributions. Authors get insightful criticism and additional incentives to avoid embarrassing errors. Publishers get quality reviews that will expand their audience. And reviewers get exposure to new work and a forum for their own ideas.

In practice, however, the system breaks down at several key junctures. First, and most obviously, reviewers are not always disinterested. They generally need some reason to spend scarce time assessing someone else's work instead of focusing on their own. Of course, not all self-interested motives are equally problematic, at least in their effect on the quality of reviews. Some authors simply enjoy the power of passing judgment; others like the attention that comes from writing in mainstream publications. For many academics, the next best thing to getting their own book reviewed in forums such as the *New York Times* is a chance to play God with someone else's.

Other motives, however, threaten independent judgment. The most common are personal relationships. The academic world is built on reciprocity, and positive reviews can serve as favors for friends or for colleagues who may be in a position to do unto others what has been done unto them. Some commentators operate on the principle that if they can't say something nice, they won't say anything at all. The fear of retaliation is undoubtedly responsible for at least some of the puff pieces that pass for scholarly assessment.[57] Book editors' own interests can compound the problem; their friendships and substantive biases can lead to selection of someone likely to provide a glowing evaluation.

Other considerations push in similar directions. For example, many feminists, myself included, do not write negative reviews of feminist work in mainstream publications. Catfights within the sisterhood get disproportionate attention, and while the field is still struggling for public legitimacy, we would rather contribute to the solution not the problem. If we have time to spend on reviews, we would prefer to find works that put feminism's best foot forward. The downside of that position, of course, is that it preempts candid criticism by those best situated to provide it.

There are, however, countervailing incentives that keep the slide into sweetness in check, but that also pose fairness concerns. As with other media commentary, the public generally prefers nasty to nice, and some editors are famous for obliging.[58] Reviewers, for their part, have their own interests in delivering "snarks"—assessments that are gratuitously mean-spirited and employ "wit for wit's sake."[59] Reviews can also be a time-honored technique of retribution by those criticized or overlooked in the work at issue. Many academics undoubtedly follow the practice of a British critic in David Lodge's novel *Small World*. His first step in writing a review was to check the book's index for his own name. What he found determined what he said.[60] Reviews are also opportunities to settle scores for other slights, as well as outlets for unprovoked envy. Critics who cannot see why the book in question is getting so much more attention than their own may seize the occasion to expose the injustice. Finally, even well-intentioned reviewers may succumb to the temptation to discuss the book that they think *should* have been written, a strategy profoundly irritating to authors and readers who would have liked some attention to what actually *was* written.[61]

Some correctives for these problems are obvious in principle but hard to realize in practice. The system would plainly work better if, as commentators often suggest, editors and reviewers were held to higher ethical standards. Most obviously, editors should not select someone criticized by the book or known to be hostile to its author or approach. Nor should they choose one of the author's friends. The deputy editor of the *New York Times* book review section uses a simple rule of thumb to determine whether the relationship between the parties is too close. If the reviewer knows the names of the author's children, "It's not good."[62] Academics should not review a work when their impartiality might reasonably be questioned. That includes circumstances in which they are paid by an interested third party, such as a conservative foundation, for writing the review.[63] Reviewers also should disclose, both to editors and readers, any obvious source of bias.[64]

The difficulty, however, is how to enforce such standards in the face of strong competing incentives.

The most effective correctives would be greater self-restraint and reputational sanctions. Public criticism, including letters to editors from disinterested parties, might help reduce the most flagrant bias and unwarranted bile. Reviewers who have not themselves been on the receiving end of poisonous critiques would benefit from more mentoring. If empathy does not come naturally, a conscientious editor's role is to remind reviewers of the costs of gratuitously snide asides, not goad them to entertaining excess.

Authors and readers alike could also profit from reminders about the fallibilities of the review system. A celebrated example is the *New York Times'* cursory dismissal of Betty Friedan's *The Feminine Mystique*: "It is superficial to blame the 'culture' . . . as she does. . . . To paraphrase a famous line, 'The fault, Mrs. Friedan, is not in the culture, but in ourselves.'"[65] Few of Western Civilization's most revered novelists and poets have lacked for venomous critics: an anthology of "rotten reviews" includes such targets as Austin, Bacon, Beckett, Bellow, Bronte, Byron, Camus, Chaucer, Chekhov, Coleridge, Dickens, Dickenson, Donne, Dreiser, Eliot, Emerson, Faulkner, Fitzgerald, Flaubert, Forester. . . . [66] A still more extensive list could undoubtedly be collected of all the truly rotten work that has received fulsome praise. For those at risk of overreaction to critics' assessments, the best advice may be along the lines of that once given to Charlton Heston. When he noted that he had finally "learned to ignore the bad reviews," Laurence Olivier reportedly responded, "Fine, now learn to ignore the good ones."[67]

The Academic in Policy Arenas

Further lessons in humility are readily available to academics who seek more direct channels of social influence. Public intellectuals, both from inside and outside the academy, have long played an important role in American politics. That role has varied over time, but in some periods, such as the founding of the Republic, the Progressive Era, the New Deal, the Cold War, and the Great Society of the 1960s, they exercised particular influence over public policy.[68] In recent decades, a substantial number of academics have cycled in and out of government as full-time public officials, part-time consultants, and occasional advisers. The major universities have contributed some of the leading architects of foreign and domestic policy: Madeleine Albright, Henry Kissinger, Daniel Patrick Moynihan, Robert Reich, Condoleezza Rice, Donna Shalala, and George Schultz are obvious examples. Even more common are scholars who serve in mid-level positions for brief periods, or work with legislative and administrative bodies on particular issues.

Such involvement can have obvious benefits for all concerned. The government receives expertise well beyond what it can attract in career civil servants, along with the independence and fresh perspectives that academics playing only temporary or part-time roles can supply. The academy also benefits from the experience and reputation that their faculty acquire in the world outside it. As George Washington University president Stephen Trachtenberg has observed, having professors visibly advising government insiders can be a highly effective and inexpensive public relations strategy; it suggests that "to be an undergraduate here is to mingle with the great, and to be on the way up . . . to America's ruling class."[69] Individual faculty members benefit as well; they gain insights, status, contacts, and, at least occasionally, the satisfaction that comes from pushing policy in a constructive direction.

Yet these potential advantages too often go unrealized. Political theorists Charles Lindblom and David Cohen's classic study, *Usable Knowledge*, chronicled the mutual dissatisfaction that can arise on both sides when faculty enter the policy arena: professors are disappointed "because they are not listened to," and decision makers are disappointed "because they do not hear much they want to listen to."[70] The expectations, values, and priorities that professors bring to the policy world are often fundamentally at odds with what they find there. In government circles, a common question, usually rhetorical, is whether everyone is "on the same page." Academics who have temporarily joined these circles may be on the same page, but it is often in a different book.

Professors who seek policy roles generally have a mix of motives: intellectual curiosity, ambition, and a desire to do some good in the world. The first objective is more readily satisfied than the others, and much of the knowledge acquired is deeply disillusioning. Professors are not necessarily naive, but neither are they always prepared for precisely how politicized the political process can be, and how far it can stray from public interests. Academics hoping to promote social welfare can frequently be frustrated by the petty personal concerns and partisan agendas that stand in the way. Those steeped in the pursuit of knowledge also may be insufficiently sensitive to the limits of their usefulness in policy arenas: their data may not be definitive, uncontested, or able to resolve complex value trade-offs.[71] And academics who are hoping for power, status, and recognition can be discomfitted by the low esteem and inadequate influence that their advice commands among politicians.

Some three-quarters of a century ago, Theodore Roosevelt complained that "our more intellectual men often shrink from the raw coarseness and the eager struggle of political life as if they were women."[72] Commentators on contemporary trends have observed the same distaste, although they identify causes other than insufficient masculinity. What seems to drive today's professors from policy arenas is not simply "coarseness" but rather the corrosive influence of money, special interests, and personal agendas. Academics are, after all, emissaries from a world of ideas, in which reasons matter and principles are, at least in principle, paramount. By contrast, as columnist Maureen Dowd once noted, political culture is often dominated by "fake morality and real hypocrisy."[73]

In *Locked in the Cabinet*, former labor secretary Robert Reich explores the disconnect between his experience as a Harvard professor of public policy and his role as the Clinton Administration's Secretary of Labor trying to implement public policy. The first inkling of the culture shock came during coaching for his confirmation hearings, when he learned that "You have to respond to [Senators'] questions. You don't have to answer them. You *shouldn't* answer them. You're not *expected* to answer them." The correct response was a variation on the theme of "Senator, you know far more about this than I do, and I look forward to hearing your views in the years to come."[74] Former governor of California Jerry Brown gives much the same advice to the political novice; "a little vagueness goes a long way in this business."[75]

The dynamics that often drive government decisions are not the ones that academic institutions most value: disinterested analysis, factual accuracy, candid dialogue, and respect for competing views. Professors who enter the fray on issues such as welfare policy or tort reform often find that popular prejudices or corporate lobbying can easily muffle the voice of reason. To be an effective insider may require complicity in unprincipled compromise.[76] Some professors resign in protest; others retreat in relief when their leave of absence is up or their project expires.[77] Many end up in the state of resigned cynicism that philosopher Richard Rorty described in a widely circulated lament titled "Intellectuals in Politics": "acting as if [they] believed not only that democracy has not been working lately but that there is no longer any point in trying to make it work."[78]

Such attitudes are further reinforced by the disdain that academics often encounter among seasoned politicians. The long-standing anti-intellectual streak in American culture is readily apparent on Capitol Hill.[79] I encountered enough for a lifetime during my own brief stint as special counsel to the House of Representatives Judiciary Committee during the Clinton impeachment hearings. One of my tasks was to coordinate a series of hearings on the meaning of the impeachment clause in the United States Constitution. Committee staff and I had no trouble convincing the nation's leading legal historians and constitutional law scholars to testify. We had less success persuading some of the congressional committee members that it was worthwhile even to show up, let alone pay attention to what was being said. The committee chair, Representative Henry Hyde, made clear his view. "We had a 'parade' of professors," Hyde announced dismissively at several press conferences. "We should get academic credit for these hearings." And in testament to the committee's forbearance, Hyde offered his own definition of an intellectual: "someone educated beyond his intelligence."[80] Many of his congressional colleagues seemed to have regarded professors' testimony in the same vein as Prussian emperor Frederick II, who confided to one of his ministers that his theory of acquiring land was to "begin by taking. I shall find scholars afterwards to demonstrate my perfect right."[81]

Part of the problem is that on many issues, governmental decision making is driven by considerations that have little to do with the merits;

decision makers are uninformed and uninterested in being informed by experts, academics or otherwise.[82] But professors often contribute to their own marginality by naive or condescending attitudes toward the policy-makers they are trying to persuade.[83] Such attitudes were also on display among some of the academic experts in the impeachment proceedings, who lectured Congressional committee members as if they were not-too-bright undergraduates who had failed to do the assigned reading. These arrogant and patronizing tones provoked a response in kind, and led some politicians to treat the hearings as pro forma photo opportunities, with no real bearing on the outcome.

In less publicized settings, the charade can be still worse. Even the most respectful, well-behaved academics frequently put in long, unpaid hours preparing legislative or administrative agency testimony that few decision makers show up to hear, and fewer still ever bother to read. Of course, the indifference of legislators and high-level administrative officials does not necessarily mean that faculty involvement is pointless. The staff who help craft policy, and the judges and law clerks who later help interpret it, often take seriously the academic expertise that politicians ignore. But prominent scholars are often unaccustomed to marginalization, and experiencing it in government settings leads many to put their time and talents elsewhere.[84]

How much direct influence academics exercise in public policy remains a matter of long-standing debate, and systematic data are unavailable.[85] It is, however, clear that researchers who want to exercise such influence need to become more realistic in their expectations and strategic in their involvement. Academics need to frame projects and present advice in ways that speak clearly to issues driving decisions.[86] Lessons are readily available from independent research institutes that have focused agendas and coordinated public relations and lobbying efforts. Universities, for their part, could also do more to help their faculty effectively reach policy audiences. Additional fellowships, stipends, workshops, and related resources could be targeted to that effort. More academic institutions could establish their own policy research centers or consortia that help to steer scholarship toward projects with socially valuable outcomes in areas such as poverty and public health.[87] There are, to be sure, limits on how far academic institutions can travel down this road without becoming, or appearing to become, overtly political. But it does not serve the public interest for universities to cede the policy terrain to nonacademic institutes that have explicit partisan ties. Nor does it make sense to have so much research and expertise on social issues wasted because professors lack the capacity to make it accessible.

ACADEMIC FREEDOM AND ACADEMIC RESPONSIBILITY

One reason that professors can make important contributions as public intellectuals is academic freedom. The general principle that faculty should be able to challenge received views without fear of retaliation is firmly rooted in American legal traditions and university policies. However, the safeguards of academic freedom are by no means absolute, and the context in which they are most contested involves public speech that is unrelated to the speaker's scholarly expertise. Such speech accounts for the vast majority of academic freedom grievances that come before the American Association of University Professors.[88] These claims raise crucial, long-standing questions concerning the role of public intellectuals. Do academics speaking in public forums deserve special constitutional or employment protections beyond those available to citizens in general? If so, do these special rights confer any special obligations? Should professors trading on their reputations as scholars adhere to scholarly standards of accuracy and restraint when they speak in nonacademic settings? Should any sanctions follow from failures to do so?

Historical Background

To address those issues, it is helpful to understand the historical origins of academic freedom. America borrowed the concept from German universities of the late nineteenth century. There, its function was to protect the free inquiry essential to the pursuit of knowledge. German protections did not, however, encompass political speech, which was thought to undermine habits of disinterested scholarship.[89] By contrast, in this country, the events that eventually helped institutionalize academic freedom concerned political expression. A pivotal 1900 case involved Edmund Ross, a Stanford professor of economics. Ross attracted ire for his outspoken support of populism, Anglo-Saxon racial purity, and restrictions on Asian immigration. Jane Stanford, who had inherited a fortune built on coolie labor, had sufficient control over the university she helped found to cause his dismissal. When the head of the history department denounced the dismissal, he, too, was ousted, which triggered a wave of faculty resignations.[90] In response to widespread criticism from newspapers and peers, Stanford's president attempted to recast the termination as a response to moral misconduct rather than speech: Ross's "erratic" behavior and his misrepresentation of confidential information had allegedly demonstrated unfitness.[91]

Many remained unconvinced. The case highlighted the vulnerability of faculty, who generally held short-term contracts and were readily subject to retaliation. Largely in response to these concerns, Arthur Lovejoy, one of the Stanford faculty members who had resigned in protest, organized a group that ultimately founded the American Association of University Professors (AAUP). Its first president promptly commissioned a report on academic freedom that Lovejoy coauthored, and in 1915 the Association issued a *Declaration of Academic Freedom and Tenure*. These twin safeguards, the report maintained, were essential to protect the distinctive role of scholars: "to impart the results of their . . . investigations and reflections, both to students and the general public, without fear or favor."[92] With respect to speech unrelated to teaching or research, the AAUP was more circumspect. Although its *Declaration* made clear that scholars should not be "debarred from giving expression to their judgments upon controversial questions," including matters outside their expertise, they were also "under a peculiar obligation to avoid hasty or unverified or exaggerated statements, and to refrain from intemperate or sensational modes of expression."[93]

In 1940, the AAUP issued a revised document, *Statement of Principles on Academic Freedom and Tenure*, which has served as the model for most American colleges and universities. It provides:

> When they speak or write as citizens, [professors] should be free from institutional censorship or discipline, but their special position in the community imposes special obligations. As scholars and educational officers,

they should remember that the public may judge their profession and their institution by their utterances. Hence they should at all times be accurate, should exercise appropriate restraint, should show respect for the opinions of others, and should make every effort to indicate that they are not speaking for the institution.[94]

A subsequent AAUP committee opinion made clear that a professor's "expression of opinion as a citizen cannot constitute grounds for dismissal unless it clearly demonstrates a faculty member's unfitness for his position. Extramural utterances rarely bear upon the faculty member's fitness for his position."[95]

The Scope of Protected Speech

Protection for statements unrelated to academic work is, however, difficult to justify under the original rationale for academic freedom. Why, as one early twentieth century *New York Times* editorial famously put it, should every professor enjoy an "inalienable right . . . to make a fool of himself and his college by . . . intemperate sensational prattle about every subject under the sun?"[96] After all, scholarly inquiry and classroom expression are not inhibited in any direct way by restraints on unrelated public speech.

The expansion of academic freedom to protect such speech has been explained on several grounds. The first is pragmatic. Law professor William Van Alstyne argues that academic freedom has served as "any old port in a storm."[97] It has filled in where constitutional principles have failed to provide adequate safeguards. By its terms, the First Amendment only limits state restrictions on speech, and therefore does not protect professors in private institutions. Moreover, not until the 1970s did the Supreme Court apply the Amendment to political expression by teachers in public institutions, well after a visible need for academic freedom had emerged.[98] Constitutional protections as currently interpreted also do not encompass speech that is "disruptive" of institutional operations. So, for example, courts have allowed universities to demote department chairs for offensive off-campus comments that might be imputed to their university.[99] Safeguards for such expression come only from academic freedom standards voluntarily adopted by educational institutions. The same is true for campus speech by professors at private colleges and universities. The growing number of untenured faculty at those institutions have no other safeguards against retaliation for unpopular expression. Unless and until courts and legislatures make safeguards for speech more broadly available, academic freedom remains a necessary foundation for open debate.

But that raises a broader question: Why should professors enjoy more protection than other individuals for expressing unwelcome views? One answer is that society benefits from having academics, who are schooled in scholarly traditions of rigorous analysis and factual accuracy, speak freely on matters beyond their specialty and in contexts beyond the classroom. Some faculty members achieve substantial public influence in those contexts. Examples include the foreign policy commentary of linguist Noam Chomsky and literary critic Edward Said, and the social criticism of legal scholar Richard Posner.[100] Moreover, the boundaries between professional and nonprofessional expression often blur. Recent highly publicized events at Columbia University are a case in point. Some allegedly inflammatory pro-Palestinian statements occurred in a professor's off-campus lecture, which a faculty investigating committee viewed as "a challenging grey zone" between classrooms and public forums.[101]

A further reason for extending academic freedom to encompass such forums is institutional; it relieves colleges and universities from the external pressure that they would face if they were responsible for all the expression that occurs in these contexts. Higher education has had ample experience with demands for faculty dismissals or disciplinary sanctions from outraged trustees, regents, donors, and other powerful constituencies. Principles of academic freedom have sometimes bent in the face of such demands. Professors' opposition to intervention during World War I, alleged sympathy toward communism during the McCarthy era, and radical activity during the 1960s were sometimes taken as evidence of unfitness for academic responsibilities.[102] Pressure for retaliation would be far greater if academic freedom were not at least in theory a shield for political speech both on and off the campus. Abbott Lawrence Lowell, one of Harvard's most distinguished presidents, underscored this concern. If a university has a right to restrain its professors, "it has a duty to do so, and it is responsible for whatever it permits. There is no middle ground."[103] And, in Lowell's view, any such institutional responsibility would unduly compromise individual freedom.

Current Controversies

In the contemporary political climate, universities can ill afford heightened accountability for unpopular expression. Academic freedom remains at risk in both campus and off-campus settings. Expression of unpopular positions, particularly those regarding terrorism, race, ethnicity, gender, and religion, continue to expose faculty to disciplinary action and to cause cancellation or disruption of public events.[104] Concerns about the suppression of conservative views have led to a range of initiatives. One is an "Academic Bill of Rights," which has been introduced in Congress and in almost a third of state legislatures, in order to protect students from "political, ideological, religious, and antireligious indoctrination."[105] To that end, the legislation calls for "a plurality of methodologies and perspectives" in faculty appointments and "a diversity of approaches to unsettled questions" in curricular matters, including adequate representation of dissenting views.[106] As currently formulated, the bill has no enforcement structure but is designed to serve as a foundation for further action if its provisions are not respected.[107]

Groups such as Campus Watch and Students for Academic Freedom have organized on over a hundred campuses to demand adoption and enforcement of such initiatives; these organizations also monitor "liberal propaganda," "unpatriotic" statements, and antireligious bias.[108] At UCLA, a conservative alumni group offered students up to $100 for tapes of lectures that documented how "radicals" on the faculty were "actively proselytizing their extreme views in the classroom." The group posted a list of objectionable professors on its Website, but its accompanying profiles of the "Dirty Thirty" included virtually no evidence of classroom misconduct. Offenses instead included open support for gay rights and affirmative action, and newspaper editorials on the Middle East.[109] In some states, legislative committees have begun investigating allegations of ideological discrimination by faculty in public colleges and universities.[110] The federal Commission on the Future of Higher Education has also held hearings that explored concerns regarding professors' "left-wing political bias."[111]

Supporters of such measures claim that they are necessary to restore intellectual balance on American campuses. According to a recent public opinion poll by the *Chronicle of Higher Education*, about half of surveyed Americans believe that colleges improperly introduce a liberal bias in teaching.[112] Some basis for concern also emerged in another poll, described in Chapter 3, involving undergraduates at the nation's fifty top-ranked schools. In that survey, commissioned by the American Council of Trustees and Alumni, almost half of students felt that presentations on political issues were almost completely one-sided and that professors frequently injected political views into the course even when they had nothing to do with the subject matter.[113]

Prominent academic leaders have also expressed concern about the obstacles to achieving candid and civil debate. In 2005, the American Council on Education (ACE), joined by twenty-seven other higher educational organizations, issued a statement affirming the importance of "intellectual pluralism" and "the free exchange of ideas"; sixteen presidents of major universities released a similar statement.[114] Academic leaders are, however, virtually united in opposing legislative efforts to enforce such values. AAUP officials express widespread views when they criticize the Academic Bill of Rights as mislabeled and misconceived: in their view, it is "really an academic bill of wrongs" that would chill the free inquiry that the statute claims to support.[115] As historian Joan Scott notes, "it's one thing to insist that differences of opinion be respected. It's another to claim that all opinions have equal weight" and are entitled to course coverage.[116] Legislatively mandated balance undermines capacities for critical thinking and evaluative judgments that higher education seeks to foster. As the ACE statement emphasizes, "government recognition and respect for the independence of colleges and universities is essential for intellectual excellence."[117]

Yet although there are compelling reasons to protect the faculty's right to speak, there are equally compelling reasons for faculty to exercise that right responsibly. The pursuit of knowledge requires not simply freedom from restraint but affirmative commitments to reason, fairness, and accuracy.[118]

Those who speak with the authority of academia have a special obligation to preserve its credibility. Professors have a strong stake not only in resisting official sanctions for speech, but also in condemning its misuse.

Case Studies

Two recent, highly publicized cases illustrate that need. The first case involved Ward Churchill, a University of Colorado professor of ethnic studies who wrote a polemical, but initially obscure, essay shortly after 9/11. His claim was that those killed in the World Trade Towers were implicated in the sins of corporate America: "True enough, they were civilians of a sort. But innocent? Gimme a break. . . . If there was a better, more effective, or in fact any other way of visiting some penalty befitting their participation upon the little Eichmanns inhabiting the sterile sanctuary of the twin towers, I'd really be interested in hearing about it."[119] He heard plenty. A professor at Hamilton College, which had invited Churchill to speak, discovered and circulated the essay. The story then reached a national television audience, courtesy of Bill O'Reilly, who thoughtfully provided contact information for Hamilton College. The college then received some eight thousand e-mails about the event, and enough death threats to force cancellation of the speech. The firestorm was further fueled by allegations concerning Churchill's academic qualifications and misconduct: plagiarism, falsification, lack of a Ph.D., and misstatements concerning his war record and Native American heritage. Colorado's governor, along with many of the state's legislators, demanded his dismissal. Once an investigation began, powerful politicians also promised that if an appropriate response was not forthcoming, they would cut the budget of Churchill's ethnic studies department.[120]

The case provoked sharp division within the academic community. The dominant view, reflected in an AAUP statement, was that Churchill had a right to make incendiary claims, and that the university had a right to investigate his possible violations of academic standards, subject to full due process protections.[121] That may be the best available compromise of competing principles, but it poses obvious concerns. Almost all of the allegations concerning Churchill had been raised previously. The university's decision to pursue them only after the 9/11 comments sent a discomfiting message. As one scholar noted, "academic freedom of speech now comes with the fear of investigation, should you say the wrong thing to the wrong group at the wrong time. Whatever the outcome for Churchill, the academy loses."[122]

The public pays a price as well. Although the function of academic freedom is to encourage full and informed debate, inflammatory polemics seldom promote it. What passed for public discourse on the substance of the issue were programs such as O'Reilly's and Bill Maher's, which pitted Churchill's extremist views against the personal outrage of relatives of World Trade Center victims.[123]

A second highly publicized controversy over the public intellectual role involved Harvard president Laurence Summers. The remarks at issue came during a conference of the National Bureau of Economic Research on Diversifying the Science and Engineering Workforce. Summers had agreed to come on the condition that he could speak "unofficially" and could offer some "attempts at provocation."[124] His attempts succeeded well beyond expectations. To account for women's underrepresentation in science and engineering, Summers ventured three explanations. The least important, in his view, was gender "socialization" and discrimination. The most important was the "near total commitment to work" expected of those in elite professional positions. The second most important was women's allegedly inferior mathematical and scientific ability at the "high end" of the performance range. Although he "would like nothing better than to be proved wrong," Summers indicated that his reading of the data revealed biological sex-based differences in "intrinsic aptitude." In support of his hypothesis, Summers referred specifically to only one study. It had found half as many female as male twelfth-graders who scored in the top 5 percent of mathematics and science aptitude tests. He also found it telling that his two-and-a-half-year-old twin daughters, when given trucks, concluded that the "daddy truck is carrying the baby truck." And, in full embrace of his provocateur role, Summers analogized the underrepresentation of women in math and engineering to the underrepresentation of white men in the National Basketball Association and of Jews in farming.[125]

Summers's remarks attracted international coverage and widespread condemnation, both because of the substance of his claims and the leadership position from which he spoke. If Summers truly believed that he was free to shed his institutional identity at will, then he was, as Stanley Fish suggested, "clueless in academe."[126] In a letter to Summers following his remarks, Harvard's Standing Committee on Women noted what should have been obvious: "The president of a university never speaks entirely as an individual, especially when that institution is Harvard."[127] Assertions about women's intellectual inferiority raise questions about an administration's professed commitment to diversity, a commitment that in Harvard's case was already in question. During Summer's previous four years in office, women's representation in tenured positions in the arts and sciences had dropped from 37 to 11 percent.[128] Given this record, even the *New York Times*'s editorial page was moved to question whether Summers was the "perfect person to free-associate on why women have trouble getting tenure."[129] A Times op-editorialist, Camille Paglia, was still blunter: Summers failed "Academic Anthropology 101."[130]

Not all agreed. Some conservative commentators became at least temporary converts to the cause of academic freedom, now that it was threatened by the "gods of political correctness" and "hysterical" "uber-feminists."[131] An *American Spectator* article lambasted universities' apparent double standard for political speech: "While Ward Churchill can tell lies about the differences between America and the terrorists, Larry Summers is forbidden to tell truths about differences between men and women."[132] Other, more liberal commentators, such as Harvard professors Alan Dershowitz and Richard Freeman, applauded Summers for departing from the usual presidential "pablum" and "babble."[133] According to Dershowitz, "if we have a problem with presidents in major universities in the United States today, . . . it's not that they're being too provocative, it's that it's the opposite." They are "too worried about tipping the boat, too worried about alienating anybody. . . . [More of them] should become intellectual leaders and provocateurs on their campus."[134]

There is, however, a profound difference between leading and provoking, and provocation is not the only alternative to pablum. Many campus leaders share the approach of Yale president Richard Levin; they speak out on issues related to higher education or to public concerns on which they have professional competence.[135] What they justifiably avoid are controversial public statements when they have no such expertise, and when their institutions will pay a substantial price. Most knowledgeable observers, including Summers himself in retrospect, wished that he had exercised such restraint.[136] His failure to do so, coupled with other, similar missteps, contributed to his forced resignation.[137] As the chair of Harvard's task force on women in science and engineering noted, the problem was not simply that Summers had been provocative, but that he had strayed beyond his competence. The difficulty with his comments was not that they were "politically incorrect, but that they were just plain incorrect."[138] His overgeneralization from selective data misrepresented gender research in ways that undermined his institution's core commitments to diversity and equal opportunity. Summers's initial unwillingness to release a transcript, while claiming academic freedom for its contents, compounded the problem.

Assertions about women's intellectual inferiority have a long and unbecoming history. For centuries, an array of "scientific data" was assembled to justify the exclusion of women from higher education and all of the elite professions.[139] In a joint editorial, the presidents of MIT, Princeton, and Stanford underscored the risk that speculation about "innate" gender differences in science and engineering "may rejuvenate old myths and reinforce negative stereotypes and biases."[140] What Summers failed to acknowledge was that many studies show no significant persistent differences between male and female aptitudes for math.[141] Nor is there evidence that small differences in scores at the top range of standardized aptitude tests predict achievement in math and science.[142] Moreover, sex differences in test scores and academic performance vary considerably across time and culture, a fact hard to square with genetic explanations.[143] Since the late 1960s, women's representation among holders of Ph.D.s has grown from under 1 percent to about 17 percent in engineering, from 2 percent to 18 percent in physics, and from 12 percent to 44 percent in biological and agricultural science.[144] What has changed is not women's "innate aptitude," but rather social attitudes. So too, a wealth of data reveals persistent and pervasive biases that impede women's advancement in traditionally male-dominated fields.[145] Summers offered no evidence for his assumption that those biases were less important than differences in aptitude, which are more contested and less consistently documented.

Yet these substantive flaws in Summers' analysis were not the focus of media coverage. Although some major news publications offered at least cursory analysis of the causes of women's underrepresentation in science and engineering, the main emphasis was on more diverting topics: political correctness; feminist harpies; sex differences in mammals; and Summers' own previous gaffes, post-conference apologia, and censure by the Harvard faculty. The *New York Times* Sunday op-ed page profiled sex differences in fruit flies and toads, and *Time* ran stories titled "Harvard's Crimson Face" and "Harvard's Hit Man," which put presidential foibles front and center.[146] Unlike the Churchill affair, however, the saga of "Summers and Smoke" at least had a silver lining; Harvard got new task forces on women and an unprecedented level of funding and accountability for gender issues.[147]

Despite their other differences, both case histories underscore a broader point. One irony of academic freedom is that if it is exercised irresponsibly, attention is diverted from the substantive debates that the protection seeks to advance. As Columbia president Lee Bollinger has noted, when controversies arise, the focus too often shifts to speakers, not their speeches, and to whether their views are protected, not whether they are persuasive on the merits.[148] Provocation attracts a spotlight, but one that can readily misdirect our gaze. Particularly in this age of instant notoriety, academic rights call for academic responsibility. Professors capable of attracting widespread attention need to consider the consequences, both for higher education in general and for their own institutions in particular. Academic freedom should prevent discipline or dismissal for offensive speech; it should not preempt criticism. Academic integrity is a common good, and faculty share a common obligation to condemn conduct that falls short.

THE INTELLECTUAL IN PUBLIC: CONFERENCES, PANELS, AND THE PURSUIT OF STATUS

Although relatively few academics play a prominent public intellectual role in speaking to mass audiences on social issues, virtually all function in more modest public settings as lecturers, panelists, and conference participants.

These occasions do not always bring out the best in the "best and brightest." The reasons have much to do with the pursuit of status, and how it subverts the pursuit of knowledge.

Conferences

Over the past half century, academic conferences have come to occupy increasing importance for both professional and personal reasons. The growing specialization of knowledge creates a corresponding demand for occasions that enable experts from different institutions or disciplines to discuss common interests and meet colleagues who will serve as collaborators, reviewers, references, and contacts. In some fields, annual meetings provide the official site for job interviews. In virtually all fields, these events serve informal employment-related functions as well; they are convenient occasions for screening potential appointments candidates, showcasing work, exchanging gossip, and courting publishers. Conferences also provide the leisure of the theory class. Particularly for underpaid junior and non-tenure-track faculty, they provide welcome employer-subsidized or tax-deductible boondoggles. In one of his biting satires of academic jet setting, British novelist David Lodge offers a prologue modeled on Chaucer's *Canterbury Tales*:

> The modern conference resembles the pilgrimage of medieval Christendom in that it allows the participants to indulge themselves in all the pleasures and diversions of travel while appearing to be austerely bent on self-improvement. To be sure, there are certain penitential exercises to be performed—the presentation of a paper perhaps, and certainly listening to the papers of others. [But mainly these excursions are a chance to] . . . eat, drink, and make merry . . . and yet, at the end of it all, return home with an enhanced reputation for seriousness of mind.[149]

They are also what law professor Julius Getman labels "rituals of prestige competition. Professors strut around . . . hotel lobbies with the assiduousness of Birds of Paradise in their display dance. . . ."[150] In-group and out-group status hierarchies are enforced with all the petty viciousness of junior high school. For those at the bottom of the pecking order, typically new entrants and embittered veterans with undistinguished credentials, the message is that "everyone but [them] knows everyone else."[151] Some arrive with determination to better their station and rub shoulders with the great or near great. They lurk in lobbies, corridors, and the front rows of conference sessions waiting to pounce. In her advice columns for academics, Emily Toth describes the behavior: up and comers gaze furtively at everyone's chests, as they try to decide "are you anybody and should I be sucking up to you?"[152] Many will relinquish their prey only when someone higher on the pecking order comes into view. Then, all but accomplished fawners may veer off gracelessly, in mid-anecdote if necessary, to secure a place among a tonier set. In chronicling this behavior, David Brooks notes that the ultimate humiliation occurs when someone is "trapped outside a conversational klatsch and cannot induce anyone in the ring to step back and let him in." The agony is compounded if "people on the other side of the klatsch see his social exclusion and observe that he lacks the celebrity to . . . [gain] entrance."[153]

Behavior is not necessarily better in the coveted inner circle. In Brooks's experience, history does not record a case of any public intellectual "who has actually become more charming as he became more successful."[154] Conferences are often occasions for celebrities to "strut and fret and rattle their statuses," while basking in the envy of lesser mortals.[155] Intellectual elites can work a conference room like medieval lords of the manor, accumulating half-minute homages from the multitudes and bestowing gracious nods in return. As Toth explains, "even when flattery is transparent, the effort is flattering."[156] So celebrities and acolytes become mutual enablers in ingratiation rituals that do not reflect well on any of the participants.

Conference dining puts all these pathologies in sharp relief. If seating is not assigned, the jockeying for position resembles childhood games of musical chairs. Many celebrities may be happy to accept brief homage in hallways and receptions, but their noblesse oblige does not extend to an entire meal. Rather than endure entrapment by the underclass, the academic aristocracy tends to bypass group dining entirely or to commandeer a corner where interlopers are plainly unwelcome. Ironically enough, those practicing the crudest elitism are often the most politically egalitarian. In law, the most notorious offenders have been from the far left. Leaders of the Critical

Legal Studies Movement were known for denouncing America's "false hierarchies" by day and re-creating them by night in their own social settings.

For the most conscientious conference social climbers, seating arrangements are, of course, only the first challenge. There is also the matter of dinner table chitchat, which must include the proper elements of erudition, name dropping, and seemingly spontaneous repartee. The conference circuit is, however, littered with "conversational overachievers."[157] Wind them up on any subject and they will never run down. Academic celebrities tend to be the worst offenders, if only because they are allowed to get away with it. Asking some of these individuals what they are working on is a rookie mistake for which everyone within earshot may pay. Accomplished raconteurs can easily work their way from appetizer through coffee without any encouragement from their dining companions, except an occasional appreciative murmur to indicate that the audience is still awake. Occasionally some hardy soul will attempt to derail the monologue with faint irony, along the lines of Mrs. Patrick Campbell's celebrated efforts with a leading British expert on insect behavior. After an entire evening focused on the army command structure of warrior ants, she inquired politely, "Do they have a navy too?"[158]

Panels

Similar egotism is also on display in substantive conference sessions, as well as in panels and lectures on other occasions. P. G. Wodehouse captured a common frustration of captive audiences: "The Agee woman told us for three quarters of an hour how she came to write her beastly book when a simple apology was all that was required."[159] The tedium is especially irritating if perpetrators have not achieved sufficient eminence to entitle them to banality. Problems can arise from both under- and overpreparation. Sins of omission tend to be readily apparent, even if speakers are not so ill-bred as to display the tiny scrap of paper on which they have jotted a few notes in the cab ride over. Speaking from the heart is almost always a mistake at any event at which substance is expected and alcohol is served. Drink and drivel are familiar companions in academic novels, and life too often imitates art.

Overpreparation can cause equal discomfort, especially if the academic is sharing impaired. Some panelists are bound and determined to get through their prepared presentation, even if it well exceeds their allotted time.[160] They also tend to pounce on every question that is not specifically directed to someone else and ponder it in tedious detail. Additional problems arise if moderators chafe at their limited role, and milk it for all it is worth. This can result in seemingly endless introductions, with every aspect of the speakers' pedigree explored in loving detail. I can still recall examples that could have passed for parody; one introduction of Supreme Court Justice Ruth Bader Ginsburg began with her junior high school cheerleading triumphs and proceeded for a leisurely quarter hour with the moderator's own assessment of the justice's subsequent judicial accomplishments.

Members of the audience can be comparable offenders, particularly if they have not had their own panel to monopolize. The most irritating "questions" make no pretense of being questions. They come from speakers who want attention, not answers. "I'm smart, you're not" is the not-so-subtle subtext. Occasionally a panelist rises to the bait, and it is not a pretty sight. In one of his more memorable exchanges, Stanley Fish interrupted a question with "Stop! I'm going to formulate your objection better than you can, because I've heard it a thousand times before."[161] From these occasions come enduring grudges. After being verbally challenged by legal theorist Ronald Dworkin, Fish titled a pair of published rebuttals "Wrong Again" and "Still Wrong After All These Years."[162]

All too often, a rigid panel format undermines the dialogue it is meant to promote. A junior professor described a representative experience. At his first presentation at a literary studies conference, the number of scholars on the panel (five) exceeded those in the audience (four). Undaunted, each panelist read his paper in its entirety, "carefully, ponderously, each syllable thudding the dead air." No one dared suggest that the participants "bag the formalities" and actually talk to each other and the audience.[163]

None of this behavior is, to be sure, unique to academics, but that should not absolve the profession of responsibility for better responses. Mentoring, role modeling, and informal reputational sanctions are the most plausible strategies. Respected professors could do more to publicly shame and satirize the most egregious conduct. Programs for graduate students and new faculty members could include discussion of panel do's and don'ts, and higher education periodicals could devote more treatment to the subject.[164]

Individuals at the early stages of their academic careers also could profit from a deeper understanding of status anxiety and better coping strategies. I wish I had known, when first attending the annual meeting of the Association of American Law Schools, that my sense of marginalization was almost universally shared. My junior colleagues are now relieved to hear that after a quarter century of attendance and a term as the Association's president, I still walk into the mass reception feeling exactly as they do: that no one there knows who I am or has any desire to find out. Many academics would also benefit from hearing early in their careers what frequently becomes obvious only later: pro forma interchanges with celebrities are vastly overrated; overt self-promotion is generally unproductive; and one of the most satisfying conference pastimes is helping a junior colleague have a less painful initiation than they once had themselves.

The Presentation of Self in Public Life

For many faculty members, a few helpful hints about personal appearance would also be in order. The conventional wisdom is that academics are the worst-dressed professionals, by a considerable margin.[165] They reportedly outdistance even the insurance sales force for "remorselessly unattractive" apparel, although there is no consensus about whether this is a problem, or even a subject worthy of discussion.[166] The tradition of frumpiness has its origins in the academic robes that symbolized the life of the mind and its distance from worldly pursuits. These black tent-styled garments covered a multitude of aesthetic sins and helped to preserve the dignity of scholars who couldn't afford, couldn't recognize, or couldn't be bothered to acquire more tasteful alternatives. Early American colleges and universities somewhat relaxed this standard by abandoning robes but requiring attire for both faculty and students in keeping with the rectitude and scholarly focus their campus hoped to encourage. In the mid-eighteenth century, departures from this standard caused Harvard College to issue an ordinance explicitly requiring its students to appear only in black, grey, and dark blue attire and prohibiting "silk nightgowns."[167]

For contemporary academics, this protective coloration is, of course, no longer enforced, and those seeking a public intellectual role cannot be entirely indifferent to what replaces it. Social science research confirms what common experience suggests: poor appearance is a professional liability, and academics are not exempt, although the bar is somewhat lower than for other occupational groups. Economists have quantified the "plainness" penalty in various workplace settings, as well as the impact of physical attractiveness on teaching evaluations of university faculty.[168] Instructors who are viewed as better looking receive significantly higher ratings, and contrary to conventional assumptions, the difference is greater for men than for women.[169] A Website, RateMyProfessors.com, gives students the option of evaluating their teachers' helpfulness, clarity, and sex appeal, and of commenting on particular features and fashion faux pas (fetching "buns," or hideous "blue fleece sweatercoat thing").[170] Teaching evaluation forms are another occasion for anonymous fashion tips. One of my colleagues received such aesthetic advice: "Professor Fisher should not wear yellow suede shoes with brown pants. But the belts are always nice." Spinster feminists have been particularly inviting targets. British novelist Dorothy Sayers offers a typical portrait: "a curious little creature" attending a Cambridge women's college reunion "dressed in unbecoming pink, who looked as though she had been carelessly packed away in a drawer all winter and put into circulation again without being ironed."[171] Conservative critic Christina Hoff Sommers is even less charitable: "There are a lot of homely women in women's studies."[172]

Appearance can also matter in hiring interviews, conference presentations, and other formal settings. Dress codes do, of course, vary across regions and disciplines. What is appropriately artsy for most art departments will raise eyebrows in business schools. But whatever the standards, a shared feature is that they matter. Small idiosyncrasies are tolerable, sometimes even charming; major deviations from prevailing norms carry a cost.

According to one school of thought, audiences should "little notice nor long remember" what professors wear on formal academic occasions.[173]

Toth's advice columns take this position and warn against being too earthy or too elegant. "Super chic" styles in job interviews make decision makers feel uncomfortable, and eccentric choices (red taffeta dress, green polyester pants) signal inadequate judgment. If candidates don't know how to dress appropriately, what else don't they know? The pro-frump faction believes it best to err on the side of graveyard green, toad brown, and funereal black.[174] Certain basic principles of hygiene and aesthetics also apply. When Willa Cather was once asked if she could give one rule to follow for aspiring writers, she reportedly paused, looked down at the questioner, and responded, "Never wear brown shoes with a blue suit."[175]

An opposing school, represented by flagrantly flamboyant dressers such as literary theorist Jane Gallup, believe that "frumpy gets you [nowhere] except forgotten."[176] Whatever choice you make, your clothes make a statement, so it might as well be one that expresses your identity. For Gallup, giving a lecture on the American West in fringed pants and cowboy boots is a way to amplify her message.[177] Such efforts are a frequent target of academic satire. In Saul Bellows's *Ravelstein*, a woman physicist is known for exotic themes; one season she features nothing but ostrich leather and ostrich feathers in boots, hats, bags, and gloves. A still more famous male cultural critic parades a $4,500 Parisian sports coat that he carelessly and irreparably stains on its inaugural wearing. To these professors, fashion autonomy is part of academic freedom; their divine right also extends to teaching in jeans or appearing tieless at formal functions.[178] After all, along with many great minds came execrable taste: Jean-Paul Sartre's coat of artificial orange fur made lasting impressions.[179] For many faculty, the absence of fashion police is a valued perk of campus life. Perhaps as other, more expensive benefits fall prey to budget freezes, higher education will join the ranks of home-employment companies that advertise this feature. Universities could lure prospective job applicants with promises that they can work in their underwear and "succeed in [their workplace] without really dressing."[180]

But if academics stray outside the campus and seek influence in public intellectual settings, the standards are less forgiving. My own experience may be typical. In my early years of teaching, I paid no attention, and my rotation of grey, black, and brown skirts hovered between drab and dowdy. I was undoubtedly viewed as my generation's version of a woman professor in Randall Jarrell's classic *Pictures from an Institution*:

> When well-dressed women met Flo they looked at her as though they couldn't believe it. She looked as if she had waked up and found herself dressed—as if her clothes had come together by chance and involved her, an innocent onlooker in the accident.... Mostly she wore, in the daytime in the winter, a tweed skirt, a sweater-set, and a necklace. The skirt looked as if a horse had left her its second best blanket ... the necklace (sometimes it had earrings to match) was made of seeds or acorns or sea-shells that had been gathered and varnished, by her children, if you were lucky—by her charities if you were unlucky.[181]

What forced my wardrobe upgrade was becoming director of a research institute, and the kindly intervention of feminist colleagues who felt that Something Must be Done.

Emergency remedial shopping was in order. Although many institutes, including my own, live in genteel poverty, their directors are not supposed to advertise that fact, and I was pushing the envelope. My conversion was undertaken with the zeal of Christian missionaries seeking to take salvation to the heathen. Colleagues temporarily appropriated my credit card, supervised its use in approved retail settings, and confiscated the worst offenders in my wardrobe rotation. In a vain effort to salvage one especially treasured item from certain destruction, I noted that it had been with me since high school. "Exactly" was the grim response. Institute staff greeted my refurbishment with such evident relief that I got the message, as well as the clothing. Or so I thought. But as I have subsequently learned on forays into more visible public intellectual roles, what passes muster on campus does not satisfy the world outside it. While serving as the chair of an American Bar Association Commission on Women in the Profession, I was taken aside by the Association's public relations staff. In the nicest possible way, they diplomatically explained that for major occasions, my skill level was inadequate; I would need professional makeup, a hair stylist, and a personal shopper.

There is, of course, a gender dimension to all of this. Men don't need to master mascara, and I doubt that any of my male colleagues in equivalent

positions were quizzed, as I was, on whether they had acquired appropriately color-coordinated accessories. But racial and ethnic minorities face
biases as well. My African-American male colleagues report that "dressing
down" is part of "white privilege"; if they turn up in jeans and sweatshirts,
they risk losing classroom authority or being mistaken for the maintenance
staff. Much as all of us might like to affect "high-minded disdain" for matters as mundane as fashion, we cannot ignore the subtext we send.[182] And
if the choice is ceding the public intellectual space to the conservative commentators who know how to dress for success, those of us who are fashion
challenged might just need to get with the program.

Rethinking the Role

The public role of academics presents multiple challenges for a profession
that traces its ideals and identity to monks' scholarly labors in secluded
monasteries. One such challenge involves a tension in values. Academic
principles of disinterested inquiry and factual rigor are chronic casualties
in media and policy settings. The skills of self-promotion and polemical
prose that often land scholars in the public spotlight can also sabotage their
performance once they arrive there. It is, in essence, hard for public intellectuals to remain intellectual.

Other concerns arise from unbecoming behaviors that are not unique to
academics. Nor are academics by any means the worst offenders. Panels and
annual meetings of other occupations reveal similar examples of arrogant,
self-aggrandizing, or fawning conduct.[183] And compared with nonacademic
pundits or "independent" researchers bankrolled by partisan policy institutes, our profession fares reasonably well. Yet the lapses of others are no
excuse for our own or for our unwillingness to assume some collective responsibility for improvement.

The most plausible strategies are those noted previously: more preparation and accountability for the public intellectual role. Universities should
provide better mentoring for graduate students and junior faculty, and
greater assistance for those seeking media and policy influence. More rewards should be available for work that reaches general audiences on matters of social importance. And more informal peer pressure should target

behaviors that may be amusing in academic novels but are profoundly irritating in actual experience. In short, both individuals and institutions need more occasions for scrutiny of their public roles. Academics love to gossip about the foibles of others. We also need to be more self-reflective about our own. Few of us can afford the luxury of the character in Oscar Wilde's *Ideal Husband* who confides, "I always pass along good advice. It is the only thing to do with it. It is never of any use to oneself."

Chapter Six

IDEALS AND INSTITUTIONS

The concluding chapters of books on universities often bear an eerie resemblance to universities' own concluding ceremonies. Academic institutions, like their graduating students, appear perennially at thresholds, confronting unprecedented challenges. As Woody Allen puts it in a celebrated parody of a commencement address: "More than any other time in history, mankind faces a crossroads. One path leads to despair and utter hopelessness. The other to total extinction. Let us pray we have the wisdom to choose correctly."[1]

Almost forty years ago, *Time* ran a cover story of this genre under the title, "The Impending Financial Crisis of Higher Education." Every university leader quoted in the article described what Columbia's president termed problems of "staggering magnitude and complexity." According to Yale's president, "the less well-endowed university is literally finding its back to the wall as it tries to be competitive in faculties, facilities and programs." With costs rising "infinitely faster than academic revenue," even the richest institutions were, in the words of Harvard's assistant dean, "reaching for the panic button."[2] Keeping up with expensive technological and research needs was essential to "build a university's prestige," but it also created "bottomless pits for funds."[3]

Four decades later, the same themes recur. The 1960s are recalled with nostalgia as a period of academic growth and prosperity, and the current crisis is presented as different in kind or degree from its predecessors. Although the basic financial problem is the same as in earlier eras—escalating demands that exceed existing revenues—the underlying causes are rooted in structural forces that now appear unlikely to change.[4] Moreover, as the preceding chapters have indicated, higher education faces other pressing challenges involving its mission, governance, and quality of life. Few of these concerns are new, but all have assumed new urgency in the face of increasing competitive, financial, and technological pressures.

Yet the most serious problem for higher education may be the widespread reluctance to come to terms with what the problems are. A profession and a public long inundated with crisis rhetoric have an understandable tendency to discount current concerns that seem variations on well-worn themes. Like a bored but dutiful commencement audience, faculty often regard exhortations about the state of higher education with polite indifference, confident that this too shall pass, and that academic institutions will somehow muddle through. And of course they will. But in what form and at what cost are the crucial questions. They deserve greater attention from a wider audience.

DEFINING THE CHALLENGES

A profession that traces its origins to the groves of "Akademia," an olive orchard outside of Athens, now does its work in institutions of increasing scale, complexity, and commercial entanglements. Maintaining academic values in this setting raises a host of challenges. They fall into several interrelated clusters: finances, competition, access, diversity, technology, and governance.

The economic problems are summarized in Chapter 1. The central difficulty arises from a growing gap between resources and revenues. Costs are escalating in areas such as scientific research, information technology, financial aid, student services, regulatory compliance, and health benefits. These increasing needs have not been matched by corresponding increases in public funding. Nor does the situation seem likely to improve, at least in the foreseeable future. The United States already spends an estimated $200 billion annually on higher education, and invests a greater proportion of its gross national product on academic institutions than any other nation.[5] As the national Commission on the Future of Higher Education has noted, "at both federal and state levels, financial support for higher education is seen, and will likely continue to be seen, as less important or urgent than other budget priorities (defense, homeland security, disaster relief . . . Medicaid, and K-12 education)."[6] In the face of these competing priorities, the conventional wisdom has been that universities must find ways to do more with less. But as one expert wryly notes, "The reality is that institutions will have to do less with less."[7]

Universities face challenges on other fronts as well. The growing importance of rankings has intensified bidding wars for talented faculty and students. The pursuit of status has not only compounded financial difficulties but also distorted academic priorities. Higher education faces a classic prisoner's dilemma, in which institutionally rational behavior leads to socially undesirable results. More resources are diverted into excessive salaries for academic celebrities, scholarships for economically advantaged students, glitzy amenities, and public relations campaigns. As both institutions and individuals face pressure to boost their reputations, other priorities can fall by the wayside. What loses out are activities such as teaching and advising, which are crucial to the academic mission but not readily evaluated in national rankings or in hiring, promotion, and compensation processes. Status hierarchies also encourage overproduction of arcane scholarship that contributes little to the discipline or the world outside it, at the expense of service and public intellectual activities.

The pursuit of status, and the price it entails, poses other concerns. What constraints should universities place on commercial activity? How should they balance quality and affordability? As the opening chapter made clear, we remain a far distance from accommodating the needs of all who could benefit from higher education, and we are failing to reduce educational inequality among income groups. Academic institutions also face related challenges in meeting the needs of an increasingly diverse student population. A declining minority of those now attending colleges and universities

are between the ages of eighteen and twenty-two, and demand is growing fastest among older Americans.[8] These students have different needs
and priorities than their younger classmates. Creating a culture that will
support a lifetime of learning and responding to those at varying career
stages will become increasingly important as the population ages. Differences across race, ethnicity, sex, class, and culture, among faculty as well as
students, pose further challenges.

Technology creates new pressures as well as possibilities. The delivery
of education online and through video hookups dissolves boundaries of
time and space. Experts such as Peter Drucker have suggested that distance
learning may make free-standing residential institutions obsolete.[9] Many
disagree, but no one doubts that the relative value of face-to-face contact
is becoming an increasingly central question. That question will assume
growing importance as nonprofit universities struggle to compete not just
with each other but also with for-profit and virtual campuses and other information service providers.[10] Opportunities for low-cost electronic communication offer enormous benefits but carry hidden costs. In a world of
growing scholarly specialization, an American linguist may have far more
contact with peers in Europe or Asia than with chemists in an adjacent
building. How the university can maintain its sense of intellectual community and institutional loyalty is an increasingly pressing concern. That concern is exacerbated by two other developments. One is the growing resource
inequality across disciplines, and the tensions involving cross-subsidization
of the "haves" by the "have nots." A central challenge involves developing a
funding structure that is fair, and appears fair, to fields in the sciences and
professions that generate a disproportionate share of tuition and external
revenues.[11] A second concern involves equitable treatment of the growing
corps of provisional and part-time untenured professors who have limited
stakes and limited leverage in their current workplaces.

RETHINKING TENURE

One of the primary ways that higher education has coped with revenue
shortfalls is by increasing its reliance on relatively low-paid, non-tenure-track

"contingent" faculty. From a financial standpoint, this is an understandable strategy. In most disciplines, the overproduction of graduates with Ph.D.s or the professional equivalent has created a buyers' market. From an educational standpoint, however, this solution raises multiple concerns and reignites long-standing controversies. The arguments for and against tenure have been aired at length elsewhere and do not require exhaustive review here.[12] But no analysis of academic life can ignore the growing reliance on contingent workers and its implications for academic values.

Current Practices

Tenure, as commonly defined, means a guarantee of continuing employment unless there is cause for dismissal. Academic handbooks and court decisions typically interpret cause to include incompetence, neglect, moral turpitude, and financial exigencies.[13] Yet despite this shared definition, practices concerning tenure vary considerably across disciplines and institutions. There are differences in the percentage of total faculty who are tenured, the percentage of eligible faculty who are promoted to tenure, and the policies toward non-tenure-track employees.[14] Yet claims about the evils or necessity of *the* tenure system often gloss over these variations and their implications for the academic culture.

Despite important differences across institutional and departmental contexts, the general trend in higher education is clear: tenure is losing ground. About two-thirds of all faculty and three-quarters of new appointments hold untenured positions.[15] Over 40 percent of professors are part-time, and only 5 percent of these have tenure.[16] The proportion of non-tenure-track faculty is likely to increase. At the close of the twentieth century, a third of surveyed professors reported recent efforts at their institution to eliminate, weaken, or modify tenure.[17] A third also thought that tenure was an outmoded concept, and half believed that it should be modified.[18] A majority of presidents of four-year institutions favored replacing tenure with long-term contracts.[19] Commenting on these trends, former Stanford University president Donald Kennedy concluded that the traditional system was "dying of natural causes."[20]

Flexibility

One of the causes is the inflexibility of tenure in a world of changing demographic, financial, and enrollment dynamics. Higher education confronts a shortage of openings for entry-level faculty, because of resource constraints, a federal ban on mandatory retirement, and a bulge of professors hired in the boom of the 1960s and 1970s. The result has been to limit universities' responsiveness to shifts in student interests, disciplinary trends, and research funding opportunities.[21] Although it is generally possible to terminate tenured professors if financial constraints force the elimination of entire programs, that is generally too drastic an option to cope with modest declines in enrollment or external project funding.[22] Short-term and part-time hiring is an easier way for universities to minimize mismatches between curricular or research needs and faculty expertise.

Non-tenure-track appointments also provide opportunities for professors to balance their personal and professional lives. Reduced academic obligations are particularly attractive to those with substantial family responsibilities. Women still assume a disproportionate share of those responsibilities, which helps account for their disproportionate share of part-time appointments.[23] Married female professors with children under six are half as likely to hold tenure-track positions as their married male counterparts.[24] Of course, unequal family responsibilities are only part of the explanation for women's unequal academic status. Gender biases and unconscious stereotypes play a well-documented role in American workplaces, and higher education is no exception.[25] But the convergence of women's biological and tenure clocks is part of the problem, because the time pressures involved in preparing new courses, producing respected scholarship, building a research agenda, and caring for young children can be impossible to reconcile. As subsequent discussion makes clear, women's overrepresentation in non-tenure-track positions is of obvious concern, given the second-class treatment of faculty who occupy them. But it is equally clear that part-time appointments respond to legitimate needs that traditional tenure systems do not meet.

Accountability

Nonpermanent positions also can increase accountability, which many find lacking in the traditional tenure structure. A long-standing complaint is that job security insulates unproductive "deadwood" faculty from review. No hard evidence is available on the extent of this problem, but about three quarters of surveyed professors believe that tenure "sometimes protects incompetent faculty."[26] The limited research available indicates that productivity, measured by quantity of publications and external funding, does tend to decline gradually with age, but there is no data indicating that the *quality* of research or teaching declines.[27]

Defenders of the current system argue that post-tenure review procedures can deal with performance concerns. About half of all institutions that grant tenure have adopted such procedures, and almost two thirds of states require them for public universities.[28] The effectiveness of these review processes is open to doubt. In general, they require faculty development plans for those with significant performance problems. Sanctions are available only in cases of serious, prolonged, and unremedied difficulties, and dismissals for cause are extremely rare. One survey of two public universities found no terminations over a ten-year period; a lawyer for the AAUP is aware of only one dismissal in any institution.[29] As economists Ryan Amacher and Roger Meiners note, there are "high costs and few rewards" for administrators who attempt to put teeth into performance reviews.[30]

In practice, the only real options for dealing with unproductive tenured professors are financial: reduce their compensation or bribe them to retire. These strategies are not always successful. One widely recounted example involving Stanford's early retirement plan suggests why. The provost thought it was an inspired solution for a notoriously unproductive faculty member; the plan would enable him to retire immediately at half salary. But, the professor wanted to know, why should he do that when he was effectively retired already on full salary?[31] Other efforts to hold faculty accountable by asking them to justify their resource allocations have met with similar resistance. In one widely reported example at Harvard, the president was informed that "Once someone is a tenured professor, they answer to God."[32]

Cases like that, both real and imagined, are lightning rods for public criticism. In a world of increased corporate downsizing and decreased job security, many taxpayers, legislators, and trustees have difficulty seeing why higher education should be different.[33] If universities need to prune departments in the face of changing priorities and budgetary constraints, why not allow them to terminate the most ineffective and inessential faculty? What entitles tenured professors to a uniquely privileged status?

Academic Freedom

The conventional answer is, of course, academic freedom. If professors "'speak truth to power' . . . they are with some regularity bound to disturb or offend those in power and therefore to require the protection of tenure."[34] As the discussion in Chapter 5 makes clear, academics' freedom to challenge received views is essential to the pursuit of knowledge. The issue, however, is whether tenure is necessary or sufficient to that end. A majority of faculty now lack tenure; they depend on contractual provisions, constitutional guarantees, and institutional cultures for protection. On the whole, those safeguards appear reasonably effective in preventing dismissals for reasons related to academic freedom.[35] Indeed, even in the days before widespread adoption of tenure systems, terminations for cause were relatively rare.[36]

There are, however, disturbing exceptions, and some evidence suggests that faculty in institutions lacking tenure are reluctant to criticize the administration.[37] But that same reluctance may also occur in many universities that have tenure systems; administrators have ways of making their displeasure felt. Studies of institutions that have abolished or done without tenure, both here and abroad, find that it is not the essential factor in securing free expression and inquiry; institutional prestige and culture are more important.[38] Where safeguards for academic freedom fall short, many experts believe that the solution is to strengthen these safeguards, not rely on tenure for a select subclass of professors.

Supporters of tenure, however, believe that it serves other socially valuable functions apart from promoting academic freedom. It enables scholars of proven ability to embark on long-term projects that might not have immediate payoffs. A system of periodic contract renewals may discourage such investment. Another justification is that, without the guarantees of tenure, established faculty would be less willing to hire talented junior professors who might threaten their position.[39] Tenure also helps attract and retain highly qualified professionals, who otherwise might choose higher-paying positions in the public and private sectors.[40] According to one proponent, "we must keep in mind that it is not the first goal of the university to avoid paying faculty for doing nothing. Indeed, given the potentially debilitating morale problems of the university, there is something to be said for paying the nonproductive faculty well."[41] That claim is hard to reconcile with the research noted in Chapter 1 documenting high levels of professional satisfaction. And it is hard to imagine making the case of overpayment with a straight face to legislators who are comparing the resource needs of higher education with other pressing social priorities. Although tenure obviously serves important values, it is by no means clear whether the benefits exceed the disadvantages or how much would be lost under a well-designed alternative structure.

Fairness

These disadvantages include not only the expense and inflexibility of the tenure system itself but also the often inequitable treatment of the academic underclass outside that system. Although the status of non-tenure-track professors varies across institutions and disciplines, it generally leaves much to be desired. They typically have higher course loads and lower salaries, and are treated like second-class citizens.[42] The majority of part-time faculty work for half the pay per course of full-time colleagues.[43] Many members of this contingent workforce lack space, resources, benefits, professional-development support, and opportunities to participate in social events and governance systems.[44] A parody of a "personals" listing for one of these lecturers captures the experience: "Lonely adjunct: Works hard, honest grader, loves the classroom and committee work (seriously). You're an accredited institution with a dental plan. Please, no more than four courses per term. All serious inquiries considered."[45] Petty discourtesies and last-minute notices of changes in employment compound the problem. A character in James Hynes's novel *The Lecturer's Tale* sums up the situation of writing instructors: these inhabitants of shabby basement cubicles are the "steerage of the English Department, the first to drown if the budget springs a leak."[46]

The tenure system does not ensure widespread job security; it simply distributes that protection to a favored minority.[47] This academic caste system carries hidden costs. It erodes morale and institutional commitment and imposes all the expenses associated with frequent turnover. The conditions under which non-tenure-track faculty teach often impair performance; low salaries force many to become "freeway flyers," juggling multiple courses at multiple institutions, where they are largely unavailable outside the classroom.[48] Part-time faculty spend 50 to 100 percent less time per course hour on teaching than their full-time counterparts, and some research finds that increasing reliance on non-tenure-track instructors translates into poorer educational outcomes for students.[49] So too, in departments that rely heavily on such part-time professors, the shrinking number of tenured faculty end up with disproportionate advising, committee, and related administrative burdens.[50] This division of the profession into haves and have nots devalues teaching and breeds resentment. Academics ineligible for tenure generally feel that they are not respected and that they lack effective channels to raise collective concerns.[51]

Reforms

Various correctives are possible. Higher education experts and associations, including the AAUP, have identified a range of best practices. They include better policies and oversight structures for non-tenure-track professors. The objective should be to ensure consistent, equitable treatment, to monitor performance and satisfaction, and to give these professors a voice in the curricular and governance decision making that affects them.[52] They should also receive salaries and benefits commensurate with their qualifications and contributions. A variety of appointment statuses should be available depending on the length and amount of service to the institution. Faculty with long-term relationships and substantial responsibilities deserve multiyear contracts, opportunities for professional development such as conferences and research funds, and minimum procedural protections against untimely or capricious terminations. All non-tenure-track faculty should be integrated into institutional events and should receive the office space, staff support, and other resources necessary for effective performance. In short, these academics should be treated in a manner consistent with their important educational role.[53] To make that happen, they will need to exert more collective pressure, through national associations, unions, and local campus organizations.[54]

In the long term, however, the entire tenure structure requires reassessment. A system that evolved in order to safeguard principles of academic freedom is less essential now that those principles are broadly recognized and protected through other legal and contractual provisions. Today, a more varied set of career trajectories could better serve the needs of both individuals and institutions. Most universities' up-or-out tenure systems, with their full-time teaching and research requirements, poorly match the preferences and capabilities of many gifted academics. Short-term extensions of the tenure clock for those with primary caretaking responsibilities are a partial response, but broader structural change is necessary. To attract the most qualified talent pool, universities should offer a range of options with different responsibilities, entry points, and job security. Many professors with substantial caretaking obligations might prefer part-time tenured status or an extended period to compile the record necessary for tenure. Academics with significant financial needs might choose higher income over permanent job security.

The most systematic recent study of faculty and graduate student preferences found that a significant percentage would accept non-tenure-track positions if the terms were right. Relevant considerations included the geographic location, the balance of teaching and research responsibilities, the quality of the department, the chances for contract renewal, and the fit with family circumstances.[55] As this and other research indicate, the attractiveness of tenure has much to do with status and self-esteem; academic freedom is a far less important concern.[56] If individuals on alternative tracks were viewed as having comparable qualifications to those with tenured positions, many more faculty would be willing to consider those positions. For example, one management school offered an option to junior faculty who were judged tenurable: a ten-year renewable appointment with a salary premium instead of tenure. About half chose higher income over job security.[57] Developing processes that could substitute for tenure in certifying merit could build support for reform.[58] One alternative would be to designate certain statuses, such as full professor, as available only to those who met the conventional criteria for tenure. Faculty in those positions could receive increased compensation and research support, but not permanent job security. If such options were widely available, or if substantial improvements were made in the treatment of non-tenure-track professors, an employment structure with more flexibility and accountability might evolve.

Such reforms would, in turn, be more attainable if academics became more informed about plausible alternatives to tenure. Research on institutions that have recently either eliminated or adopted tenure suggests that the changes make far less practical difference than is commonly supposed. Where faculty lack opportunities for tenure, the vast majority, typically on the order of 90 percent, are renewed under long-term contracts.[59] Complaints concerning academic freedom are few, and faculty satisfaction rates are high.[60] Yet such findings seldom figure in debates over tenure. Most of those who have obtained the status reflexively resist reform. The system works well for them, so why should they support a change?[61] The reason, of course, is that the system is not working as well for everyone else. Bringing that point home will require more external pressure and structures of accountability along the lines discussed below.

In short, the stakes in the battle over tenure may be far less than is often supposed by both the public and the profession. In institutions at which tenure has become a major issue, enormous energy has been invested with little practical effect.[62] To large extent, the problems with the current system are symptomatic of a broader structural problem in higher education: inadequate accountability for performance. Addressing that issue directly may be the best way to secure a wide range of reforms, including those that involve tenure and the treatment of faculty who lack its protection.

Promoting Institutional Accountability

Addressing the challenges facing higher education raises a final set of issues concerning accountability. How can we ensure that universities are sufficiently responsive to their diverse constituencies? And how can we engage and enable faculty to participate more effectively in decisions that shape their professional futures?

Academic accountability is an enduring and elusive objective. In medieval Bologna, students contracted directly with scholars for their services and insisted on getting what they paid for. Professors had to post deposits or swear to cover the advertised syllabus and to lecture for the full class period.[63] In today's academic structure, students have no such leverage, but a growing number of governing bodies are becoming more vigilant on students' behalf. Accrediting agencies impose basic requirements that primarily concern process and resources, such as facilities, services, and faculty qualifications. However, as the federal Commission on the Future of Higher Education notes, these requirements do not address learning outcomes.[64] Nor do they ensure cost-effectiveness or prevent what some legislative decision makers consider to be faculty shirking. In one celebrated case, accounts of a University of Washington professor mowing her lawn at 10 A.M. on a weekday morning aroused widespread indignation. Why wasn't she in her office or in the classroom? Such concerns have prompted legislative initiatives to require faculty to report their hours or to be on campus for the full work week.[65]

By the turn of the twenty-first century, almost three-quarters of states were using some form of performance-based assessments in funding decisions for public institutions. Criteria included faculty workloads; retention and graduation rates; licensing test scores; and incorporation of technology, telecommunications, and distance learning.[66] These measures have provoked frequent resistance, and contributed to what the president of the American Association of Higher Education has labeled a "crisis" in accountability.[67]

The desire for more objective ways of evaluating both individual and institutional performance is rooted in broader cultural trends. Over the past quarter century, a wide range of accountability initiatives has emerged in corporate, public, and nonprofit sectors. Prominent examples that have been adapted for higher education include student test scores, along lines originally developed for elementary and secondary schools, and the Baldridge National Quality Program standards, based on models initially designed to assess business performance. Administered by the National Institute of Standards and Technology, the Baldridge Program identifies criteria for organizational effectiveness, promotes best practices, and recognizes outstanding achievement.[68] As modified for higher education in the mid-1990s, the Baldridge framework encourages institutional self-evaluation in areas such as leadership, strategic planning, workforce accomplishments, and organizational achievements as compared with peer institutions.[69] Other recent accountability initiatives include the National Survey on Student Engagement described in Chapter 3 and the "Measuring Up" report card financed by the Pew Charitable Trusts. The Measuring Up framework grades state performance on the "educational capital" of their college graduates, including test performance in reading, math, and graphics; licensing exam results; and postgraduate admissions exam scores.[70] Some institutions have also formalized internal performance review systems for faculty and departments.

Such initiatives have met with mixed but often unenthusiastic reactions. In principle, accountability is impossible to oppose, but in practice, many recent mandates yield dubious payoffs. Beleaguered administrators are already awash in reporting requirements. Virtually all university operations are subject to regulatory oversight. State and federal agencies, legislative budget committees, accrediting organizations, licensing authorities, and government and foundation funders all demand detailed data. Reporting obligations are an increasingly burdensome feature in academic life, particularly for deans, center directors, department heads, committee chairs, and principal investigators. Some institutions even prepare reports on reporting, which analyze the completeness and timeliness of submissions.[71]

Unsurprisingly, academics tend to view further oversight with skepticism, especially when the measures chosen to assess performance offer only partial, and sometimes misleading, pictures. For example, neither standardized test scores nor graduation rates are necessarily indicative of educational quality; they may have more to do with the capabilities of incoming students than with their classroom experiences.[72] Tying institutional budgets to performance on these criteria can encourage teaching to the tests or diluting graduation standards. Such financial reward structures also unjustly penalize institutions with the least qualified students and withhold the resources necessary for improvement.[73] Attempting to police faculty work hours is likely to prove similarly unproductive. Professors' self-reports are, as a practical matter, impossible to police, and time spent in the office is not a good predictor of effectiveness as teachers or scholars. Nor do surveyed faculty generally believe that current performance reviews significantly improve teaching or scholarly productivity.[74] Most important educational activities are not amenable to the simple quantitative assessments that politicians and governing boards have increasingly demanded.[75]

Yet the answer to flawed or incomplete information is better information, not less. The reflexive resistance to accountability among many faculty is part of the problem. The impulse behind most efforts is constructive, even if the means are not. Where policies are misguided, the response should be to devise better ones, and to identify more clearly the limits of recent measures. Despite increased reporting requirements, most institutions do not conduct comprehensive evaluations of educational effectiveness, and those that do often fail to make the results public. As the Federal Commission on the Future of Higher Education has concluded, both consumers and policymakers lack a sufficient factual basis to make informed decisions.[76]

The absence of adequate performance measures ill serves all concerned. Higher education is, after all, a public good. Even private institutions are heavily subsidized through tax exemptions, student aid, and research grants. The public deserves concrete measures of the return on its investment, and institutions themselves have much to gain from well-designed evaluation systems. Not all external oversight is what some faculty regard as "intellectual McCarthyism."[77] Despite their limitations, some reporting requirements are responsible for much of higher education's recent progress in areas such as conflicts of interest and equal employment opportunity. As the philosopher William James noted, "No priesthood ever reformed itself."[78] Many of the sophisticated accountability initiatives recently developed by higher education experts could be catalysts for more effective self-evaluation and accreditation standards.[79]

What these accountability approaches generally have in common is reliance on multiple factors, both quantitative and qualitative, that are widely accepted as gauges of performance. So, for example, a variation of the Baldridge framework for evaluating teaching and learning includes a wide range of indicators, including the qualifications of instructors; the coherence and comprehensiveness of course materials; the adequacy of support services; and the test performance, engagement, and satisfaction of students.[80] Some institutions have developed their own, equally varied criteria to assess departmental performance. One large university took several years to design a process that was widely accepted by faculty and administrators. Departments could veto particular proposed measures, but then had to devise alternatives. What eventually emerged was a framework that gauged departmental standing in multiple areas, including undergraduate and graduate teaching; scholarly productivity and reputation; external funding; and contributions to the university, state, and society in general. Performance on each of these dimensions was assessed through a variety of measures. For example, criteria for evaluating undergraduate teaching included the number of student majors and course enrollments per faculty member, student course ratings, and the percentage of departmental majors who gained admission to graduate and professional schools.[81]

Comparable assessment processes could be useful for many university functions. Preceding chapters have identified areas in which greater accountability or better performance criteria are necessary. With respect to scholarship, evaluation should focus less on quantity and provide more recognition for a wider range of contributions. In many disciplines, social relevance, accessible prose, and practical impact should carry greater weight. Publications for a nonscholarly audience deserve more respect, but they should also be held to more rigorous standards of academic responsibility, such as fairness, accuracy, and disclosure of conflicts of interest.

At research universities, contributions other than scholarship also should assume greater priority in performance reviews, as well as in promotion, compensation, and appointments processes. Most obviously, faculty should be more accountable for their teaching and service. That, in turn, will require better evaluation structures. Chapters 3 and 4 have suggested a number of possibilities. For example, peer review of classroom performance could be more frequent, informed, and disinterested. Universities also could establish more systematic processes for evaluating faculty committee and administrative service. They also could make such evaluations more central in allocating workloads and determining compensation.

Another area in which greater accountability is necessary involves misconduct in research and teaching. As discussion in Chapters 2 and 3 made clear, the absence of adequate information and enforcement structures concerning ethical violations is itself an ethical problem. So is the absence of clarity about whether certain conduct rises to the level of a sanctionable offense. Norms concerning the need for attribution of authority or credit for authorship are often fuzzy, as are disclosure requirements for research funded by third parties. Effective oversight structures are frequently lacking. Misconduct in teaching typically escapes sanctions unless it rises to the level of moral turpitude or violates legal as well as ethical standards, such as those governing sexual harassment and racial bias. Universities, professional associations, accrediting bodies, and scholarly journals all must do more to clarify ethical standards and to hold academics responsible for violations.

Finally, higher education needs broader concepts of accountability. Universities generally gauge their success in terms of academic excellence and focus attention on academic performance criteria. Yet academic achievement is highly dependent on organizational support. The ability of faculty and students to function effectively turns on the responsiveness, capacities, and efficiency of university administrative operations. Performance along these dimensions can materially affect institutional reputation, morale, recruitment, and development efforts. Obvious as this point seems, its importance is seldom fully registered in academic priorities.[82] Faculty are generally more willing to vent their frustrations than to invest energy in solutions. Perfunctory reviews of individual staff performance too often substitute for systematic assessments of organizational effectiveness and comparisons with other institutions. Well-designed evaluation is necessary for all university functions, not simply the narrow subset singled out by legislative initiatives or media rankings. No profession enjoys so much autonomy in determining the terms of its own work. Academic freedom rests on academic responsibility, and institutions that do not establish adequate systems of holding themselves accountable will find that others are doing it for them.

RETHINKING ACADEMIC PRIORITIES: THE PURSUIT OF PRESTIGE AND THE PURSUIT OF KNOWLEDGE

In eighteenth-century Florence, a man of literature took the life of a cousin who accused him of not understanding Dante.[83] That impulse will be well understood by most contemporary scholars. Academics are, of course, scarcely unique in their concerns about reputation. Indeed, as Alain de Botton's *Status Anxiety* makes clear, such concerns are endemic to the human condition.[84] But the desire for intellectual recognition is particularly pronounced among faculty, who, by definition, have built their careers by excelling on traditional measures of academic achievement. While the pursuit of status can be a constructive spur to excellence, it also can become an end in itself and subvert other more crucial values. Many of the problems chronicled in preceding chapters stem from the overvaluation of prestige by academics and their institutions.

At the institutional level, much of the problem stems from increasing competition and increasing reliance on rankings as a measure of achievement. Neither trend is likely to be reversed, but both need somehow to be cabined or redirected. If we cannot reduce competitive pressures, we can at least rethink what is worth competing for, and how we might change the terms of the competition. Collective action is obviously needed. Academic institutions, professional associations, foundations, and other nonprofit groups must work together to improve existing rating systems and to design alternatives. Modifying criteria, publishing comparative data without a bottom-line ranking, and rating different rating systems are all worth pursuing.[85] Another possibility, proposed by the federal Commission on the Future of Higher Education, would be a database enabling consumers to evaluate an institution based on their own priorities. Instead of relying on the arbitrary weighting of various measures by publications such as *U.S. News and World Report*, applicants could customize rankings to reflect the importance that they attach to factors such as financial aid, graduation rates, student engagement, and so forth.[86] If adequate information on institutional performance was included, such a database could help counteract the worst aspects of the current ranking structure.

Better public education about higher education is also essential. Empirical research suggests that most Americans share inaccurate assumptions about the cost structure of colleges and universities, and that fuller information would increase popular support for raising tuition for those who could afford it.[87] However, effective communication about costs has to go in both directions. Even a highly knowledgeable public may well prefer different trade-offs between excellence and affordability than many institutions are pursuing. Just as middle-class Victorians once wanted a pianoforte in the parlour regardless of whether anyone in the family could play, academics have often wanted programs that embellish their reputations, irrespective of societal demand. In today's economic climate, we need a more candid public dialogue on fundamental resource issues. How much expertise, in how many fields, and in how many institutions, can we realistically afford?

Individual faculty also need to think more deeply about how the pursuit of knowledge relates to the pursuit of status, and what forms of recognition are worth the price. In his mid-eighteenth-century *Theory of Moral Sentiments*, Adam Smith posed the fundamental question: "To what purpose is all the toil and bustle of this world? What is the end of avarice and ambition, of the pursuit of wealth, of power and preeminence?" Beyond meeting the basic "necessities of nature," what is "that great purpose of human life which we call *bettering our condition*?" Smith's answer would resonate with contemporary academics: "To be observed, to be attended to, to be taken notice of with sympathy . . . and approbation."[88] Our self-respect is intimately bound up in the respect of others and in the sense that what we do matters to the world. In many ways, this is all to the good. As de Botton notes, it is hard to imagine a satisfying life that is free of such concerns; they are part of the price we pay for having aspirations, wanting communities, and caring about those besides ourselves.[89] The problem arises when we lose sight of what forms of recognition matter most, and when we make our own values unduly captive to the judgments of others.

Status hierarchies carry special costs in university life. For most faculty, one of the main motivations for choosing an academic career, and one of its main satisfactions, is intellectual freedom.[90] Professors value having control over their own time, agendas, and priorities. Yet that freedom is diminished when the pursuit of prestige becomes controlling. Moreover, because academic recognition is to some extent a relative good, a large percentage of the profession is bound to come up short. Much of the unhealthy behavior chronicled in the preceding chapters stems from undue preoccupation with status.

The solutions are obvious in principle and elusive in practice. The fundamental challenge is for academics to stay focused on their own values, and to make the best use of their abilities in the service of goals that they find most meaningful. Rewards can come from many sources, and not all of them register prominently on the conventional pecking order. Harvard philosopher William James once claimed that "to give up pretensions is as blessed a relief as to get them gratified."[91] Whether or not the satisfactions are truly equivalent, letting go of certain status needs is often far preferable to the alternative. In an essay on academic success and failure, sociologist Gary Marx similarly suggests that the most dependable rewards come from practicing the craft itself, independent of external validation: "I came to realize that I got pleasure from finding partial answers to questions I wondered about, turning a clever phrase, ordering a set of ideas. In a competitive world of uncertain [payoffs,] . . . there is much to be said for valuing the process of production as an end in itself."[92] Teaching a good class, mentoring a junior colleague, advising a student in difficulty, even shouldering one's fair share of administrative housekeeping can be a source of internal satisfaction, if not external recognition. Enabling others to carry on the pursuit of knowledge is a task worthy of our talents.

A common homily at commencement ceremonies is that graduates should remember as they leave why they came. Most students enter universities with more than vocational interests. Many hope to find intellectual challenge and the skills to leave some corner of the world slightly better than they found it. Many of us enter the academic life with similar motivations, and the advice we give to graduates is also worth taking ourselves. What defines our profession is a commitment to learning: our own, our students, our readers. We need more occasions to consider how well our daily activities advance our deepest aspirations and what institutional structures get in the way. Our pursuit of knowledge should always include self-knowledge, and a commitment to connect our principles with our practices.

REFERENCE MATTER

Notes

CHAPTER ONE

1. John Gardner, *Mickelsson's Ghosts* (New York: Knopf, 1982), 16.

2. United States Department of Education, National Center for Education Statistics, *Education Directory, Colleges and Universities* (Washington, DC: United States Department of Education, 2002), 295, Table 243.

3. Donald Kennedy, *Academic Duty* (Cambridge, MA: Harvard University Press, 1997), 4.

4. James J. Duderstadt, *A University for the 21st Century* (Ann Arbor: University of Michigan Press, 2000), 48; Carnegie Classification Website, www.carnegiefoundation. org/classifications.

5. Derek Bok, *Higher Education* (Cambridge, MA: Harvard University Press, 1986), 31.

6. *London Times, The Times Higher Education Supplement* (London: Times Newspapers Ltd., 2004).

7. Derek Bok, *Our Underachieving Colleges* (Princeton, NJ: Princeton University Press, 2006), 11.

8. Elaine Showalter, *Faculty Towers: The Academic Novel and Its Discontents* (Philadelphia: University of Pennsylvania Press, 2005), 121.

9. Richard Levin, *The Work of the University* (New Haven, CT: Yale University Press, 2003), 89; "Remember Detroit," The Economist, March 9, 2006, 11.

10. Jeffrey Selingo, "U.S. Public's Confidence in Colleges Remains High," *Chronicle of Higher Education*, May 7, 2004, A1.

11. Jaroslav Pelikan, *The Idea of the University: A Reexamination* (New Haven, CT: Yale University Press, 1992), 210–11.

12. Alexander W. Astin, *What Matters in College? Four Critical Years Revisited* (San Francisco: Jossey-Bass, 1993), 276.

13. Higher Education Research Institute, *The American College Teacher: National Norms for the HERI Faculty Survey* (Los Angeles: Higher Education Research Institute, University of California at Los Angeles, 2005) (78 percent); Allen Sanderson, Voon Chin Phua, David Herda, *The American Faculty Poll* (Chicago: National Opinion Research Center, 2000), 13 (90 percent). See also Philip C. Wankat, *The Effective, Efficient Professor* (Boston: Allyn and Bacon, 2001), 2 (discussing the 1998 UCLA Higher Education Research Institute faculty survey).

14. For Europe, see Donald E. Hall, "The Grass Isn't Greener," *Chronicle of Higher Education*, July 8, 2005, C1, C4.

15. Peter Keane, "Interloper in the Fields of Academe," *Toledo Law Review* 35 (2003): 119, 121.

16. Selingo, "U.S. Public's Confidence in Colleges," A1.

17. Sanderson, Phua, and Herda, *The American Faculty Poll*, 37, 32, 28.

18. John Henry Newman, *The Idea of a University*, ed. Martin J. Suaglie (Notre Dame, IN: Notre Dame Press, 1900), discussed in Levin, *The Work of the University*, 13.

19. Stanley Aronowitz, *The Knowledge Factory* (Boston: Beacon Press, 2000), 117 (citing data indicating that those with B.A. degrees average about twice the incomes of those with only a high school education).

20. Bill Readings, *The University in Ruins* (Cambridge, MA: Harvard University Press, 1996), 23.

21. Sanderson, Phua, and Herda, *The American Faculty Poll*, 23.

22. Dominic J. Brewer, Susan M. Gates, and Charles A. Goldman, *In Pursuit of Prestige* (New Brunswick, NJ: Transaction, 2002), 134.

23. Thorstein Veblen, *Higher Education in America* (New York: B. W. Huebsch, 1918), 168.

24. Lawrence K. Pettit, "Problems of Ethics in Higher Education," *Educational Record* 71 (1990):34, 36. See also Bok, *Higher Education*, 14; Sheila Slaughter and Larry L. Leslie, *Academic Capitalism* (Baltimore: Johns Hopkins University Press, 1997), 122; Martin Trow, "On the Accountability of Higher Education in the United States," in *Universities and Their Leadership*, eds. William G. Bowen and Harold T. Shapiro (Princeton, NJ: Princeton University Press, 1998), 15, 22. Some experts on higher education often distinguish between two status-related measures. *Reputation* is the broader term, which refers to an institution's ability to consistently meet the specific demands of its primary constituencies. *Prestige* refers to the opinion that those constituencies have of the institution's relative quality. Brewer, Gates, and Goldman, *In Pursuit of Prestige*, 27–29.

25. Paul Boyer, *College Rankings Exposed* (Lawrenceville, NJ: Thomson Peterson, 2003), 36.

26. Colin Diver, "Is There Life After Rankings?" *Atlantic Monthly*, November 2005, 136–37; Jan Hoffman, "Judge Not, Law Schools Demand of a Magazine That Ranks Them," *New York Times*, February 19, 1998, A1; Leigh Jones, "Ranking Time Brings Rain of Promos," *Legal Times*, November 3, 2005, 6 (quoting Paul Caron). For discussion of this problem in the context of teaching, see Chapter 3.

27. Stephen P. Klein and Laura Hamilton, *The Validity of the* U.S. News and World Report *Rankings of ABA Law Schools* (Washington, DC: Association of American Law Schools, 1998); Terry Carter, "Rankled by the Rankings," *ABA Journal*, March 1998, 46, 48–49; Roger L. Geiger, *Knowledge and Money* (Stanford, CA: Stanford University Press, 2004), 149.

28. Brewer, Gates, and Goldman, *In Pursuit of Prestige*, 31, 86; Michael Sauder and Ryon Lancaster, "Do Rankings Matter? The Effects of *U.S. News & World Report* Rankings on the Admissions Process of Law Schools," *Law and Society Review* 40 (2006): 125–29.

29. Derek C. Bok, "Markets and Mindwork," *Washington University Journal of Law and Policy* 10 (2002): 1, 4; Nicholas Confessore, "What Makes a College Good?" *Atlantic Monthly*, November 2003, 118, 126, 128.

30. Boyer, *College Rankings Exposed*, 43; Ann Hulburt, "Exile in Guidesville?" *New York Times Magazine*, September 19, 2004, 19, 20; Nicholas Thompson, "The Best, The

Top, The Most," *New York Times*, August 3, 2003, A4; Carl Bialik, "Small Change by *U.S. News* Leads to New Controversy in Rankings," The Numbers Guy, *Wall Street Journal*, April 7, 2005, available at numbersguy@wsj.com; Sauder and Lancaster, "Do Rankings Matter?" 112–15; Leigh Jones, "Law Schools Play the Rank Game," *National Law Journal*, April 18, 2005, A10; Robin Wilson, "Deep Thought, Quantified," *Chronicle of Higher Education*, May 20, 2005, 8.

31. For examples, see Thomas E. Corts, "Let's Stop Trivializing the Truth," *Trusteeship* 5 (January–February 1997): 6, 7; Diver, "Is There Life After Rankings?" 137; Alex Wellen, "The $8.78 Million Maneuver," *New York Times*, July 31, 2005, Section 4A, 18–19.

32. See Jones, "Law Schools Play the Rank Game," A10; Ronald G. Ehrenberg, "Reaching for the Brass Ring: The *U.S. News and World Report* Rankings and Competition," *Review of Higher Education* 26 (2002): 145, 150–51; Brian Leiter, "The *U.S. News* Law School Rankings: A Guide for the Perplexed," May, 2003, available at www.utexas.edu/law/faculty/bleiter/rankings/guide.html.

33. Wellen, "The $8.78 Million Maneuver," 18, 19; see also Jones, "Law Schools Play the Rank Game," A10.

34. Clara M. Lovett, "The Perils of Pursuing Prestige," *Chronicle of Higher Education*, January 21, 2005, available at http://chronicle.com/prm/weekly/v51/i20/20b02001.htm.

35. Brewer, Gates, and Goldman, *In Pursuit of Prestige*, 27; Geiger, *Knowledge and Money*, 230; Anne K. Walters, "Magazine Rankings of Business Schools Hurt M.B.A. Programs, Scholars Argue," *Chronicle of Higher Education* (August 8, 2005): 58.

36. Diver, "Is There Life After Rankings?" 137; Jones, "Ranking Time Brings Rain of Promos," 6; Norman Bradburn, "Outranked and Underrated," *Legal Affairs*, November–December, 2005, 24; Jan Hoffman, "Judge Not, Law Schools Demand of a Magazine That Ranks Them," A1; Carter, "Rankled by the Rankings," 48–49.

37. Walters, "Magazine Rankings of Business Schools Hurt M.B.A. Programs, Scholars Argue," A58; "The Washington Monthly College Guide," *Washington Monthly*, September 2005, 24, 26.

38. Jones, "Ranking Time Brings Rain of Promos," 6 (quoting Robert Morse).

39. James Axtell, *The Pleasures of Academe* (Lincoln: Nebraska University Press, 1998), 123.

40. Veblen, *Higher Education in America*, 172; Derek Bok, *Universities in the Marketplace: The Commercialization of Higher Education* (Princeton: Princeton University Press, 2003), 18 (quoting Veblen); Veblen, Higher Education in America, 106.

41. For "upward drift," see David Riesman, *Constraint and Variety in American Education* (Lincoln, NE: University of Nebraska Press, 1956), 14. For "mission creep," see Duderstadt, *A University for the 21st Century*, 26, 57; Robert M. Diamond, "Some Final Observations," in *A Field Guide to Academic Leadership*, ed. Robert M. Diamond (San Francisco: Jossey Bass, 2002), 483.

42. Paul J. DiMaggio and Walter Powell, "The Iron Cage Revisited: Institutional Isomorphism and Collective Rationality in Organizational Fields," *American Sociological Review* 48 (1983): 147, 152–53; John W. Meyer, "The Charter: Conditions of Diffuse Socialization," in *Social Process and Social Structures*, ed. W. Richard Scott (New York: Holt, Rinehart, and Winston, 1970), 564, 565–68.

43. Henry Ward Beecher, *Norwood: Or, Village Life in New England* (New York: Charles Scribner, 1868), 181.

44. Paul Fussell, "Schools for Snobbery," *New Republic,* October 4, 1982, 25.

45. Stephen Stigler, "Competition and Research Universities," in *The Research University in Time of Discontent,* eds. Jonathan R. Cole, Elinor Barber, and Stephen R. Graubard (Baltimore: Johns Hopkins University Press, 1994), 115, 148.

46. Report of the Wingspread Group on Higher Education, *An American Imperative: Higher Expectations for Higher Education* (Racine, WI: The Johnson Foundation, Wingspread, 1993), 81 (quoting Robert Hutchins).

47. James Engel and Anthony Dangerfield, "Humanities in the Age of Money," *Harvard Magazine,* May–June 1998, 48, 50, 52; Eyal Press and Jennifer Washburn, "The Kept University," *Atlantic,* March, 2000.

48. Jane Tompkins, *A Life in School: What the Teacher Learned* (Cambridge, MA: Perseus Books, 1996), 216.

49. Pierre Bourdieu, *Homo Academicus,* trans. Peter Collins (Stanford, CA: Stanford University Press, 1988).

50. Charles J. Sykes, *ProfScam: Professors and the Demise of Higher Education* (Washington, DC: Regnery Gateway, 1988); Frank H. T. Rhodes, "The Advancement of Learning: Prospects in a Cynical Age," *Proceedings of the American Philosophical Society* 142 (1998): 218, 219.

51. Ronald G. Ehrenberg and Michael Rizzo, "Financial Forces and the Future of American Higher Education," *Academe* (July–August 2004): 28, available at www.aaup. org/publications/Academe/2004/04ja/04jaehre.htm; Kennedy, *Academic Duty;* John B. Bennett, *Collegial Professionalism: The Academy, Individualism, and the Common Good* (New York: American Council on Education, Oryx Press, 1998); Kenneth Eble, "Conflicts Between Scholarship and Teaching," in *A Professor's Duties: Ethical Issues in College Teaching,* ed. Peter J. Markie (New York: Rowman and Littlefield, 1994), 209.

52. Zachary Karabell, *What's College For? The Struggle to Define American Higher Education* (New York: Basic Books), 13. See also Gerald Graff, *Clueless in Academe: How Schooling Obscures the Life of the Mind* (New Haven, CT: Yale University Press, 2003), 150.

53. John Kenneth Galbraith, *A Tenured Professor* (Cambridge: MA: Houghton Mifflin, 1990), 78.

54. John W. Aldridge, *The Party at Cranton* (New York: David McKay, 1960), 15.

55. Aldridge, *The Party at Cranton,* 28.

56. Louis Menand, "How to Make a Ph.D. Matter," *New York Times Magazine,* September 22, 1996, 78, 79.

57. Bourdieu, *Homo Academicus,* 85.

58. Gerald Warner Brace, *The Department* (New York: Norton, 1968), 280.

59. Gary Marx, "Reflections on Academic Success and Failure: Making it, Forsaking It, Reshaping It," in *Authors of Their Own Lives,* ed. Bennett M. Berger (Berkeley, CA: University of California Press, 1990), 267–68.

60. C. P. Snow, *The Masters* (London: MacMillan, 1951), 48.

61. Brewer, Gates, and Goldman, *In Pursuit of Prestige,* 140.

62. Axtell, *The Pleasures of Academe,* 215; John N. Pully, "The Big Squeeze," *Chronicle of Higher Education,* December 19, 2003; Derek Bok, "Academic Values and the Lure of Profits," *Chronicle of Higher Education,* April 4, 2003.

63. Ehrenberg and Rizzo, "Financial Forces and the Future of American Higher Education."

64. Greg Winter, "Why the Cost of College Keeps Going Up," *New York Times*, October 26, 2003, E2; College Board, *Trends in College Pricing, Trends in Higher Education Series* (New York: College Board Publications, 2005), sections 2.2 and 2.3, available at www.collegeboard.com;prod_downloads/press/cost04/041264TrendsPricing2004.FINAL.pdf; Richard Vedder, *Going Broke by Degree: Why College Costs Too Much* (Washington, DC: American Enterprise Institute Press, 2004), 3, 6.

65. Mark Dudzic and Aldoph Reed Jr., "Free Higher Ed!" *The Nation*, February 23, 2004, 16.

66. Jeffrey Selingo and Jeffrey Brainard, "The Rich-Poor Gap Widens for Colleges and Students," *Chronicle of Higher Education*, April 7, 2006, A1, A13; Charles Miller and Geri Malandra, *Accountability/Assessment: Issue Paper by the Secretary of Education's Commission on the Future of Higher Education* (Washington, DC: United States Department of Education, April 4, 2006), available at www.ed.gov/about/bdcomm/list/hiedfuture/reports.html.

67. Michael Janofsky, "College Leaders' Earnings Top $1 Million," *New York Times*, November 14, 2005, A12; Sam Dillon, "Ivory Tower Executive Suite Gets C.E.O.-Level Salaries," *New York Times*, November 15, 2004, A17; Kennedy, *Academic Duty*, 171–72; Julianne Basinger, "High Pay, Hard Questions," *Chronicle of Higher Education*, Nov. 19, 2004, available at http://chronicle.com/weekly/v51/il3/13b00301.htm.

68. Paul Fain, "The Federal Lens Focuses on College Chiefs' Pay," *Chronicle of Higher Education*, November 18, 2005, B13; John L. Pulley, "A Fallen President Breaks His Silence," *Chronicle of Higher Education*, October 22, 2004, A38; Thomas Sowell, *Inside American Education* (New York: Maxwell Macmillan International, 1993), 272.

69. Robert C. Dynes, letter to the editor, *San Francisco Chronicle*, November 16, 2005, B8.

70. Timothy R. Tangherlini, letter to the editor, *San Francisco Chronicle*, November 16, 2005, B8.

71. Committee on Education and the Workforce, U.S. House of Representatives, "College Cost Central: A Resource for Parents, Students, and Taxpayers Fed Up with the High Cost of Higher Education," at http://edworkforce.house.gov/issues/108th/education/highereducation/collegecostcentral/htm.

72. Martin Anderson, *Imposters in the Temple* (New York: Simon & Schuster, 1992), 38.

73. Adam Smith, "Experience of the Institutions for the Education of Youth," in *An Inquiry into the Nature and Causes of the Wealth of Nations*, eds. Roy H. Campbell and Andrew S. Skinner (Indianapolis: Library Classics, 1976), 764.

74. John Hechinger, "Higher Education Bill Aims to Stir Up Academia," *Wall Street Journal*, March 30, 2006, A8.

75. Stanley Fish, "Give Us Liberty or Give Us Revenue" (quoting Lyall), *Chronicle of Higher Education*, October 31, 2003, C4.

76. Dennis Cauchon, "Grants More Than Offset Soaring University Tuition," *USA Today*, June 28, 2004, A4.

77. Frank H. T. Rhodes, "The Advancement of Learning: Prospects in a Cynical Age," *Proceedings of the American Philosophical Society*, 139; James O. Freedman, *Liberal Education and the Public Interest* (Iowa City: University of Iowa Press, 2003), 33–34.

78. Ehrenberg and Rizzo, "Financial Forces and the Future of American Higher Education."

79. Axtell, *The Pleasures of Academe*, 213 (reporting Department of Education find-ings of an average fifty-three-hour work week for faculty and fifty-seven hours in re-search universities); Trow, "On the Accountability of Higher Education in the United States," 41 (estimating that faculty in research universities spend about sixty hours in institutional obligations); Wankat, *The Effective, Efficient Professor*, 1 (citing range of fifty-five to sixty-two hours a week); Ray Delgado, "Faculty Survey Shows Most Like Their Quality of Life," *Stanford Campus Report*, December 10, 2003, 1, 4 (noting that Stanford faculty report an average work load of sixty hours a week).

80. "What Professors Earn," *Chronicle of Higher Education*, April 18, 2003 (noting that instructors averaged between $36,000 and $39,000 and lecturers between $43,00 and $44,000). See Cary Nelson and Stephen Watt, *Academic Keywords: A Devils Diction-ary for Higher Education* (New York: Routledge, 1999), 93, 123.

81. Lila Guterman, "Research Inc.," *Chronicle of Higher Education*, November 25, 2005, A13, A14.

82. Frederick Rudolph, *The American College and University* (Athens, Georgia: Uni-versity of Georgia Press, 1990), 158–70, 194–96; Laurence R. Veysey, *The Emergence of the American University* (Chicago: University of Chicago Press, 1965), 6.

83. *Addresses at the Inauguration of Charles William Eliot as President of Harvard Col-lege* (Cambridge, 1869), 48.

84. Claude Charleton Bowman, *The College Professor in America: An Analysis of Ar-ticles Published in the General Magazines, 1890–1938* (New York, Arno, 1977, (c. 1938)), 54 (quoting *New Republic*).

85. Rudolph, *The American College*, 196.

86. Rudolph, *The American College*, 194. See also Burton Bledstein, *The Culture of Professionalism: The Middle Class and the Development of Higher Education in America* (New York: Norton 1976), 274–81.

87. Beecher, *Norwood*, 26.

88. Ernest L. Boyer, *Scholarship Reconsidered* (Princeton, NJ: Carnegie Foundation for the Advancement of Teaching, 1990) (quoting Cather), 5.

89. Upton Sinclair, *The Goose-Step* (Pasadena, CA: Upton Sinclair, 1922), 390.

90. Veysey, *Emergence of the American University*, 390.

91. Harold Wave Whicker, "Doctors of Dullness," *North American Review* CXV (1929).

92. Andrew Carnegie, quoted in *U.S. Commission of Education Report* (Washington, DC 1889–1890), Vol. II, 1143. See Veysey, *Emergence of the American University*, 14.

93. David L. Kirp, *Einstein, Shakespeare, and the Bottom Line* (Cambridge, MA: Har-vard University Press, 2003) (quoting the Yale Report), 258.

94. The statement, perhaps apocryphal, is commonly attributed to Jeremiah Day.

95. Veblen, *Higher Education in America*, 155.

96. Veysey, *Emergence of the American University* (quoting Wilson), 242.

97. Rudolph, *The American College*, 256.

98. Rudolph, *The American College*, 280.

99. Jaroslav Pelikan, *The Idea of the University: A Reexamination* (New Haven, CT: Yale University Press, 1992) (quoting Robert Maynard Hutchins), 104.

100. Boyer, *Scholarship Reconsidered*, 6.

101. See Bennett, *Collegial Professionalism*, 3–4. See also Daniel Cottom, *Why Education Is Useless* (Philadelphia: University of Pennsylvania Press, 2003), 9.

102. See Veysey, *Emergence of American Universities*, 350, 398–406. For other examples, see Sinclair, *The Goose-Step*.

103. Veysey, *Emergence of the American University*, 388–89.

104. Veysey, *Emergence of the American University*, 327; Kirp, *Shakespeare, Einstein, and the Bottom Line*, 6; Bok, *Universities in the Marketplace*, 2.

105. "The Perplexities of a College President," *Atlantic Monthly* LXXXV (1900): 483, 493; Veysey, *Emergence of the American University*, 352–53.

106. Veysey, *Emergence of the American University*, 351 (quoting Princeton Trustee).

107. Bok, *Universities in the Marketplace*, 19 (quoting John Jay Chapman).

108. Sinclair, *Goose-Step*, 23–29, 63; Veblen, *Higher Education in America*, 167–72.

109. Kirp, *Shakespeare, Einstein, and the Bottom Line*, 3. See Bok, *Universities in the Marketplace*, 2; Kennedy, *Academic Duty*, 11–12; Jennifer Washburn, *University, Inc.* (New York: Basic Books, 2005).

110. Kirp, *Shakespeare, Einstein, and the Bottom Line*, 36 (quoting Hutchins).

111. Bok, *Universities in the Marketplace;* Sheila Slaughter, "Professional Values and the Allure of the Market," *Academe* (January 13, 2004); Clark Kerr, "Knowledge Ethics and the New Academic Culture," *Change*, January–February, 1994, 12; Slaughter and Leslie, *Academic Capitalism*, 129–32, 230; Washburn, *University, Inc.*, 136–41.

112. Sykes, *Profscam*, 230.

113. Jules Getman, *In the Company of Scholars: The Struggle for the Soul of the University* (Austin, Texas: University of Texas Press, 1992), 209.

114. Sykes, *Profscam*, 229, n. 9.

115. James L. Shulman and William G. Bowen, *The Game of Life: College Sports and Educational Values* (Princeton, Princeton University Press, 2001).

116. Welch Sugos, "Sports as the University's 'Front Porch'? The Public Is Skeptical," *Chronicle of Higher Education*, May 2, 2003, available at http://chronicle.com/weekly/v49/i34/34a01701.htm.

117. Sykes, *Profscam*, 239 (quoting Parajo Dunes Conference Statement).

118. Bok, *Universities in the Marketplace*, 115–16.

119. Richard Vedder, *Going Broke by Degree: Why College Costs Too Much* (Washington, DC: American Enterprise Institute Press, 2004), 160–77.

120. Joe Berry, *Reclaiming the Ivory Tower: Organizing Adjuncts to Change Higher Education* (New York: Monthly Review Press, 2005), 3.

121. John Hechinger, "Battle Over Academic Standards Weighs on For-Profit Colleges," *Wall Street Journal*, September 30, 2005, A1; Anya Kamenetz, "The Profit Chase," *Slate*, November 16, 2005, available at www.slate.com/toolbar.aspx?action=print&id=2130516.

122. David F. Noble, *Digital Diploma Mills: The Automation of Higher Education* (New York: Monthly Review Press, 2001); Nelson and Watt, *Academic Keywords*, 116–17.

123. Hechinger, "Battle Over Academic Standards," A1, A16. Kamenetz, "The Profit Chase."

124. *Kropinski v. World Plan Executive Council-U.S.*, 853 F. 2d 948, 950–53 (D.C. Cir. 1988). The appellate court reversed a jury verdict of $137,890 and remanded for a new trial. No record of a final settlement was reported. For recent litigation, see Kamenetz, "The Profit Chase."

125. Richard Matasar, "A Commercialist Manifesto: Entrepreneurs, Academics, and the Purity of Heart and Soul," *Florida Law Review* 46 (1996): 805.

126. Bennett, *Collegial Professionalism*, 4; Jonathan R. Cole, "Balancing Acts: Dilemmas of Choice Facing Research Universities," in *The Research University in a Time of Discontent*, eds. Jonathan R. Cole, Elinor G. Barber, and Stephen R. Graubard (Baltimore: Johns Hopkins Press, 1994), 1; Stuart Palmer, *The Universities Today: Scholarship, Self-Interest, and Politics* (Lanham, MD: University Press of America, 1998), 172–73.

127. Bennett, *Collegial Professionalism*, viii.

128. Kennedy, *Academic Duty*, 33.

129. Piper Fogg, "The Gap That Won't Go Away," *Chronicle of Higher Education*, April 18, 2003, A12.

130. United States Department of Education, *Staff in Postsecondary Institutions, Fall 2003, and Salaries of Full-Time Instructional Faculty, 2003–04* (Washington, DC: United States Department of Education, National Center for Education Statistics, May 2005).

131. Barbara Ehrenreich, "Class Struggle 101," *The Progressive*, November, 2003, 1.

132. Pully, "The Big Squeeze;" Bok, *Academic Values;* Slaughter and Leslie, *Academic Capitalism*, 21, 129.

133. The Commission on the Academic Presidency, Association of Governing Boards of Universities and Colleges, *Renewing the Academic Presidency* (Association of Governing Boards of Universities and Colleges, 1996), 2; Harold M. Williams, "The Economics of Higher Education in the United States" in *Challenges Facing Higher Education at the Millenium*, eds. Werner Z. Hirsch and Luc E. Weber (New York and Oxford, UK: International Association of Universities Press, 1999), 65; Alan E. Gusken and Mary B. Marcy, "Pressures for Fundamental Reform," in *Field Guide to Academic Leadership*, ed. Robert M. Diamond (San Francisco: Jossey Bass, 2002), 3, 4–8.

134. Duderstadt, *A University for the 21st Century*, 189.

135. Piper Fogg, "When Private Colleges Come Knocking," *Chronicle of Higher Education*, November 12, 2004, available at http://chronicle.com/weekly/v5/i12/`12a020001.htm.

136. Kirp, *Einstein, Shakespeare, and the Bottom Line*, 66–78; Mary A. Burgan, "The Faculty Superstar Syndrome," *Academe* (May, June 1988): 10, 13.

137. David Lodge, *Small World* (New York: Macmillan, 1984), 42.

138. Regina Warwick, "To Spurn a Star," *Chronicle of Higher Education*, January 16, 2004, C2. For the demand for basketball tickets, see Stuart Rojstaczer, *Gone for Good: Tales of University Life after the Golden Age* (New York: Oxford University Press, 1999), 103.

139. Kirp, *Einstein, Shakespeare, and the Bottom Line*, 5. See also Alison Schneider, "Recruiting Academic Stars: New Tactics in an Old Game," *Chronicle of Higher Education*, May 29, 1998, A12–14.

140. Barbara Smaller, *New Yorker*, April 4, 2005, 63.

141. Dean of Student Services at Babson College, quoted in Kirp, *Einstein, Shakespeare, and the Bottom Line*, 23. See also Elizabeth Warren and Amalia Warren Tyagi, *The Two-Income Trap* (New York: Basic Books, 2003), 43.

142. Ehrenberg and Rizzo, "Financial Forces and the Future of American Higher Education."

143. Matthew Quirk, "The Best Class Money Can Buy," *Atlantic*, November 2005, 128–30.

144. Alice Gomstyn, "U.S. Faces a College-Access Crisis, Education-Policy Group

Warns," *Chronicle of Higher Education*, October 10, 2003, A35, available at http://chronicle.com/prm/weekly/v50/i07/07a03501.htm.

145. Ehrenberg and Rizzo, "Financial Forces and the Future of American Higher Education." For inequality in general, see Miller and Malandra, *Accountability/Assessment*. For selective institutions, see Ross Douthat, "Does Meritocracy Work?," *Atlantic Monthly*, November, 2005, 120, 122, 124. See also William Bowen, Martin A. Kurzweil, and Eugene M. Tobin, *Equity and Excellence in American Higher Education* (Charlottesville: University of Virginia Press, 2005).

146. Donald Kennedy, "Making Choices in the Research University," in *Research Universities in a Time of Discontent, eds.* Jonathan R. Cole, Elinor G. Barber, and Stephen R. Graubard (Baltimore: Johns Hopkins University Press, 1994) 85, 97. See also Cole, "Balancing Acts: Dilemmas of Choice Facing Research Universities," in id., 1.

147. Bennett, *Collegial Professionalism*, 125; Getman, *In the Company of Scholars*, 266.

148. Allan Bloom, *The Closing of the American Mind* (New York: Simon & Schuster, 1987). See also Bok, *Our Underachieving Colleges*, 40–45.

149. Slaughter, "Professional Values." See also David Damrosh, *We Scholars: Changing the Culture of the University* (Cambridge, MA: Harvard University Press, 1995), 41.

150. Mark Oppenheimer, "Higher Learning, A Tutorial," *Wall Street Journal*, February 16, 2006, W9.

151. Damrosh, *We Scholars*, 41.

152. Bennett, *Collegial Professionalism*, 116.

153. Bruce Wilshire, *The Moral Collapse of the University* (New York: State University of New York Press, 1990), 126 (quoting Emerson).

Chapter Two

1. James Axtell, *The Pleasures of Academe* (Lincoln, NE: University of Nebraska Press, 1998), 35; David P. Hamilton, "Trivia Pursuit," *Washington Monthly*, March 1991, 36.

2. David P. Hamilton, "Research Papers: Who's Uncited Now?," *Science* 251 (1991): 25; Lynne V. Cheney, "Mélange: Foolish and Insignificant Research in the Humanities," *Chronicle of Higher Education*, July 17, 1991, B2.

3. Axtell, *The Pleasures of Academe*, 235–36; Charles J. Sykes, *ProfScam: Professors and the Demise of Higher Education* (Washington, DC: Regnery Gateway, 1988), 5; Martin Anderson, *Imposters in the Temple* (New York: Simon & Schuster, 1992), 97.

4. George Ade, "Fables in Slang," quoted in the *Oxford Dictionary of Literary Quotations*, ed. Peter Kemp, 1997, 202.

5. Richard A. Posner, "The Deprofessionalization of Legal Teaching and Scholarship," *Michigan Law Review* 91 (1993): 1921, 1928.

6. E-mail from David Luban, professor of law and philosophy, Georgetown University Law Center, to Deborah L. Rhode, November 8, 2001.

7. Ernest L. Boyer, *Scholarship Reconsidered* (Princeton, NJ: Carnegie Foundation for the Advancement of Education, 1990), 62.

8. Boyer, *Scholarship Reconsidered*, 15.

9. William G. Bowen, *Ever the Teacher: William G. Bowen's Writings as President of Princeton* (Princeton, NJ: Princeton University Press, 1987), 238; Axtell, *The Pleasures of*

Academe, 53. See also Roger L. Geiger, *Knowledge and Money* (Stanford, CA: Stanford University Press, 2004), 1, 5.

10. Charles M. Vest, *Research Universities: Overextended, Underfocused, Overstressed, Underfunded,* Speech delivered at the Cornell University Conference on the American University, May 25, 1995, 4.

11. Thomas J. Tighe, *Who's in Charge of America's Research Universities? A Blueprint for Reform* (Albany, NY: State University of New York Press, 2003), 91.

12. Axtell, *The Pleasures of Academe,* 237.

13. Fiona Cownie, *Legal Academics: Culture and Identities* (London: Hart Publishing, 2004), 134.

14. Margaret Edson, *Wit* (New York: Farrar, Straus, and Giroux, 1999), 20.

15. Tom Stoppard, *The Real Thing, rev. ed.* (London and Boston: Faber and Faber, 1983), 54.

16. Fred Rodell, "Goodbye to Law Reviews," *Virginia Law Review* 23 (1936): 36, 38.

17. Rene Denfield, *The New Victorians* (New York: Warner, 1995), 5.

18. Judith Butler, "A Bad Writer Bites Back," *New York Times,* March 20, 1999, A27.

19. Jonathan Culler and Kevin Lamb, "Introduction: Dressing Up and Dressing Down," in *Just Being Difficult,* eds. Jonathan Culler and Kevin Lamb (Stanford, CA: Stanford University Press, 2003), 1.

20. H. L. Mencken, quoted in Sykes, *ProfScam,* 4 n. 2.

21. Culler and Lamb, "Introduction," 1; see Denis Dutton, "Bad Writing Contest: Results for Round Three," posted at www.miami.edu/phi/misc/badwrit3.htm.

22. Martha Nussbaum, "The Professor of Parody," *The New Republic,* February 22, 1999, 37, 38.

23. Camille Paglia, quoted in Daniel Harris, "Nieztsche Does Downtown," *The Nation,* November 21, 1994, 615.

24. Butler, "A Bad Writer Bites Back," A27.

25. Herbert Marcuse, quoted in Butler, "A Bad Writer Bites Back," A27.

26. Culler and Lamb, "Introduction," 8.

27. David Palumbo-Liu, "The Morality of Form; or What Is 'Bad' About 'Bad Writing,'" in Culler and Lamb, *Just Being Difficult,* 171, 176.

28. Jonathan Franzen, "Mr. Difficult," *New Yorker,* September 30, 2002, 100.

29. Nussbaum, "The Professor of Parody," 38.

30. Robert W. Gordon, "Lawyers, Scholars, and the 'Middle Ground,'" *Michigan Law Review* 91 (1993): 2075, 2076; Kenneth Lasson, *Trembling in the Ivory Tower: Excess in the Pursuit of Truth and Tenure* (Baltimore: Bancroft Press, 2003), 23.

31. Deborah L. Rhode, "Legal Scholarship," *Harvard Law Review* 115 (2000): 1327, 1337. In one survey, over two-thirds of surveyed attorneys had consulted law reviews on average less than once a month; a third had not consulted them at all in the preceding six months. Max Stier, Kelly M. Klaus, Dan L. Bagatell and Jeffrey J. Rahlinski, "Law Review Usage and Suggestions for Improvement: A Survey of Attorneys, Professors and Judges," *Stanford Law Review* 44 (1992): 1467, 1484 table 4.

32. C. Wright Mills, "On Intellectual Craftsmanship," in *The Sociological Imagination,* ed. Tom Gitlin (New York: Oxford University Press, 2000), 7.1.

33. Examples include Terry Eagleton, *Literary Theory: An Introduction,* 2nd ed. (Minneapolis: University of Minnesota Press, 1996); Terry Eagleton, *After Theory* (London:

Allen Lane, 2003); and Raymond Geuss, *The Idea of a Critical Theory: Habermas and the Frankfurt School* (Cambridge: Cambridge University Press, 1983).

34. George Orwell, quoted in James Miller, "Is Bad Writing Necessary?," *Lingua Franca*, December–January, 2000, 33, 35, 44.

35. Denis Dutton, "Language Crimes," *Wall Street Journal*, February 5, 1999, W11.

36. W. S. Gilbert, "Am I Alone and Unobserved?" in *Patience*, ed. Edmond W. Rickett (New York; G. Schirmer, 1950), 52.

37. Nussbaum, "Professor of Parody," 39.

38. John Kenneth Galbraith, *A Tenured Professor* (Boston: Houghton Mifflin, 1990), 50.

39. Page Smith, *Killing the Spirit* (New York: Viking, 1990), 263.

40. Charles W. Collier, "The Use and Abuse of Humanistic Theory in Law: Reexamining the Assumptions of Interdisciplinary Legal Scholarship," *Duke Law Journal* 41 (1991): 191, 201–206; Arthur Austin, "Footnote Skulduggery and Other Bad Habits," *University of Miami Law Review* 44 (1990): 1009.

41. Arnold S. Jacobs, "An Analysis of Section 16 of the Securities Exchange Act of 1934," *New York Law School Law Review* 32 (1987): 209; see Lasson, *Trembling in the Ivory Tower*, 50.

42. Rhode, "Legal Scholarship," 1335.

43. Kenneth Lasson, "Scholarship Amok, Excesses in the Pursuit of Knowledge," *Harvard Law Review* 103 (1990): 926, 936.

44. Austin, "Footnote Skulduggery," 1025.

45. Andrew J. McClurg, The World's Greatest Law Review Article," in *Amicus Humoriae, An Anthology of Legal Humor*, eds. Robert M. Jarvis, Thomas E. Baker, and Andrew J. McClurg (Durham, NC: Carolina Academic Press, 2003), 201.

46. Steven Bradford, "As I Lay Writing: How to Write Law Review Articles for Fun and Profit," *Journal of Legal Education* 44 (1994): 13, 17.

47. David Brooks, *Bobos in Paradise: The New Upper Class and How They Got There* (New York: Simon & Schuster, 2000), 170.

48. Lasson, *Trembling in the Ivory Tower*, 15.

49. Lynne V. Cheney, quoted in Martin Anderson, *Impostors in the Temple* (New York: Simon & Schuster, 1992), 97.

50. Lasson, "Scholarship Amok," 936.

51. Sandra M. Gilbert and Susan Gubar, *Masterpiece Theatre: An Academic Melodrama* (New Brunswick, NJ: Rutgers University Press, 1995), xvii. See also John Ellis, *Against Deconstruction* (Princeton, NJ: Princeton University Press, 1989).

52. *Journals of Ralph Waldo Emerson*, eds. Edward Waldo Emerson and Waldo Emerson Forbes (Boston: Houghton Mifflin, 1909–1914), 553.

53. See Loran L. Lewis, "The Law of Icy Sidewalks in New York State," *Yale Law Journal* 6 (1897), 258; and sources cited in Rhode, "Legal Scholarship," 1329.

54. George Eliot, *Middlemarch* (New York: Oxford University Press, 1999 [1871]); for discussion, see A. D. Nuttall, *Dead from the Waist Down: Scholars and Scholarship in Literature and Popular Imagination* (New Haven, CT: Yale University Press, 2003).

55. Kingsley Amis, *Lucky Jim* (New York: Viking Press, 1953), 16.

56. Stevie Davies, *Four Dreamers and Emily* (New York: The Women's Press, 1993), 82.

57. Rachel Maines, "The Evolution of the Potholder: From Technology to Popular Art," *Journal of Popular Culture* 19, no. 1 (Summer 1985): 3, cited in Sykes, *ProfScam*, 102; Mary Ellen Brown, "The Dialectic of the Feminine: Melodrama and Commodity in the Ferraro Pepsi Commercial," *Communication Journal* 9 (1987): 335, cited in Sykes, *ProfScam*, 112; Michael J. Ryan, "Does Foraging Success Determine the Mating Behavior of the Male Tundra Frog?," *Chronicle of Higher Education*, October 7, 1987, cited in *Sykes, ProfScam*, 104. For "Aspects of Ionicity," see Anne Matthews, "Deciphering Victorian Underwear and Other Seminars," *New York Times*, February 10, 1991, 43 (describing papers at the Modern Language Association Annual Meeting). For Pacific salmon, see Lasson, *Trembling in the Ivory Tower*, 37.

58. The awards listed are from 2005 and 2002; see www.improb.com/ig/what-are. html.

59. C. Noe, "End Cash-Cow Scapegoating and Get Back to Basics," *Clearing Up*, March 20, 2006, 5.

60. Deborah L. Rhode, *Speaking of Sex* (Cambridge, MA: Harvard University Press, 1997), 75.

61. Harvey Brooks, "Current Criticisms of Research Universities," in *The Research University in a Time of Discontent*, eds. Jonathan R. Role, Elinor G. Barber, and Stephen R. Graubard (Baltimore: Johns Hopkins University Press, 1994), 231, 236.

62. Derek Bok, quoted in Boyer, *Scholarship Reconsidered*, 76.

63. Anderson, *Imposters in the Temple*, 94–95.

64. Anderson, *Imposters in the Temple*, 95.

65. Ian Shapiro, *The Flight from Reality in the Human Sciences* (Princeton, NJ: Princeton University Press, 2005).

66. Shapiro, *The Flight from Reality*, 2, 203 (discussing desires for rigor and theoretical sophistication); Sanford F. Schram, "A Return to Politics," in *Perestroika, The Realists' Rebellion in Political Science*, ed. Kristin Renwick Monroe (New Haven, CT: Yale University Press, 2005), 103, 108. See also Bent Flyvbjerg, *Making Social Science Matter: Why Social Inquiry Fails* (Cambridge, UK: Cambridge University Press, 2001); Stephen Toulmin, *Return to Reason* (Berkeley, CA: University of California Press, 2002).

67. Ian Shapiro, "Problems, Methods and Theories in the Study of Politics, or What's Wrong with Political Science and What to Do About It," in *Problems and Methods in the Study of Politics*, eds. Ian Shapiro, Rogers M. Smith, and Tarek E. Masoud (New York and Cambridge: Cambridge University Press, 2004); Monroe, *Perestroika*, 66, 69; Schram, "A Return to Politics," 105.

68. Shapiro, *The Flight from Reality*, 203.

69. Edward A. Fox, quoted in John H. Byrne, "Research in the Ivory Tower: Fuzzy, Irrelevant, Pretentious?," *Business Week*, October 29, 1990: 62.

70. Warren G. Bennis and James O'Toole, "How Business Schools Lost Their Way," *Harvard Business Review*, May, 2005, available at www.hbsp.org.

71. Mills, "On Intellectual Craftsmanship" 7-1, 7-6.

72. Peter H. Schuck, "Why Don't Law Professors Do More Empirical Research?," *Journal of Legal Education* 39 (1989): 323, 333.

73. Schuck, "Empirical Research," 333.

74. Stephen Carter, quoted in "Forum: The Future of the Public Intellectual," *The Nation*, February 12, 2001: 28; Byrne, "Research in the Ivory Tower," 62.

75. Russell Jacoby, *The Last Intellectuals* (New York: Basic, 1987), 198.

76. Allan Bloom, *The Closing of the American Mind* (New York: Simon & Schuster, 1987), 370.

77. David Lodge, *Changing Places* (Bath, UK: Chivers Press, 1986), 59.

78. Axtell, *Pleasures of Academe*, 238.

79. Donald Kennedy, *Academic Duty* (Cambridge, MA: Harvard University Press, 1997), 193. For the tendency to judge quantity rather than quality, see Derek Bok, "Markets and Mindwork," *Washington University Journal of Law and Policy* 10 (2002): 1, 5; Rudolph H. Weingartner, *The Moral Dimensions of Academic Administration* (Lanham, MD: Rowman and Littlefield, 1999), 71.

80. Boyer, *Scholarship Reconsidered*, 33.

81. Eyal Press and Jennifer Washburn, "The Kept University," *Atlantic*, March 2000, 54 (quoting Paul Berg).

82. Lila Guterman, "Occupational Hazards," *Chronicle of Higher Education*, June 24, 2005, A15, A16. See also Jeffrey Brainard, "A More Social Science," *Chronicle of Higher Education*, November 18, 2005, available at http://Chronicle.com/weekly/v52/i13/13a/0220/htm.

83. David Blumenthal, Eric G. Campbell, Nancyanne Causino, and Karen Seashore Louis, "Participation of Life-Science Faculty in Research Relationships with Industry," *New England Journal of Medicine* 335 (December 1996): 1734, 1736–37.

84. Marcia Angell, "Is Academic Medicine for Sale?" *New England Journal of Medicine*, 342 (May 2000): 1516.

85. Catherine Diamond and Thomas J. Ruane, letters to the editor, *New England Journal of Medicine* 343 (2000): 508.

86. Lynne V. Cheney, *Tyrannical Machines* (Washington, DC: National Endowment for the Humanities, 1990), 25.

87. Sykes, *Profscam*, 5.

88. Steven M. Cahn, *Saints and Scamps: Ethics in Academia* (Totowa, NJ: Rowman and Littlefield, 1986), 3–8.

89. James Monroe Taylor, "The Neglect of the Student in Recent Education Theory," quoted in Laurence R. Veysey, *The Emergence of the American University* (Chicago: University of Chicago Press, 1965), 296.

90. Cheney, *Tyrannical Machines*, 27.

91. Tighe, *Who's in Charge of America's Research Universities?* 91.

92. Robin Wilson, "Widespread Complaints: Undergraduate Students Are Found Increasingly Dissatisfied," *Chronicle of Higher Education*, Jan. 9, 1991, A1.

93. Cahn, *Saints and Scamps*, 3.

94. Axtell, *The Pleasures of Academe*, 241.

95. For an early exposition, see William James, "The Ph.d. Octopus," *Harvard Monthly* 36 (March 1903): 1–8. For a contemporary view, see Anderson, *Imposters in the Temple*, 117–18.

96. Stuart Palmer, *The Universities Today: Scholarship, Self-Interest, and Politics* (Lanham, MD: University Press of America, 1998), 48; James Freedman, *Liberal Education and the Public Interest* (Iowa City, IA: University of Iowa Press, 2003), 43; Axtell, *Pleasures of Academe*, 61–68, 240–41; Peter J. Markie, *A Professor's Duties: Ethical Issues in College Teaching* (Lanham, MD: Rowman and Littlefield, 1994), 5; Frank H. T. Rhodes,

The Creation of the Future: The Role of the American University (Ithaca, NY: Cornell University Press, 2001), 163; Jaroslav Pelikan, *The Idea of the University* (New Haven, CT: Yale University Press, 1992).

97. Freedman, *Liberal Education*, 48.

98. George Stigler, *The Intellectual and the Market Place* (Cambridge: Harvard University Press, 1984), 16.

99. Lewis Elton, "Research and Teaching: Conditions for a Positive Link," *Teaching in Higher Education* 6 (2001): 40, 50–51.

100. Axtell, *The Pleasures of Academe*, 241.

101. For no adverse effect, see Axtell, *The Pleasures of Academe*, 237, 240–41. For adverse effects, see Philip C. Wankat, *The Effective, Efficient Professor: Teaching, Scholarship and Service* (Boston: Allyn and Bacon, 2001), 211; and Arthur W. Astin, *What Matters in College? Four Critical Years Revisited* (San Francisco: Jossey-Bass, 1993), 66–67, 410–23.

102. Axtell, *Pleasures of Academe*, 241; Wankat, *The Effective, Efficient Professor*, 211. See also Tighe, *Who's in Charge of America's Research Universities?* 93–94, 114.

103. Hazard Adams, *The Academic Tribes*, 2nd ed. (Urbana, IL: University of Illinois Press, (1988), 95.

104. Wankat, *The Effective Efficient Professor*, 211; Alexander W. Astin, *What Matters in College?: Four Critical Years Reconsidered* (San Francisco: Jossey Bass, 1993), 66–67, 410–23; Burton R. Clark, *Places of Inquiry: Research and Advanced Education in Modern Universities* (Berkeley, CA: University of California Press, 1995), 135, 227.

105. Tighe, *Who's in Charge of America's Research Universities?* 105.

106. Rosemary Chalk, Mark S. Frankel, and Sallie B. Chafer, *Professional Ethics Activities in the Scientific and Engineering Societies* (Washington, DC: American Association for the Advancement of Science, 1980), 101, 102. See American Association for the Advancement of Science [AAAS], *The Role and Activities of Scientific Societies in Promoting Research Integrity, Report of a Conference* (Washington, DC: United States Office of Research Integrity, September, 2000), 1. For other disciplines, see Nicholas H. Steneck, "Research Universities and Scientific Misconduct," *Journal of Higher Education* 65 (1994): 311.

107. American Association of University Professors, *Statement on Professional Ethics, 1966* (Washington, DC: American Association of University Professors, 1966).

108. AAAS, *Research Integrity*, 3.

109. AAAS, *Research Integrity*, 3; Judith P. Swazey, Melissa S. Anderson, and Karen Seashore Louis, "Ethical Problems in Academic Research," *American Scientist* 81 (November–December, 1993): 42; John M. Braxton and Alan E. Bayer, "Perceptions of Research Misconduct and an Analysis of Their Correlates," *Journal of Higher Education* 65 (1994): 351, 352; Mary Frank Fox and John M. Braxton, "Misconduct and Social Control in Science," *Journal of Higher Education* 65 (1994): 374, 378–79.

110. *Federal Register* 56 (May 14, 1991): 22286, 22287–88.

111. Francis L. Macrina, *Scientific Integrity* (Washington, DC: ASM Press, 1995), 4; National Academy of Sciences, Panel on Scientific Responsibility and the Conduct of Research, Committee on Science, Engineering, and Public Policy, *Responsible Science: Ensuring the Integrity of the Research Process, Volume I* (Washington, DC: National Academy Press, 1992); Institute for the Study of Applied and Professional Ethics (Corporate Author), reprinted in Deni Elliott and Judy E. Stern (eds.), *Research Ethics: A Reader*

(Boston: New England University Press, 1997), 213, 214; Edward J. Hackett, "A Social Control Perspective on Scientific Misconduct," *Journal of Higher Education* 65 (1994): 242, 243.

112. Melissa Anderson, "Misconduct and Departmental Context," *Journal of Information Ethics* 5 (1996): 15; Neil W. Hamilton, *Academic Ethics* (Westport, CT: Praeger, American Council on Education, 2002), 7.

113. Chris M. Golde and Timothy M. Dore, *At Cross Purposes: What the Experiences of Today's Doctoral Students Reveal About Doctoral Education* (Philadelphia: Pew Charitable Trusts, 2001).

114. Sheldon Krimsky and L. S. Rothenberg, "Conflict of Interest Policies in Science and Medical Journals: Editorial Practices and Author Disclosures," *Science and Engineering Ethics* 7 (2001): 205, 208. See also Henry Thomas Stelfox, Grace Chua, Keith O'Rourke, and Allan S. Detsky, "Conflict of Interest in the Debate Over Calcium Channel Antagonists," *New England Journal of Medicine* 338 (January 1998): 101 (noting that 63 percent of authors of surveyed articles had a financial relationship, but fewer than 4 percent disclosed it). See the discussion in Richard B. Schmitt, "Rules May Require Law Professors to Disclose Fees," *Wall Street Journal*, January 31, 2000, B1.

115. Swazey, Anderson, and Louis, "Ethical Problems," 545.

116. Swazey, Anderson, and Louis, "Ethical Problems," 547; Anderson, "Misconduct," 24.

117. Brian C. Martinson, Melissa S. Anderson, and Raymond de Vries, "Scientists Behaving Badly," *Nature*, June 2005, 737.

118. Martinson, Anderson, and de Vries, "Scientists Behaving Badly," 738.

119. See AAAS, *Research Integrity;* Swazey, Anderson, and Louis, "Ethical Problems"; Braxton and Bayer, "Perceptions of Research Misconduct"; Fox and Braxton, "Misconduct and Social Control"; Elliot and Stern, *Research Ethics;* Harold J. Noah and Max A. Eckstein, *Fraud and Education: The Worm in the Apple* (Lanham, MD: Rowman and Littlefield, 2001), 16; Jon Wiener, *Historians in Trouble: Plagiarism, Fraud, and Politics in the Ivory Tower* (New York: The New Press, 2005); Peter Charles Hoffer, *Past Imperfect: Facts, Fictions, Frauds: American History from Bancroft and Parkman to Ambrose, Bellesiles, Ellis, and Goodwin* (New York: Public Affairs, 2004); Scott Smallwood, "Former Scientist at U. Of Vermont to Plead Guilty to Vast Research Fraud," *Chronicle of Higher Education*, March 18, 2005, available at http://chronicle.com/daily/2005/03/2005031802n.htm.

120. For examples, see Elliott and Stern, *Research Ethics;* Hamilton, *Academic Ethics;* Macrina, *Scientific Integrity;* Jonathan Knight and Carol J. Auster, "Faculty Conduct: An Empirical Study of Ethical Activism," *Journal of Higher Education* 70 (March-April 1999): 188.

121. Noah and Epstein, *Fraud and Education;* Kennedy, *Academic Duty*, 224; National Academy of Sciences, Panel on Scientific Responsibility, 221–22; Hackett, "A Social Control Perspective on Scientific Misconduct," 246–48.

122. Braxton and Bayer, "Perceptions of Research Misconduct," 353; Fox and Braxton, "Misconduct and Social Control," 380.

123. Swazey, Anderson, and Louis, "Ethical Problems," 551.

124. Fox and Braxton, "Misconduct and Social Control," 380; Steneck, "Research Universities and Scientific Misconduct," 324; Noah and Eckstein, *Fraud and Education*.

125. For various definitions, see Scott McLemee, "What Is Plagiarism?" *Chronicle of Higher Education*, December 17, 2004, 9.

126. Kennedy, *Academic Duty*, 215.

127. Suzy Hansen, "Dear Plagiarists: You Get What You Pay For," *New York Times*, August 22, 2004, Section 7, page 11.

128. For slight modifications, see Bernard E. Whitley Jr. and Patricia Keith-Speigel, *Academic Dishonesty: An Educator's Guide* (Mahway, NJ, 2002), 18–20. For borrowing primary source material, see Hoffer, *Past Imperfect: Fact, Fictions, Fraud?* 188, 197; Wiener, *Historians in Trouble*, 188–90. See also Steneck, "Research Universities," 319. For borrowing conceptual schemes, see Stepanie C. Ardito, "Plagiarism, Fabrication, and Lack of Attribution," *Information Today*, July–August, 2002, 16; David Glen, "Copycat Allegations Roil Sociologists at Penn, Raising Questions Whether Analytic Schemes Can Be Plagiarized," *Chronicle of Higher Education*, Oct. 7, 2005, available at http://chronicle.com/daily/2005/10/2005/1000704n.html.

129. See McLemee, "What Is Plagiarism?" 9 (quoting Emerson).

130. For recent examples see Elizabeth Mehren, "Professor Admits Not Crediting Author," *Los Angeles Times*, September 29, 2004, A24; Scott Smallwood, "The Fallout: What Happened to Six Scholars Accused of Plagiarism," *Chronicle of Higher Education*, December 17, 2004, A12; Sara Rimer, "When Plagiarism's Shadow Falls on Admired Scholars," *New York Times*, November 24, 2004, A23; Malcolm Gladwell, "Something Borrowed," *New Yorker*, November 22, 2004, 41; Wiener, *Historians in Trouble*, 195.

131. Ari Posner, "The Culture of Plagiarism," *The New Republic*, April 18, 1985, 19.

132. Francis L. Macrina, "Authorship and Peer Review," in Macrina, *Scientific Integrity*, 69; National Academy of Science, Panel on Scientific Responsibility, 220; Kennedy, *Academic Duty*, 196.

133. John B. Bennett, *Collegial Professionalism* (Phoenix: American Council on Education, Oryx Press, 1998), 57.

134. Michael Thompson, "Hidden in Plain Sight," *Chronicle of Higher Education*, December 2, 2005, B5.

135. David Glenn, "Judge or Judge Not," *Chronicle of Higher Education*, December 17, 2004, A16.

136. Glenn, "Judge or Judge Not," A16.

137. Glenn, "Judge or Judge Not," A16. For an example of an association that does conduct such inquiries, see Thomas Bartlett, "Theology Professor Plagiarized Passages in His Book on Ethics, Professional Group Finds," *Chronicle of Higher Education*, January 7, 2005, http://chronicle.com/prm/daily/2005/01/2005010703n.htm (discussing Boston Psychoanalytic Society).

138. For example, W.W. Norton & Co., the press that published Charles Ogletree's book *All Deliberate Speed*, inserted an errata sheet. Rimer, "When Plagiarism's Shadow Falls on Admired Scholars," A12.

139. AAAS, *Research Integrity*, 10.

140. Nicholas Wade, "Lowering Expectations at Science's Frontier," *New York Times*, January 15, 2006, 14.

141. Sanctions by an institution could include denials of tenure or termination of employment, as well as demotions, reduced compensation, and denial of status as a principal investigator. Scholarly journals and publishers could also refuse to consider

future submissions by a plagiarist for a prescribed period. See David Glen, "The Price of Plagiarism," *Chronicle of Higher Education*, December 17, 2004, 17.

142. Kennedy, *Academic Duty*, 204; Charles W. McCutcheon, "Peer Review: Treacherous Servant, Disastrous Master," in Eliot and Stern, *Research Ethics*, 151, 163; Ellen K. Coughlin, "Concerns About Fraud, Editorial Bias, Prompt Scrutiny of Journal Practices," *Chronicle of Higher Education*, February 15, 1989, A4.

143. Douglas P. Peters and Stephen J. Ceci, "Peer Review Research Practices of Psychological Journals: The Fate of Published Articles, Submitted Again," *Behavioral and Brain Sciences* 5 (June 1982): 187, 190.

144. Patricia Werhane and Jeffrey Doering, "Conflicts of Interest and Conflicts of Commitment," in Eliot and Stern, *Research Ethics*, 166; Derek Bok, *Universities in the Marketplace* (Princeton, NJ: Princeton University Press, 2003); Alan V. Munck, "Examples of Scientific Misconduct," in Eliot and Stern, *Research Ethics*, 31.

145. "U.S. National Institute of Health Announces Tighter Ethics Rules," *Health Insurance Law Weekly*, Feb. 27, 2005, 7.

146. "Information for Contributors," *Science* 259 (1993): 41.

147. Angell, "Is Academic Medicine for Sale?" 1516, 1518; Hamilton Moses III, Eugene Braunwald, Joseph B. Martin, and Samuel O. Thier, "Collaborating with Industry: Choices for the Academic Medical Center," *New England Journal of Medicine* 347 (2002): 1371, 1373–75.

148. Angell, "Is Academic Medicine for Sale?" 1518; Michelle M. Mello, Brian R. Clarridge, and David M. Studdert, "Academic Medical Centers' Standards for Clinical Trial Agreements with Industry," *New England Journal of Medicine*, 352 (May 2005): 2202; Kevin A. Schulman, Damon M. Seils, Justin W. Timbie, Jeremy Sugarman, Lauren A. Dame, Kevin P. Weinfurt, Daniel B. Mark, and Robert M. Califf, "A National Survey of Provisions in Clinical-Trial Agreements Between Medical Schools and Industry Sponsors," *New England Journal of Medicine* 347 (October 2002): 1335.

149. Noah and Eckstein, *Fraud and Education*, 119.

150. Lisa A. Bero, Alison Galbraith, and Drummond Rennie, "The Publication of Sponsored Symposiums in Medical Journals," *New England Journal of Medicine* 327 (1992): 1135–40; Thomas Bodenheimer, "Uneasy Alliance—Clinical Investigators and the Pharmaceutical Industry," *New England Journal of Medicine* 342 (200): 1538–44; Mildred Cho and Lisa A. Berg, "The Quality of Drug Studies Published in Symposium Proceedings," *Annals of Internal Medicine* 124 (1996): 485–89; Stelfox, Chua, O'Rourke, and Detsky, "Conflict of Interest in the Debate Over Calcium-Channel Antagonists," 101–106.

151. Mark Friedberg, Bernard Saffran, Tammy J. Stinson, Wendy Nelson, and Charles. L. Bennett, "Evaluation of Conflict of Interest in Economic Analysis of New Drugs Used in Oncology," *Journal of American Medical Association* 282 (1999): 1453, 1455.

152. For similar findings, see Cho and Berg, "The Quality of Drug Studies," 485–89; Stelfox, Chua, O'Rourke, and Detsky, "Conflict of Interest," 101, 102; and Bodenheimer, "Uneasy Alliance," 1539. For funding, see Bodenheimer, "Uneasy Alliance," 1539, and Jennifer Washburn, *University, Inc.* (New York: Basic Books, 2004), 237.

153. Washburn, *University, Inc.*, 113; Bodenheimer, "Uneasy Alliance," 1541–42; Guterman, "Occupational Hazards," A15, A16; Bryn Williams-Jones, "Knowledge Commons

or Economic Engine—What's a University For?" *Journal of Medical Ethics*, October, 13, 2005: 249.

154. "Manipulating a Journal Article," *New York Times*, Dec. 11, 2005, E1 (discussing research on Vioxx published in the *New England Journal of Medicine*).

155. Blumenthal, Campbell, Causino, and Louis, "Participation of Life-Science Faculty," 1734, 1736–37; Washburn, *University, Inc.*, 74–75.

156. Rory K. Little, "Law Professors as Lawyers: Consultants, of Counsel, and the Ethics of Self-Flagellation," *South Texas Law Review* 42 (2001): 345. The Association of American Law School's "Statement of Good Practices by Law Professors in the Discharge of their Ethical and Professional Responsibilities," as amended in 2003, requires professors to disclose "material facts" relating to financial support of research but does not require disclosure of the amount of funding. Nor does the Association attempt to enforce these practices.

157. Alan Zarembo, "Funding Studies to Suit Need," *Los Angeles Times*, December 3, 2003: A1. See also Elizabeth Amon, "Exxon Bankrolls Critics of Punitives," *National Law Journal*, May 17, 1995, A1.

158. Bodenheimer, "Uneasy Alliance," 1540. See also Annetine C. Gelijns and Samuel O. Thier, "Medical Innovation and Institutional Interdependence: Rethinking University-Industry Connections," *Journal of the American Medical Association* 287 (January 2002): 72, 74.

159. Mello, Clarridge, and Studdert, "Academic Medical Centers' Standards," 2209; Michael M. E. Johns, Mark Barnes, and Patrik S. Florencio, "Restoring Balance to Industry-Academia Relationships in an Era of Institutional Conflicts of Interest," *Journal of the American Medical Association* 299 (February 2003): 41, 743–45.

160. Angell, "Is Academic Medicine for Sale?" 1518; Washburn, *University, Inc.*, 235–37; Johns, Barnes, and Florencio, "Restoring Balance," 746.

161. Mello, Clarridge, and Studdert, "Academic Medical Centers' Standards," 2209; Bodenheimer, "Uneasy Alliance," 1540.

162. For disclosure standards and enforcement see Stelfox, Chua, O'Rourke, and Detsky, "Conflict of Interest," 104; Mello, Clarridge, and Studdert, "Academic Medical Centers' Standards," 2209; AAAS, *Report on Research Integrity*, 13–15. For collaborative funding arrangements see Guterman, "Occupational Hazards," A18; Moses, Braunwald, Martin, and Thier, "Collaborating with Industry," 1373.

163. Guterman, "Occupational Hazards," A18.

164. Personal Interview, Margaret Eaton, Fellow, Stanford Bioethics Center, August 5, 2005.

165. AAAS, *Report on Research Integrity*, 8–9.

Chapter Three

1. See Martin Anderson, *Imposters in the Temple* (New York: Simon & Schuster, 1992), 45, 46, discussed in James Axtell, *The Pleasures of Academe: A Celebration and Defense of Higher Education* (Lincoln, NE: University of Nebraska Press, 1998), 242, n. 69.

2. Jennifer Washburn, *University, Inc.* (New York: Basic Books, 2004), 207; Derek Bok, *Our Underachieving Colleges* (Princeton, NJ: Princeton University Press, 2006), 4, 48–51. Forty percent of faculty at four-year public universities believed that research

was valued more than teaching. Allen Sanderson, Voon Chin Phua, David Herda, *The American Faculty Poll* (New York and Chicago: TIAA-CREFF, and National Opinion Research Center, 2000), 33.

3. See Charles J. Sykes, *ProfScam: Professors and the Demise of Higher Education* (Washington, DC: Regnery Gateway, 1988); Thomas Sowell, *Inside American Education: The Decline, the Deception, the Dogmas* (New York: Maxwell Macmillan International, 1993), 205–206; Scott Heller, "Teaching Award: Aid to Tenure or Kiss of Death?," *Chronicle of Higher Education* 16 (March 1988): A14; Axtell, *The Pleasures of Academe*, 242, n. 69.

4. Arthur Levine, "How the Academic Profession Is Changing," *Daedelus* 126 (1997): 1, 10.

5. Lynne V. Cheney, *Tyrannical Machines* (Washington, DC: National Endowment for the Humanities, 1990), 32. See also Bok, *Our Underachieving Colleges*, 2, 40–48.

6. Derek Bok, *Universities in the Marketplace* (Princeton, NJ: Princeton University Press, 2003), 160. See also Bok, *Our Underachieving Colleges*, 48–51; Boyer Commission on Educating Undergraduates in the Research Universities, *Reinventing Undergraduate Education: A Blueprint for America's Research Universities* (Princeton, NJ: Carnegie Foundation for the Advancement of Teaching, 1996).

7. Quoted in Adolf Brodbeck, *The Ideal of Universities* (New York: Metaphysical Publishing, 1896), n.p.

8. See Ronald Barnett, *Higher Education: A Critical Business* (Bristol, PA: Open University Press, 1997); William B. Allen and Carol M. Allen, *Habits of Mind: Fostering Access and Excellence in Higher Education* (New Brunswick, NJ: Transaction Publishers, 2003), 23; Martha Nussbaum, *Cultivating Humanity: A Classical Defense of Reform in Liberal Education* (Cambridge, MA: Harvard University Press, 1997).

9. Stephen Joel Trachtenberg, *Reflections on Higher Education* (Westport, CT: Oryx, 2002), 73.

10. Brent D. Rubin, *Pursuing Excellence in Higher Education* (San Francisco: Jossey-Bass, 2004), 66–67; Frank H. T. Rhodes, "The Place of Teaching in the Research University," in *The Research University in a Time of Discontent*, eds. Jonathan R. Cole, Elinor G. Barber, and Stephen R. Graubard (Baltimore: Johns Hopkins University Press, 1994), 179, 183; Bok, *Our Underachieving Colleges*, 58–81.

11. See Bok, *Universities in the Marketplace*, 161; Axtell, *The Pleasures of Academe*, 263.

12. Roger Benjamin et al., *The Redesign of Governance in Higher Education* (Los Angeles: Rand Corporation, 1993), 9.

13. Justin D. Baer, Andrea L. Cook, and Stephane Baldi, *The Literacy of America's College Students* (Washington, DC: American Institutes for Research, 2006), 19; Clifford Adelman, *Tourists in Our Own Land: Cultural Literacies and the College Curriculum* (Washington, DC: United States Department of Education, 1992); Rudolph H. Weingartner, *The Moral Dimensions of Academic Administration* (Lanham, MD: Rowman and Littlefield, 1999), 6.

14. Cheney, *Tyrannical Machines*, 32.

15. Mark Bauerlein, "A Very Long Disengagement," *Chronicle of Higher Education*, January 6, 2006, B6. See also Center for Survey Research and Analysis, *Elite College History Survey* (Washington, DC: American Council of Trustees and Alumni, 2000).

16. Bauerlein, "A Very Long Disengagement," B7.

17. Derek Bok, "The Critical Role of Trustees in Enhancing Student Learning," *Chronicle of Higher Education*, Dec. 16, 2005, B12; Association of American Colleges and Universities (AACU), *Liberal Education Outcomes* (Washington, DC: Association of American Colleges and Universities, 2005), 16.

18. AACU, *Liberal Education Outcomes*, 6.

19. See Howard R. Bowen, *Investment in Learning: The Individual and Social Value of American Higher Education* (San Francisco: Jossey-Bass, 1977), 63–136, discussed in Derek Bok, *Higher Learning* (Cambridge, MA: Harvard University Press, 1986), 56.

20. See www.usnews.com/usnews/edu/college/rankings/about/05rank_brief.php. For discussion, see Axtell, *The Pleasures of Academe*, 89; Cheney, *Tyrannical Machines*, 39.

21. Derek Bok, "Markets and Mindwork," *Washington University Journal of Law and Policy* 10 (2002): 1, 4.

22. Bok, *Universities in the Marketplace*, 180; Nicholas Confessore, "What Makes a College Good?" *Atlantic Monthly*, November 2003, 118, 124.

23. Alexander W. Astin, "To Use Graduation Rates to Measure Excellence, You Have to Do Your Homework," Chronicle of Higher Education, October 22, 2004, B20. For similar claims, see Thomas J. Tighe, *Who's in Charge of America's Research Universities? A Blueprint for Reform* (Albany, NY: State University of New York Press, 2003), 130; Edward P. St. John, Kimberley A. Klein, and Eric H. Asker, "The Call for Public Accountability: Rethinking the Linkages to Student Outcomes," in *Affordability, Access, and Accountability*, ed. Donald E. Heller (Baltimore: Johns Hopkins University Press, 2001), 219, 222.

24. William Zumeto, "Public Policy and Accountability in Higher Education: Lessons from the Past and Present for the New Millenium," in Heller (ed.), *Affordability, Access, and Accountability*, 185.

25. Jay Mathews, "Measure by Measure: A New Effort to Determine How Well Schools Teach," *Atlantic Monthly*, October 2004, 134. See also Richard H. Hirsh, "What Does College Teach?" *Atlantic Monthly*, November 2005, 140, 142.

26. Mathews, "Measure by Measure," 134. Reports on the test are available on the Website for the Council for Aid to Education, www.cae.org. For other assessment strategies, see Hirsch, "What Does College Teach?" 140, 142; St. John, Klein, and Askin, "The Call for Public Accountability," 222–25.

27. Jobs for the Future, *By the Numbers: State Goals for Increasing Post-Secondary Attainment* (Boston: Jobs for the Future, 2006). For the general lack of evaluation, see Charles Miller and Geri Malandra, *Accountability/Assessment: Issue Paper by the Secretary of Education's Commission on the Future of Higher Education* (Washington, DC: United States Department of Education, April 4, 2006), available at www.ed.gov/about/bdcomm/list/hiedfuture/reports.html.

28. Charles E. Glassick, Mary Taylor Huber, and Gene I. Maeroff, *Scholarship Assessed: Evaluation of the Professoriate* (San Francisco: Jossey Bass and Carnegie Foundation for the Advancement of Teaching, 1997), 20.

29. For a literature review, see Michael Theall, "Leadership in Faculty Evaluation," in *Field Guide to Academic Leadership*, eds. Robert M. Diamond and Bronwyn Adam (San Francisco, Jossey-Bass, 2002); Jane E. Harrison, "The Quality of University Teaching: Faculty Performance and Accountability, a Literature Review," *Canadian Society for the Study of Higher Education*, Spring 2002, 1, 6. For an overview of best practices, see Raoul

Arreola, *Developing a Comprehensive Faculty Evaluation System* (Bolton, MA: Anker Publishing, 2000).

30. For an overview of the research, see James A. Kulik, "Student Ratings: Validity, Utility, and Controversy," *New Directions for Institutional Research* 109 (2001): 9; John C. Ory and Katherine Ryan, "How Do Student Ratings Measure Up to a New Validity Framework?" *New Directions for Institutional Research* 109 (2001): 7; Wendy M. Williams and Stephen J. Ceci, "'How'm I Doing?': Problems with Student Ratings of Instructors and Courses," *Change*, September–October 1997, 13; and Sylvia D'Apollonia and Philip C. Abrami, "In Response," *Change*, September–October, 1997, 18. For physical appearance, see Daniel S. Hamermesh and Amy M. Parker, "Beauty in the Classroom: Professors' Pulchritude and Putative Pedagogical Productivity," NBER working paper no. 9853, July 2003. For an example of physical attractiveness ratings, see James M. Lang, "RateMyBuns.com," *Chronicle of Higher Education*, December 1, 2003, http://chronicle.com/weekly/v50/i15/15c00201.htm.

31. Michael Theall and Jennifer Franklin, "Looking for Bias in All the Wrong Places: A Search for Truth or a Witch Hunt in Student Ratings of Instruction?" *New Directions for Institutional Research* 109 (2001): 45; Ory and Ryan, "How Do Student Ratings Measure Up?" 38, 41; Bok, *Our Underachieving Colleges*, 315. For concerns about uninformed assessments by students who may have axes to grind, see Stanley Fish, "Who's in Charge Here?" *Chronicle of Higher Education*, February 4, 2005, available at http://chronicle.com/jobs/2005/02/2005020401c.htm.

32. Nalini Ambady and Robert Rosenthal, "Half a Minute: Predicting Teacher Evaluations from Thin Slices of Nonverbal Behavior and Physical Attractiveness," *Journal of Personality and Social Psychology* 64 (1993): 431. For related research see Malcolm Gladwell, *Blink: The Power of Thinking Without Thinking* (New York: Little, Brown, 2004).

33. See Theall and Franklin, "Looking for Bias," 50.

34. Nancy Van Note Chism, *Peer Review of Teaching: A Sourcebook* (Bolton, MA: Anker Publishing, 1999).

35. Kulik, "Student Ratings," 11; Donald Kennedy, *Academic Duty* (Cambridge, MA: Harvard University Press, 1997), 73.

36. Bok, *Our Underachieving Colleges*, 315–16.

37. John Gardner, *Mickelsson's Ghosts* (New York: Knopf, 1982), 100.

38. See the codes summarized in Weingartner, *The Moral Dimensions of Academic Administration*, 51.

39. See sources cited in Chapter 2 on research ethics.

40. John N. Braxton and Alan E. Bayer, *Faculty Misconduct in Collegiate Teaching* (Baltimore: Johns Hopkins University Press, 1999). See Kennedy, *Academic Duty*, 68.

41. Anne Neal, "Professors Who Preach," *The American Enterprise*, June 2005, 30.

42. Eric Hoover, "Students Study Less Than Expected, Survey Finds," *Chronicle of Higher Education*, November 26, 2004, A1, A31.

43. Weingartner, *The Moral Dimensions of Academic Administration*, 5; Cheney, *Tyrannical Machines*, 32; Warren Bennis and Hallam Movius, "Why Harvard Is So Hard to Lead," *Chronicle of Higher Education*, March 3, 2006, B4.

44. Bok, *Our Underachieving Colleges*, 37–38, 41–42; Higher Education Research Institute, *Spirituality and the Professoriate* (Los Angeles: University of California Higher Education Research Institute, 2006), 1.

45. Hoover, "Students Study Less," A1.

46. Lois Roney, *Academic Animals: A Bestiary of Higher-Education Teaching and How It Got That Way* (Philadelphia: Xlibris, 2002), 253–54. For a discussion of the incentives to dumb down course content, see Roger L. Geiger, *Knowledge and Money: Research Universities and the Paradox of the Marketplace* (Stanford, CA: Stanford University Press, 2004), 99.

47. John D. Kirwan, "Catalog of Courses: Aquarius U. Non Campus Mentis," in *Hail to Thee Okoboji!: A Humor Anthology on Higher Education*, ed. Mark C. Ebersole (New York: Fordham University Press, 1992), 114, 115–16.

48. Bok, *Universities in the Marketplace*, 161; Bok, "Markets and Mindworks," 1, 5; Derek Bok, *Higher Learning*, 181. See also Bok, *Our Underachieving Colleges*; Washburn, *University, Inc.*, 207.

49. Dominic J. Brewer, Susan M. Gates, and Charles A. Goldman, *In Pursuit of Prestige: Strategy and Competition in Higher Education* (New Brunswick, NJ: Transaction, 2002), 60.

50. Bok, *Higher Learning*, 67; Bok, *Universities in the Marketplace*, 26; Theall, "Leadership in Faculty Evaluation," 259; Harrison, "The Quality of University Teaching," 10.

51. For similar versions, see Kennedy, *Academic Duty*, 61; Professor X, *This Beats Working for a Living* (New Rochelle, NJ: Arlington Press, 1974), 15.

52. Jaroslav Pelikan, *The Idea of the University: A Reexamination* (New Haven: Yale University Press, 1992), 94–95.

53. David D. Perlmutter, "Teaching the 101," *Chronicle of Higher Education*, September 10, 2004, C1, C4.

54. Axtell, *The Pleasures of Academe*, 247.

55. John B. Bennett, *Collegial Professionalism* (Phoenix, AZ: American Council on Education and Oryx Press, 1998), 118.

56. Axtell, *The Pleasures of Academe*, 247; see Chapter 2 of this book; Boyer Commission, *Reinventing Undergraduate Education*, 16.

57. See the research discussed in Confessore, "What Makes a College Good?" 120.

58. Sanderson, Phua, and Herda, *The American Faculty Poll*, 33.

59. Bok, *Universities in the Marketplace*, 89 (quoting studies); Sowell, *Inside Higher Education*, 222; Robin Wilson, "Widespread Complaints: Undergraduate Students Are Found Increasingly Dissatisfied," *Chronicle of Higher Education*, Jan. 9, 1991, A15 (quoting student).

60. See Bok, *Higher Learning*, 180;, Boyer Commission, *Reinventing Undergraduate Education*, 15–16, 20; Barbara Gross Davis, *Tools for Teaching* (San Francisco: Jossey-Bass, 1993); Gerald F. Hess, "Heads and Hearts: The Teaching and Learning Environment in Law School," *Journal of Legal Education* 52 (2002): 84, 101–109; Lori J. Vogelgesang and Alexander W. Astin, "Comparing the Effects of Community Service and Service-Learning," *Michigan Journal of Community Service and Service Learning* 7 (Fall 2000): 25–34; Lion F. Gardiner, "Why We Must Change: The Research Evidence, Thought and Action," *The NEA Higher Education Journal* 16 (1998): 72, 76–77.

61. John Kenneth Galbraith, *A Tenured Professor* (Boston: Houghton Mifflin, 1990), 39.

62. F. M. Cornford, *Microcosmographia Academica: Being a Guide for the Young Academic Politician*, 4th ed. (Cambridge, England: Bowes and Bowes, 1906, 1949).

63. William James, "The Ph.D. Octopus," *Harvard Monthly* 36 (March 1903): 1, 3.

64. Jonathan R. Cole, "Balancing Acts: Dilemmas of Choice Facing Research Universities," in Cole, Barber, and Grumbard (eds.), *The Research University*, 27; see also Miller and Malandra, *Accountability/Assessment;* Gardiner, "Why We Must Change," 75.

65. Boyer Commission, *Reinventing Undergraduate Education*, 29; Chris M. Golde and Timothy M. Dore, *At Cross Purposes: What the Experiences of Today's Doctoral Students Reveal About Doctoral Education* (Philadelphia: Pew Charitable Trusts, 2001), 21–23.

66. Jeffrey R. Young, "Students Say Technology Has Little Impact on Teaching," *Chronicle of Higher Education*, August 13, 2004, A28. See Educourse Center for Applied Research, Survey Data 2005, at www.educourse.edu/ecar; Kelly Field, "Federal Panel on Higher Education Appears Likely to Call for Testing of College Students," *Chronicle of Higher Education*, December 9, 2005, A39.

67. Golde and Dore, *At Cross Purposes*, 21–23.

68. Emily Toth, *Ms. Mentor's Impeccable Advice for Women in Academia* (Philadelphia: University of Pennsylvania Press, 1997), 8.

69. Bob Boice, "Classroom Incivilities," *Research in Higher Education* 37 (1996): 453, 459–60 (finding uncivil behavior in two-thirds of surveyed classrooms at one institution and a high frequency of ineffective response). For examples, see Thomas Bartlett, "Taking Control of the Classroom," *Chronicle of Higher Education*, September 17, 2004, available at http://chronicle.com/weekly/v51/i04/04a00801.htm.ra page; Jill Carroll, "Dealing with Nasty Students: The Sequel," *Chronicle of Higher Education*, May 2, 2003, available at http://chronicle.com/weekly/v49/i34/34c00501.htm.

70. Boice, "Classroom Incivilities," 469.

71. Steven L. Carter, *The Emperor of Ocean Park* (New York: Knopf, 2002), 111–12.

72. Jonathan D. Glater, "To Professor@University.edu: Subject: Why It's All About Me," *New York Times*, February 21, 2006, A1, A14; Diane L. Wolf, "Letter to the Editor," *New York Times*, February 23, 2006, A26.

73. Darby Dickerson, "Cyberbullies on Campus," *University of Toledo Law Review* 37 (2005): 51; Mark Franek, "Rise of the Cyberbully Demands New Rules," *Christian Science Monitor*, May 10, 2004, 9.

74. Dickerson, "Cyberbullies," 62. See also Nathanial J. Bray and Mariett Del Favero, "Sociological Explanations for Faculty and Student Classroom Incivilities," *New Directions for Teaching and Learning* 99 (Fall 2004): 9.

75. For examples, see Dickerson, "Cyberbullies," 66–74; Glater, "To Professor," A14.

76. Piper Fogg, "Etiquette 101," *Chronicle of Higher Education*, April 7, 2006, A64.

77. Denise Nitterhouse, "Plagiarism—Not Just an Academic Problem," *Teaching Business Ethics* 7 (2003): 215, 216; Jennifer Merritt, "You Mean Cheating is Wrong?" *Business Week*, December 9, 2002, 8 (59 percent of some 1100 surveyed students on twenty-seven campuses admit cheating). See also Suzy Hansen, "Dear Plagiarists: You Get What You Pay For," *New York Times*, August 22, 2004, Section 3, 11 (noting that almost 40 percent of college students admit plagiarizing from the Internet).

78. See Bernard E. Whitely Jr., and Patricia Keith-Speigel, *Academic Dishonesty: An Educators's Guide* (Mahwah, NJ: Lawrence Ehrlbaum Associates, 2002), 2–6, 12; Hansen, "Dear Plagiarists," 11.

79. Whitely and Keith-Spiegel, *Academic Dishonesty*, 12; Bok, *Our Underachieving Colleges*, 165.

80. Billy Collins, "Introduction to Poetry," in *Sailing Alone Around the Room* (New York: Random House, 2001), 16.

81. See Thomas Gilovich, *How We Know What Isn't So: The Fallibility of Human Reason in Everyday Life* (New York: Free Press, 1991), 77–84. In general, everyone believes that they are above average, and that any failures are attributable to forces beyond their control.

82. Axtell, *The Pleasures of Academe*, 245.

83. Grant Gilmore, "What Is a Law School?" *Connecticut Law Review* 15 (1983): 1.

84. See studies cited in Deborah L. Rhode and David Luban, *Legal Ethics* (New York: Foundation Press, 2004), 1001–1002, 1025–26.

85. Joanne Martin and Bryant Garth, "Clinical Education as a Bridge Between Law School and Practice: Mitigating the Misery," *Clinical Education* 1 (1994): 443.

86. Deborah L. Rhode, *In the Interests of Justice* (New York: Oxford University Press, 2000), 203; Rhode and Luban, *Legal Ethics*, 1031.

87. Bok, *Our Underachieving Colleges*, 169. For professional programs, see Deborah L. Rhode, *Pro Bono in Principle and in Practice: Public Service and the Professions* (Stanford, CA: Stanford University Press, 2005), 22–25, 73–99.

88. Ann Colby, Thomas Ehrlich, Elizabeth Beaumont, and Jason Stephens, *Educating Citizens: Preparing America's Undergraduates for Lives of Moral and Civic Responsibility* (San Francisco: Jossey-Bass, 2003), 3.

89. Jane Tompkins, *A Life in School: What the Teacher Learned* (Cambridge: Perseus Books, 1996), 214, 221.

90. Higher Education Research Institute, *Spirituality and the Professoriate*, 6.

91. See research summarized in Rhode, *In the Interests of Justice*, 204; James R. Rest, "Can Ethics Be Taught in Professional Schools? The Psychological Research," *Ethics: Easier Said Than Done*, 1 (1988), 22, 23–24; Albert Bandura, "Social Cognitive Theory of Moral Thought and Action," in *Handbook of Moral Behavior and Development*, eds. William M. Kurtines and Jacob L. Gewirtz (Hillsdale, NJ: Lawrence Erlbaum Associates, 1991) 45, 53.

92. For clinics, see David Luban and Michael Millemann, "Good Judgment: Ethics Teaching in Dark Times," *Georgetown Journal of Legal Ethics* 9 (1995): 31. For service learning, see Colby, Ehrlich, Beaumont, and Stephens, Educating Citizens, 137–38; Diane P. Hedin, "The Power of Community Service," *Proceedings of the Academy of Political Science* 37 (1989): 201, 207; Vogelgesang and Astin, "Comparing the Effects of Community Service and Service-Learning," 25–34.

93. Colby, Ehrlich, Beaumont, and Stephens, *Educating Citizens*, 14.

94. C. Daniel Batson, *The Altruism Question: Toward a Social-Psychological Answer* (Hillsdale, NJ: Lawrence Erlbaum Associates, 1991), 18–19, 22–23, 25, 26–27, 35–36; and sources cited in Deborah L. Rhode, *Pro Bono in Principle and in Practice*, 68–69; and Dean A. Pribbenow, "The Impact of Service-Learning Pedagogy on Faculty Teaching and Learning," *Michigan Journal of Community Service Learning* 33 (2005): 25.

95. Stephen D. Papamarcos, "The 'Next Wave' in Service-Learning: Integrative, Team-based Engagements with Structural Objectives," *Review of Business* 23 (2002): 31, 37; Bok, *Our Underachieving Colleges*, 190.

96. Thomas Anthony Angelo, "A Teacher's Dozen: Fourteen General Research-Based Principles for Improving Higher Learning in Our Classrooms," *American Association for Higher Education Bulletin* 45 (April 1993), 3 (quoting George Stoddard).

97. See Rhode, *Pro Bono in Principle and in Practice*, 69.

98. Committee on Developments in the Science of Learning and Committee on Learning Research and Educational Practice, Commission on Behavioral and Social Sciences and Education, National Research Council, *How People Learn: Mind, Experience, and School*, eds. John D. Bransford, Ann L. Brown, and Rodney R. Cocking (Washington, DC: National Research Council, 1999), 131–54; Lewis Elton, "Research and Teaching: Conditions for a Positive Link," *Teaching in Higher Education*, 6 (2001), 3, 49; Gardiner, "Why We Must Change," 76–77; Robert B. Barr and John Tagg, "From Teaching to Learning—A New Paradigm for Undergraduate Education," *Change*, November–December 1995, 13, 21–22; James Eison, "Teaching Strategies for the Twenty-First Century," in Diamond and Adams, eds., *Field Guide*, 157–65. For a bibliography see www.active-learning-site.com/bib1.htm.

99. See www.active-learning-site.com/bib1.htm.; Angelo, "A Teacher's Dozen," 3–13.

100. Eison, "Teaching Strategies," 161–65; Barr and Tagg, "From Teaching to Learning," 14–22; Arthur W. Chickering and Zelda F. Gamson, "Development and Adaptations of the Seven Principles for Good Practice in Undergraduate Education," in *Teaching and Learning on the Edge of the New Millennium*, ed. Marilla D. Sevinicki (San Francisco: Jossey Bass, 1999).

101. National Survey of Student Engagement, available at www.usnews.com/usnews/edu/college/rankings/ranknsse_brief.php.

102. About 850 schools have participated, but only 7 percent have made responses to selected questions available to *U.S. News and World Report*. Confessore, "What Makes a College Good?" 124.

103. Donald Kennedy, quoted in Ernest L. Boyer, *Scholarship Reconsidered* (Princeton, NJ: Carnegie Foundation for the Advancement of Teaching, 1990), 46. See Cole, "Balancing Acts," 26, and Eison, "Teaching Strategies," 166.

104. Boyer, *Scholarship Reconsidered*, 40.

105. Braxton and Bayer, *Faculty Misconduct in College Teaching*, 179–80.

106. Chism, *Peer Review of Teaching*, 87–94.

107. Miller and Malandra, *Accountability/Assessment*.

108. Tighe, *Who's in Charge*, 61; David G. Evans, "How Not to Reward Outstanding Teachers," *Chronicle of Higher Education*, May 20, 2005, available at http://chronicle.com/free/v51/i37/37b020001.htm.

109. Cheney, *Tyrannical Machines*, 37; Bok, *Universities in the Marketplace*, 181; Frank H. T. Rhodes, "The Place of Teaching in the Research University," in Cole, Barber, and Graubard, *The Research University*, 179, 184.

110. See Boyer Commission, *Reinventing Undergraduate Education*, 20. For example, Stanford University provides grants of between $3000 and $6000 to provide stipends, travel expenses, and materials for undergraduates who are involved in a faculty member's research project. John Bravman, "Memorandum to Faculty and Research Center Affiliates," Faculty Grants for Undergraduate Research, September 9, 2004.

111. David Damrosch, *We Scholars: Changing the Culture of the University* (Cambridge, MA: Harvard University Press, 1995), 134.

112. Weingartner, *The Moral Dimension of Academic Administration*, 57.

113. Rita Bernstein, "The Nature and Nurture of Presidents," *Chronicle of Higher Education*, November 4, 2005, B10.

114. Bok, "The Critical Role of Trustees in Enhancing Student Learning," B12.

115. Peter Smith, *The Quiet Crisis: How Higher Education Is Failing America* (Bolton, MA: Anker Publishing, 2004), 136–40.

116. Harrison, "The Quality of University Teaching," 11.

117. Karen W. Arenson, "Panel Explores Standardized Tests for Colleges," *New York Times*, February 9, 2006, A1, A20; Kelly Field, "Panel to Give Colleges Gentle Shove Toward Testing," *Chronicle of Higher Education*, April 7, 2006, A33.

118. AACU, *Liberal Education Outcomes*; Donald E. Heller, "Technology and the Failure of Higher Education Policy," in *The States and Higher Education Policy: Affordability, Access, and Accountability*, ed. Donald E. Heller (Baltimore: Johns Hopkins University Press, 2001), 243, 246–50, 254–55.

119. Tompkins, *A Life in School*, 200.

Chapter Four

1. For variations of the Hutchins quote, see Bruce Wilshire, *The Moral Collapse of the University* (Albany, NY: State University of New York Press, 1992), 86; George Dennis O'Brien, *All the Essential Half-Truths about Higher Education* (Chicago: University of Chicago Press, 1998), 30.

2. Lawrence R. Veysey, *The Emergence of the American University* (Chicago: University of Chicago Press, 1965), 306.

3. Jonathan R. Cole, "Balancing Acts: Dilemmas of Choice Facing Research Universities," in *The Research University in a Time of Discontent*, eds. Jonathan R. Cole, Eleanor G. Barber, and Stephen R. Gaubard (Baltimore: Johns Hopkins University Press, 1994), 35, n. 11; W. Allen Wallis, "Unity in the University," *Daedalus* 104 (1975): 72.

4. Thomas J. Tighe, *Who's in Charge of America's Research Universities? A Blueprint for Reform* (Albany, NY: State University of New York Press, 2003), 39; Jeffrey J. Williams, "Franchising the University" in *Beyond the Corporate University*, eds. Henry A. Giroux, and Kostas Myrsiades (New York: Rowman and Littlefield, 2001), 195.

5. Sheila Slaughter, "Professional Values and the Allure of the Market," *Academe Online*, September–October 2001, www.aaup.org/publications/Academe. See sources cited in note 4.

6. Brent D. Rubin, *Pursuing Excellence in Higher Education: Eight Fundamental Challenges* (San Francisco: Jossey Bass, 2004), 289; Erin Strout, "Back on Campus, for Eternity," *Chronicle of Higher Education*, November 30, 2005, A6.

7. See the AAUP description of shared governance available at www.aaup.org/governance; Association of Governing Boards of Universities and Colleges, Report of the Commission on the Academic Presidency, *Renewing the Academic Presidency: Stronger Leadership for Tougher Times* (Washington, DC: Association of Governing Boards of Universities and Colleges, 1996), 19–26.

8. Richard P. Chait, Thomas P. Holland, and Barbara E. Taylor, "Improving the Performance of Governing Boards," quoted in "The Role of Governing Boards: Issues, Rec-

ommendations, and Research," in *Field Guide to Academic Leadership*, ed. Robert M. Diamond (San Francisco: Jossey Bass, 2002), 375.

9. Tighe, *Who's in Charge*, 36. See also Association of Governing Boards of Universities and Colleges, Frequently Asked Questions, available at www.agb.org/content/browse/zrc6.cfm.

10. Association of Governing Boards of Universities and Colleges, *Renewing the Academic Presidency*, 30; Sara Hebel, "State Regents: Should They Be Elected or Appointed?" *Chronicle of Higher Education*, October 15, 2004, 1.

11. Association of Governing Boards of Universities and Colleges, *Renewing the Academic Presidency*, 12; Hebel, "State Regents," A21; Tighe, *Who's in Charge*, 37–40; James J. Duderstadt, *A University for the 21st Century* (Ann Arbor, MI: University of Michigan Press, 2000), 46, 55.

12. Tighe, *Who's in Charge*, 36; Benjamin E. Hermalin, "Higher Education Boards of Trustees," in *Governing Academia*, ed. Ronald G. Ehrenberg (Ithaca, NY: Cornell University Press, 2004), 28, 47.

13. For a discussion of the value conflicts, see Tighe, *Who's in Charge*, 46–52; Paul J. Olscamp, *Moral Leadership: Ethics and the College Presidency* (Lanham, MD: Rowman and Littlefield, 2003), 111–12.

14. Olscamp, *Moral Leadership*, 109.

15. Tighe, *Who's in Charge*, 47.

16. Tighe, *Who's in Charge*, 47; Joan Wallach Scott, "Defending the Tradition of Shared Governance," *Chronicle of Higher Education*, August 9, 1996, B1.

17. James O. Freedman, "Presidents and Trustees," in *Governing Academia*, ed. Ronald G. Ehrenberg (Ithaca, NY: Cornell University Press, 2004), 9; Richard P. Chait, "When Trustees Blunder," *Chronicle of Higher Education*, February 17, 2006, 36. For trustees' overreliance on presidents and senior administrators for information, see Piper Fogg, "A Working Relationship: Trustees and Professors, Often at Odds, Search for Common Ground," *Chronicle of Higher Education*, February 24, 2006, 20.

18. Martin Anderson, *Imposters in the Temple* (New York: Simon & Schuster, 1992), 200; Association of Governing Boards of Universities and Colleges, *Renewing the Academic Presidency*, 11.

19. Derek Bok, "The Critical Role of the Trustees in Enhancing Student Learning," *Chronicle of Higher Education*, December 16, 2005, B12.

20. Randall Jarrell, *Pictures from an Institution* (London: Faber and Faber, 1954), 11.

21. Frederick Rudolph, *The American College and University* (Athens, GA: University of Georgia Press, 1990), 170; John S. Brubacher and Willis Rudy, *Higher Education in Transition* (New Brunswick, NJ: Transition, 1997), 365.

22. Harold T. Shapiro, "University Presidents—Then and Now," in *Universities and Their Leadership*, eds. William G. Bowen and Harold T. Shapiro (Princeton, NJ: Princeton University Press, 1998), 65, 78–80.

23. Shapiro, "University Presidents," 89 (quoting Wilson).

24. Shapiro, "University Presidents," 83, 92; Dennis M. Barden, "The Age of Reason," *Chronicle of Higher Education*, November 8, 2005, C2.

25. Upton Sinclair, *The Goose-Step: A Study of American Education* (Pasadena: Upton Sinclair, 1923), 352.

26. Theodore M. Hesburgh, "Where Are College Presidents' Voices on Important Public Issues?" in Olscampf, *Moral Leadership*, 153.

27. James O. Freedman, *Liberal Education and the Public Interest* (Iowa City: University of Iowa Press, 2003), 13.

28. Derek Bok, *Higher Learning* (Cambridge, MA: Harvard University Press, 1986), 195.

29. Karin Fisher, "Running for a Different Kind of Office," *Chronicle of Higher Education*, May 13, 2005, available at http://chronicle.com/weekly/v51/i136/36a01801.htm.

30. American Council on Education, "College Presidents Say Planning, Fundraising, Budgeting and Personnel Issues Occupy Much of Their Time," *Higher Education and National Affairs*, October 9, 2000, 2.

31. Jeffrey Selingo, "Leaders' Views About Higher Education, Their Jobs, and Their Lives," *Chronicle of Higher Education*, November 4, 2005, A26.

32. Ryan C. Amacher and Roger E. Meiners, *Faulty Towers: Tenure and the Structure of Higher Education* (Oakland, CA: Independent Institute, 2004), 31 (quoting Gerhard Casper).

33. Michael Cohen and James March, *Leadership and Ambiguity: The American College President*, 2nd ed. (Cambridge, MA: Harvard University Press, 1988), 150.

34. Hesburgh, "Where Are College Presidents' Voices?" 153.

35. Freedman, *Liberal Education*, 19 (quoting A. Bartlett Giamatti).

36. Duderstadt, *A University for the 21st Century*, 66–67; Joseph L. Dionne and Thomas Kean, *Breaking the Social Contract: The Fiscal Crisis in Higher Education, Report of the Commission on National Investment in Higher Education* (New York: Council for Aid to Education, 1997), 14.

37. Roper Center for Public Opinion Research, Harris Poll, March 10, 2004, available at www.harrisinteractive.com/harris_poll/index.asp?PID=-447 (37 percent reported a great deal of confidence in people running major educational institutions such as colleges and universities).

38. Association of Governing Boards of Universities and Colleges, *Renewing the Academic Presidency*, 10. See Rita Bornstein, "The Nature and Nurture of Presidents," *Chronicle of Higher Education*, November 4, 2005, B10.

39. Cohen and March, *Leadership and Ambiguity*, 3–5, 195–203; Association of Governing Boards of Universities and Colleges, *Renewing the Academic Presidency*, 10, 17.

40. Selingo, "Leaders' Views," A26.

41. Gabriel E. Kaplan, "How Academic Ships Actually Navigate," in Ehrenberg, *Governing Academia*, 165, 191.

42. Goldie Blumenstyk, "Outside Chance for Insiders," *Chronicle of Higher Education*, November 4, 2005, A28.

43. Selingo, "Leaders' Views," A26.

44. Sam Dillon, "Ivory Tower Gets C.E.O. Level Salaries," *New York Times*, November 15, 2004, A17.

45. Donald Kennedy, *Academic Duty* (Cambridge, MA: Harvard University Press, 1997), 139.

46. Hazard Adams, *The Academic Tribes*, 2nd ed. (Urbana, IL: University of Illinois Press, 1988), 11.

47. Tighe, *Who's in Charge?*, 45.

48. Cohen and March, *Leadership and Ambiguity*, 121.

49. Association of Governing Boards of Universities and Colleges, *Renewing the Academic Presidency*, 26; Duderstadt, *A University for the 21st Century*, 256.

50. Ryan C. Amacher and Roger E. Meiners, *Faulty Towers: Tenure and the Structure of Higher Education* (Oakland, CA: The Independent Institute, 2004), 40.

51. Alan Finder, Patrick D. Healy, and Kate Zernike, "President of Harvard Resigns, Ending Stormy 5-Year Tenure," *New York Times*, February 22, 2006, A1.

52. For examples, see the Report of the Provost's Committee on the Status of Women Faculty, Stanford University, May, 2004, available at www.stanford.edu/dept/provost/womenfacultyreport/PACSWF appendices.pdf-2004-06-01.

53. John B. Bennett, (Phoenix, AZ: American Council on Education: Oryx Press, 1998), 85; Bornstein, "The Nature and Nurture of Presidents," B11.

54. Rubin, *Pursuing Excellence*, 293, 302.

55. Rubin, *Pursuing Excellence*, 305.

56. Stanley Aronowitz, *The Knowledge Factory* (Boston: Beacon Press, 2000), 164.

57. Jarrell, *Pictures from an Institution*, 119–20.

58. Emily Toth, "Ms. Mentor: Am I Really Stuck?" *Chronicle of Higher Education*, July 20, 2004, available at http://chronicle.com/jobs/2004/07/2004072001c.htm. In one survey of women chief academic officers, slightly over a third mentioned the possibility of advancement as a motivating factor. Karen Doyle Walton and Sharon A. McDade, "At the Top of the Faculty: Women as Chief Academic Officers," in *Women Administrators in Higher Education: Historical and Contemporary Perspectives*, eds. Jana Nidiffer and Carolyn Terry Bashaw (Albany: State University of New York Press, 2001) 91.

59. C. P. Snow, *The Masters* (London: MacMillan, 1951), 111.

60. The dominant reasons for the move to administration cited by women chief academic officers were challenge (86 percent) and change (65 percent). Walton and McDade, "At the Top of the Faculty," 91.

61. Adams, *The Academic Tribe*, 139.

62. Robert Grudin, *Book: A Novel* (New York: Random House, 1992), 10.

63. John Gardiner, *Mickelsson's Ghosts* (New York: Knopf, 1982), 272.

64. Professor X, *This Beats Working for a Living* (New Rochelle, NY: Arlington House, 1973), 142.

65. Rubin, *Pursuing Excellence*, 294.

66. Walton and McDade, "At the Top of the Faculty," 91.

67. Adams, *The Academic Tribes*, 94.

68. James M. Kouzes and Barry Z. Posner, *The Jossey-Bass Academic Administrator's Guide to Exemplary Leadership* (San Francisco: Jossey-Bass, 2003), 2–14.

69. Jay Mathews, "It's Lowly at the Top: What Became of the Great College Presidents," *Washington Post*, June 10, 2001, B1, discussed in Clara M. Lovett, "The Dumbing Down of College Presidents," in Olscamp, *Moral Leadership*, 159.

70. George Dowdall and Jean Dowdall, "Crossing Over to the Dark Side," *Chronicle of Higher Education*, September 9, 2005, C1.

71. Ernest Franklin, "Interim and Untenured," *Chronicle of Higher Education*, October 6, 2005, available at http://chronicle.com/jobs/2005/10/2005100601c.htm; Rob Jenkins, "Getting into Administration," *Chronicle of Higher Education*, April 21, 2005, available at http://chronicle.com/jobs/2005/04/200542101c.htm.

72. Stephen Joel Trachtenberg, *Reflections on Higher Education* (Westport, CT: Oryx Press, 2002), 17.

73. Bok, *Higher Learning*, 24; Gordon C. Winston, "Why Can't a College Be More Like a Firm," in *New Thinking on Higher Education*, ed. Joel W. Meyerson (Bolton, MA: Anker Publishing, 1998), 2.

74. Clark Kerr, *The Uses of the University* (Cambridge, MA: Harvard University Press, 1982).

75. Kerr, *The Uses of the University*, 54. See also Charles J. Sykes, *ProfScam: Professors and the Demise of Higher Education* (Washington, DC: Regnery, 1988), 27, n. 39.

76. Stuart Rojstaczer, *Gone for Good: Tales of University Life After the End of the Golden Age* (New York: Oxford University Press, 1999), 107. See also Richard Levin, "Yale's Fourth Century" (1996), discussed in id., 108.

77. Adams, *The Academic Tribes*, 11. See also Leo M. Lambert, "Chief Financial Officers," in Diamond, *Field Guide to Academic Leadership*, 425, 433.

78. Henry Rosovsky, *The University: An Owner's Manual* (New York: Norton, 1990), 42–47.

79. Rosovsky, *The University*, 42.

80. Rosovsky, *The University*, 42.

81. Rosovsky, *The University*, 43.

82. Alexander Astin and Helen Astin, *Leadership Reconsidered: Engaging Higher Education in Social Change* (Battle Creek, MI: W.K. Kellogg Foundation, 2000), 40; report in "Turning Point," *Pew Policy Perspectives*, May 1997, 7(2), 4; Rubin, *Pursuing Excellence*, 294; Ben Tryon, "The Divide," *Chronicle of Higher Education*, October 21, 2005, C1.

83. Robert M. Diamond, "Some Final Observations," in Diamond, *Field Guide to Academic Leaderhips*, 476; Cynthia Berryman-Fink, "Can We Agree to Disagree? Faculty-Faculty Conflict," in *Mending the Cracks in the Ivory Tower*, ed. Susan A. Holton (Bolton, MA: Anker Publishing, 1998), 145–46.

84. Diamond, "Some Final Observations," 476.

85. The first quote in various forms is attributed to Fred Allen—see Des McHale, *Wit* (Kansas City: Andrew McNeil, 2003); the second to Carl C. Byers—see *The Penguin Dictionary of Modern Humorous Quotations, 2nd ed.*, ed. Fred Metcalf (New York: Penguin, 2001), 55.

86. Stuart Palmer, *The Universities Today* (Lanham, MD: University Press of America, 1998), 55.

87. Astin and Astin, *Leadership Reconsidered*, 5, 42–43; Piper Fogg, "So Many Committees, So Little Time," *Chronicle of Higher Education*, December 19, 2003, A14.

88. Lawrence Douglas and Alexander George, *Sense and Nonsensibility: Lampoons of Learning and Literature* (New York: Simon & Schuster, 2004), 101.

89. Andrew Furman, "Measure Professors' Real Service, Not Lip Service," *Chronicle of Higher Education*, November 5, 2004, B20; Fiona Cownie, *Legal Academics* (London: Hart Publishing, 2004), 144, 147.

90. Emily Toth, "Ms. Mentor, Fear of Committee-ment," *Chronicle of Higher Education*, November 16, 2001, http://chronicle.com/jobs/2001/1/2001111602c.htm; Fogg, "So Many Committees." See also Emily Toth, "Ms. Mentor, Don't Be Docile," *Chronicle of Higher Education*, January 11, 2006, http://chronicle.com/jobs/2005/01//2005011101c.htm.

91. Toth, "Fear of Committee-ment."

92. Frank Midler, "Entering the Fog," *Chronicle of Higher Education*, November 4, 2005, available at http://chronicle.com/jobs/2005/11/2005110401c.htm.

93. Stanley Fish, "Real Meetings," *Chronicle of Higher Education*, January 9, 2004, C2.

94. Gerald Warner Brace, *The Department* (New York: W.W. Norton, 1968), 228–32.

95. Brace, *The Department*, 232.

96. Dave Barry, *Claw Your Way to the Top* (Emmaus, PA: Rodale, 1986), 25–26.

97. John Kenneth Galbraith, *Ambassador's Journal* (Boston: Houghton Mifflin, 1969).

98. Barry, *Claw Your Way to the Top*, 25.

99. Fish, "Real Meetings," C2.

100. Edith Wharton, *Hudson River Bracketed* (New York: Appleton, 1929), 216.

101. McHale, *Wit*, 257 (quoting McLaughlin).

102. F. M. Cornford, *Microcosmographia Academica Being a Guide for the Young Academic Politician, 4th ed.* (Cambridge: Bowes and Bowes, 1949 [1908]), 15.

103. Edward B. Fiske, "Education: Lessons," *New York Times*, October 18, 1989, B8 (quoting Sayre).

104. Fiske, "Education," B8 (quoting Kennedy).

105. Berryman-Fink, "Can We Agree to Disagree?" 141, 142–43.

106. Emily Toth, *Ms. Mentor's Impeccable Advice for Women in Academia* (Philadelphia: University of Pennsylvania, 1997), 60; Emily Toth, "Bored by Department Meetings," *The Chronicle of Higher Education*, September 19, 2005, available at http://chronicle.com/jobs/2005/09/2005091901c.htm.

107. For examples as well as analysis, see Michael L. Siegel, "On Collegiality," *Journal of Legal Education* 54 (2004): 406, 420–24.

108. Charles Sykes, *ProfScam*, 260; Kenneth A. Shaw, "Creating Change: Suggestions for the New President," in Diamond, *Field Guide to Academic Leadership*, 391, 392.

109. Hermalin, "Higher Education Boards of Trustees," 31, 39; Gabriel E. Kaplan, "How Academic Ships Actually Navigate," in Ehrenberg, *Governing Academia*, 165, 167; Donald E. Heller, "State Oversight of Academia," in Ehrenberg, *Governing Academia*, 30, 60–65.

110. Thomas E. Corts, *Institutional Ethics and Values* (Washington, DC: Association of Governing Boards of Universities and Colleges, 1998), 3–4.

111. Joel M. Douglas, "Conflict Resolution in the Academy: A Modest Proposal," in Holton, *Mending the Cracks*, 206; William C. Warters, "Conflict Management in Higher Education: A Review of Current Approaches," in *Conflict Management in Higher Education*, ed. Susan A. Holton (San Francisco: Jossey-Bass, 1995), 77.

112. Rubin, *Pursuing Excellence*, 305.

113. Duderstadt, *A University for the 21st Century*, 254–56.

114. C. Jackson Grayson, Jr., "Benchmarking in Higher Education," in Meyerson, *New Thinking on Higher Education*, 105.

115. Bornstein, "Nature and Nurture of Presidents," B11.

116. Tighe, *Who's in Charge?*, 78–84; George Dennis O'Brien, *All the Essential Half-Truths About Higher Education* (Chicago: University of Chicago Press, 1998), 133–34.

117. Fish, "Real Meetings," C2; Ann E. Lucas, "Spanning the Abyss: Managing Conflict Between Deans and Chairs," in Holton, *Mending the Cracks*, 60, 77.

118. Furman, "Measure Professor's Real Service, Not Lip Service"; Toth, "Ms. Mentor, Don't Be Docile."

Chapter Five

1. Richard A. Posner, *Public Intellectuals: A Study of Decline* (Cambridge, MA: Harvard University Press, 2001), 23, 35; Russell Jacoby, *The Last Intellectuals: American Culture in the Age of Academe* (New York: Basic Books, 1987), 235. Cynthia Ozick, *Quarrels and Quandry: Essays By Cynthia Ozick* (New York: Knopf, 2001), 120–26.

2. See the historical discussion in Chapter 1.

3. See Ron Eyerson, *Between Culture and Politics* (Cambridge, MA: and Oxford, Polity Press, 1994), 130 (discussing race); Charlotte Allen, "Feminist Fatale," *Los Angeles Times*, February 13, 2005, M1, M2 (discussing women).

4. For an overview, see Charles Diggins, "The Changing Role of the Public Intellectual in American History," in *The Public Intellectual: Between Philosophy and Politics*, eds. Arthur M. Melzer, Jerry Weinberger, and M. Richard Zinman (Lanham, MD: Rowman and Littlefield, 2003), 91.

5. David Damrosh, *We Scholars: Changing the Culture of the University* (Cambridge, MA: Harvard University Press 1995), 7; Thomas Bender, *Intellect and Public Life: Essays on the Social History of Academic Intellectuals in the United States* (Johns Hopkins Press, 1993), 131; Joseph Joffe, "The Decline of the Public Intellectual and the Rise of the Pundit," in Melzer, Weinberger, and Zinman, *The Public Intellectual*, 113.

6. Jacoby, *The Last Intellectuals*, 7.

7. See Thorstein Veblen, *Higher Education in America* (1918), discussed in Chapter 2, and in Jacoby, *The Last Intellectuals*, 142.

8. Pierre Bordieu, *Homo Academicus*, Peter Collier, trans. (Stanford, CA: Stanford University Press, 1988), 119; Posner, *Public Intellectuals*, 34–35.

9. Posner, *Pubic Intellectuals*, 54–55.

10. Charles Kadushin, *The American Intellectual Elite* (Boston: Little, Brown, 1974), 19, 339.

11. Bruce Robbins, *Secular Vocations: Intellectuals, Professionalism, Culture* (New York, London: Verso, 1993), ix (quoting unnamed commentators); Joseph Epstein, "Intellectuals: Public and Otherwise," *Commentary Magazine*, May 2000, 51.

12. Posner, *Public Intellectuals*, 56–57.

13. W. Lance Bennett, *News: The Politics of Illusion*, 3rd ed. (New York: Longman, 1996), 143.

14. Deborah L. Rhode, "A Bad Press on Bad Lawyers: The Media Sees Research, Research Sees the Media," in *Social Science, Social Policy, and the Law*, eds. Patricia Ewick, Robert A. Kagan, and Austin Sarat (New York: Russell Sage, 1999), 157.

15. William Halton and Michael McGann, *Distorting the Law* (Chicago: University of Chicago Press, 2004), 100–101.

16. Bennett, *News: The Politics of Illusion*, 143.

17. Dan Rather, quoted in Bennett, *News: The Politics of Illusion*, 1.

18. Bennett, *News: The Politics of Illusion*, 39; Neil Postman, *Amusing Ourselves to Death* (New York: Viking Penquin, 1985), 76.

19. Halton and McGann, *Distorting the Law*, 103.

20. Ronald Goldfarb, "The End of Civilization," *Washington Lawyer*, February, 2004, 30, 32. The advice is long-standing. See Kadushin, *The American Intellectual Elite*, 59 (noting that an "acid tone is helpful" in getting published in leading journals).

21. This phrase came from a high-powered agent hoping to help me produce a sequel to Susan Faludi's *Backlash*. I have heard similar counsel from other agents and from colleagues with comparable experiences.

22. For the need for this role, see Posner, *Public Intellectuals*, 46, quoting Jean Bethke Elshtain, and Edward W. Said, *Representations of the Intellectual* (New York, Pantheon, 1994), 11, 21, 100.

23. Leah Bowman, "The New Blacklists," *Chronicle of Higher Education*, April 14, 2006, C2.

24. James E. McWilliams, "Just Another Leftist Loon," *Chronicle of Higher Education*, January 8, 2004, available at http://chronicle.com/jobs/2004/01/2004018o1c.htm.

25. Deborah L. Rhode, "Terrorists and Their Lawyers," *New York Times*, April 16, 2002, A31.

26. Personal correspondence from Tom Shaw, April 16, 2002, and personal correspondence from Robert Held, April 16, 2002.

27. Personal correspondence, Tom Shaw.

28. Deborah L. Rhode, "Step, Wince, Step, Wince," *New York Times*, October 18, 2000, 31.

29. In an interview on National Public Radio, the editorial page editor of the *New York Times* reported that the paper receives about a thousand op-eds a month. National Public Radio, San Francisco Morning Edition, interview with Gail Collins, March 28, 2005.

30. Laurie I. Levenson, "TV or Not TV," *California Lawyer*, July 1997, 96. See also Jennifer Jacobson, "Loving the Limelight," *Chronicle of Higher Education*, April 21, 2006, A12.

31. Jacobson, "Loving the Limelight," A12.

32. Jacoby, *The Last Intellectuals*, 139.

33. Posner, *Public Intellectuals*, 184. For a critique of Posner's methodology, see Alan Wolfe, *An Intellectual in Public Life* (Ann Arbor: University of Michigan Press, 2005), 363–74.

34. Aaron Wildavsky, *Craftways*, 2nd ed. (New Brunswick, NJ: Transaction Publishers, 1993), 5.

35. Paul Johnson, *Intellectuals* (London: Weidenfeld and Nicolson, 1988), 197, 220.

36. David Brooks, *Bobos in Paradise* (New York: Simon & Schuster, 2000), 174.

37. Brooks, *Bobos in Paradise*, 150.

38. Brooks, *Bobos in Paradise*, 164.

39. Bourdieu, *Homo Academicus*, 120.

40. Posner, *Public Intellectuals*, 80.

41. For examples, see Posner, *Public Intellectuals*, 128–47, 341–42.

42. George Orwell, quoted in Epstein, "Intellectuals," 49.

43. Jean Bethke Elshtain, quoted in Karen R. Long, "Ethicist Decries Clinton's 'Cavalier Disdain' for Rules," *Cleveland Plain Dealer*, September 9, 1998, 1F.

44. Edward Shils, *The Academic Ethic: The Report of the Study Group of the International Council on the Future of the University* (Chicago: University of Chicago Press, 1984), 86.

45. Kadushin, *The American Intellectual Elite*, 300.

46. Henry Kissinger, *New York Times*, January 24, 1988, quoted in Bruce Robbins, *Secular Vocations: Intellectuals, Professionalism, Culture* (New York and London: Verso, 1993), 22.

47. Robbins, *Secular Vocations*, 22.

48. Tod Gitlin, *The Intellectuals and the Flag* (New York: Columbia University Press, 2006), 4–5.

49. Arthur M. Melzer, "What Is an Intellectual?" in Melzer, Weinberger, and Zinman, *The Public Intellectual*, 11.

50. Posner, *Public Intellectuals*, 33. See also Brooks, *Bobos in Paradise*, 148.

51. Eric Lott, *The Disappearing Liberal Intellectual* (New York: Basic, 2006).

52. Learned Hand, *The Spirit of Liberty: Papers and Addresses of Learned Hand*, ed. Irving Dilliard (New York: Alfred A. Knopf, 1952), 136–37.

53. Posner, *Public Intellectuals*, 389–90. For other initiatives, see Kayan P. Parsi and Karen E. Geraghty, "The Bioethicist as Public Intellectual," *American Journal of Bioethics* 4 (2004): 17, 18–19.

54. Bill Henderson and Andre Bernard, *Rotten Reviews and Rejections* (New York: Pushcart Press, 1998), 13.

55. Richard B. Woodward, "Reading in the Dark," *Village Voice*, October 26, 1994, 12.

56. George Orwell, *Essays*, ed. John Carey (New York: Knopf, 1968), 107.

57. Laura Miller, "The Hunting of the Snark," *New York Times Magazine*, October 5, 2003, 31.

58. Heidi Julavits, "Rejoice! Believe! Be Strong and Read Hard!" *The Believer*, March 2003, 13.

59. Julavits, "Rejoice!" 13; Miller, "The Hunting of the Snark," 31.

60. David Lodge, *Small World* (New York: Macmillan, 1984), 100.

61. Professor X, *This Beats Working for a Living* (New Rochelle: Arlington House, 1974).

62. Byron Calame, "The Book Review: Who Critiques Whom—and Why?" *New York Times*, February 18, 2006, Book Review 12 (quoting Robert Harris).

63. Max Blumenthal, "Princeton Tilts Right," *The Nation*, March 13, 2006, 14, 16.

64. Posner, *Public Intellectual*, 392.

65. Lucy Freeman, "The Feminine Mystique," *New York Times*, April 7, 1963, 46.

66. Henderson and Bernard, *Rotten Reviews*, 1–43.

67. Charlton Heston and Laurence Olivier, quoted in Stanley Fish, "Aim Low," *Chronicle of Higher Education*, May 16, 2003, C5.

68. John Patrick Diggins, "The Changing Role of the Public Intellectual in American History," in Melzer, Weinberger, and Zinman, *The Public Intellectual*, 91, 92–111.

69. Stephen Joel Trachtenberg, *Reflections on Higher Education* (Westport, CT: Oryx, 2002), 72.

70. Charles Edward Lindblom and David K. Cohen, *Usable Knowledge: Social Science and Social Problem Solving* (New Haven, CT: Yale University Press, 1979), 1, 2.

71. Lindblom and Cohen, *Usable Knowledge*, 34–49.

72. Theodore Roosevelt, "Citizenship in a Republic," in *The Works of Theodore Roosevelt*, ed. Hermann Hagedorn (New York: Scribners, 1926), XIII, 32. The behavior of women intellectuals was apparently of no concern.

73. Maureen Dowd, "Last Tango in D.C.," *New York Times*, October 14, 1998, A23.

74. Robert D. Reich, "Locked in the Cabinet," excerpted in the *New Yorker*, April 21, 1997, 47.

75. Leo Rosten, *Leo Rosten's Carnival of Wit* (New York: Penguin, 1996), 208 (quoting Brown).

76. Kadushin, *The American Intellectual Elite*, 302.

77. Several Clinton appointees resigned over welfare reform, among them Mary Jo Bane of Harvard and Michael Wald of Stanford. David Ellwood of Harvard left when his leave expired.

78. Richard Rorty, "Intellectuals in Politics," *Dissent* 39 (Fall 1991): 483, 486.

79. For a historical overview, see Richard Hofstadter, *Anti-Intellectualism* (New York: Knopf, 1962).

80. "United States Senate Continues Impeachment Trial of President Clinton," available in Federal Document Clearing House, January 26, 1999 (referring to Hyde's January 26 testimony before the United State Senate); News Conference of Representative Henry Hyde, Washington, DC. Available in *Federal News Service*, December 7, 1998. I have chronicled other problematic aspects of the hearings in Deborah L. Rhode, "Conflicts of Commitment: Legal Ethics in the Impeachment Context," *Stanford Law Review* 52 (2000): 269, 343–45.

81. Leonard Roy Frank, ed. *Webster's Quotationary* (New York: Random House, 1999), 752.

82. For recent examples in the tort reform context, see Halton and McGann, *Distorting the Law*, 102–05, and Deborah L. Rhode, "Frivolous Litigation and Civil Justice Reform: Miscasting the Problem, Recasting the Solution," *Duke Law Journal* 54 (2004): 471.

83. Posner, *Public Intellectuals*, 35.

84. Kadushin, *The American Intellectual Elite*, 330.

85. See Kadushin, *The American Intellectual Elite*, 308–31, 353–58.

86. Lindblom and Cohen, *Usable Knowledge*, 87.

87. Jeffrey Brainard, "A More Social Science: Daniel Sarewitz Wants Researchers to Serve Society Better by Looking for Beneficial Results," *Chronicle of Higher Education*, November 18, 2005, A 22.

88. Robert Post, "The Structure of Academic Freedom," in *Academic Freedom After September 11*, ed. Beshara Doumani (New York: Zone Books, 2006); Walter P. Metzger, "Profession and Constitution: Two Definitions of Academic Freedom in America," *Texas Law Review* 66 (1988): 1265, 1276; Cary Nelson and Stephen Watt, *Academic Keywords: A Devil's Dictionary for Higher Education* (New York, Routledge, 1999), 23.

89. Richard Hofstadter and Walter Metzger, *The Development of Academic Freedom in the United States* (New York: Columbia University Press, 1955), 367–412; John R. Searle, "Two Concepts of Academic Freedom," in *The Concept of Academic Freedom*, ed. Edmund L. Pincoffs (Austin, TX: University of Texas Press, 1975): 86, 90; John S. Brubacher and Willis Rudy, *Higher Education in Transition* (New Brunswick, NJ: Transition, 1997) 315–16.

90. Thomas L. Haskell, "Justifying the Rights of Academic Freedom in the Era of 'Power/Knowledge,'" in *The Future of Academic Freedom*, ed. Louis Menand (Chicago: University of Chicago Press, 1996), 43, 48–53.

91. Julie A. Reuben, *The Making of the Modern University* (Chicago: University of Chicago Press, 1996), 197–98.

92. American Association of University Professors (AAUP), *General Report of the Committee on Academic Freedom and Academic Tenure* (1915), quoted in Haskell, "Justifying the Rights of Academic Freedom," 58–59.

93. AAUP, *1915 Declaration of Principles on Academic Freedom and Academic Tenure*, reprinted in AAUP, *Policy Documents and Reports* 9th ed., 2001, 291.

94. AAUP, *1940 Statement of Principles on Academic Freedom and Tenure*, reprinted in AAUP, *Policy Documents and Reports*. Some three-quarters of surveyed institutions use some or all of the AAUP Statement in their own codes. Cathy A. Trower, "What Is Current Policy?" in *The Questions of Tenure*, ed. Richard P. Chait (Cambridge, MA: Harvard University Press, 1992): 32, 34.

95. "Committee Statement on Extramural Utterances," reprinted in AAUP, *Policy Documents and Reports*, 41.

96. Brubacher and Rudy, *Higher Education in Transition*, 320.

97. William Van Alstyne, "The Specific Theory of Academic Freedom and the General Issue of Civil Liberty," in Pincoffs, *The Concept of Academic Freedom*, 59, 61.

98. *Perry v. Sinderman*, 408 U.S. 593 (1972); *Pickering v. Board of Education* 391 U.S. 563 (1968).

99. *Waters v. Churchill*, 511 U.S. 611 (1994); *Jeffries v. Harleston*, 52 F.3d 9, 14-15 (2d Cir. 1995).

100. Robert Post, in *The Structure of Academic Freedom*, makes this claim and cites Chomsky as an example.

101. Karen W. Arenson, "Columbia Panel Reports No Proof of Anti-Semitism," *New York Times*, March 31, 2005, A1, C20.

102. Ellen Schrecker, *No Ivory Tower: McCarthyism and the Universities* (New York: Oxford University Press, 1986); Julius G. Getman, *In the Company of Scholars: The Struggle for the Soul of Higher Education* (Austin, TX: University of Texas Press, 1992), 77–89; Lee Bollinger, *Cardozo Lecture on Academic Freedom* (New York: Association of the Bar of the City of New York, March 23, 2005), available at http://columbia.edu/cu/news/05/03/cardozo_lecture.html; Russell Jacoby, "The New PC: Crybaby Conservatives," *The Nation*, April 4, 2005, 11.

103. Henry Aaron Yeomans, *Abbott Lawrence Lowell, 1856–1943* (Cambridge, MA: Harvard University Press, 1948), 311–12.

104. AAUP, "Report of a Special Committee on Academic and National Security in a Time of Crisis," *Academe*, 89 (November–December, 2003), 34, 51–56; Donald Alexander Downs, *Restoring Free Speech and Liberty on Campus* (Oakland, CA: The Independent Institute and New York: Cambridge University Press, 2005), xvi-vii; Jonathan R. Cole, "The New McCarthyism," *Chronicle of Higher Education*, September 9, 2005, B7, B8; Katha Pollitt, "Brooklyn Prof in Godless Shocker," *The Nation*, June 27, 2005, 11.

105. Academic Bill of Rights, Concurrent Resolution (H.R. 318), 108 Congress (2003). See David Horowitz, "College Professors Should Be Made to Teach, Not Preach," *USA Today*, March 24, 2005, 13A; http://studentsforacademicfreedom.org/; Jennifer Jacobson, "What Makes David Run?" *Chronicle of Higher Education*, May 6, 2005, A9.

106. Academic Bill of Rights.

107. June Kronholz, "Congress Wades into Campus Politics," *Wall Street Journal*, October 4, 2005, A4.

108. Jacoby, "The New PC," 15; Roger W. Baitlen, general secretary of the AAUP, quoted in Jacobson, "What Makes David Run," A9. For sponsors' concerns about "liberal propaganda," see Cheryl A. Cameron, Laura E. Meyers, and Steven G. Olswang, "Academic Bills of Rights: Conflict in the Classroom," *Journal of College and University Law* 31 (2005): 243, 288. For concerns about unpatriotic statements, see Downs, *Restoring Free Speech*, xvi.

109. Jon Wiener, "UCLA's Dirty Thirty," *Nation*, February 13, 2006, 23, 24; Saree Makdisi, "Witch Hunt at UCLA," *Los Angeles Times*, January 22, 2006, M1.

110. Sara Hebel, "Patrolling Professors' Politics," *Chronicle of Higher Education*, February 13, 2004, A18 (describing inquiry by Colorado Senate); Jennifer Jacobson, "Pennsylvania Lawmakers Open Hearings on Political Bias in State's Public Classrooms," *Chronicle of Higher Education*, November 10, 2005, available at http://chronicle.com/daily/2005/11/2005111001n.htm; David Horowitz, "Ideologues at the Lectern," Los Angeles Times, January 22, 2006, M1, M6 (describing state legislation and hearings).

111. Kelly Field, "'Political Rigidity' in Academe Undermines Federal Support for Higher Education, Senator Tells Commission," *Chronicle of Higher Education*, December 13, 2005, available at http://chronicle.com/daily/2005/12/2005121201n.htm.

112. Mark Bauerlein, "Liberal Groupthink is Anti-Intellectual," *Chronicle of Higher Education*, November 12, 2004, B6.

113. Ann Neal, "Professors Who Preach," *American Enterprise*, June, 2005, 30, 31.

114. American Council on Education, "Statement on Academic Rights and Responsibilities," June 2005; "Forum: A Chilly Climate on Campus," *Chronicle of Higher Education*, September 9, 2005, B13.

115. Baitlen, general secretary of the AAUP, quoted in Jacobson, "What Makes David Run?" A9; "Statement Issued by the AAUP Committee A on Academic Freedom and Tenure," March 2, 2004, http://www.aaup.org/statements/SpchState/Statements/comaclass.htm.

116. Joan W. Scott, "Professors as Liberators," *Los Angeles Times*, January 22, 2006, M6.

117. American Council on Education, "Statement on Academic Rights and Responsibilities."

118. Bernard Williams, *Truth and Truthfulness: An Essay in Genealogy* (Princeton, NJ: Princeton University Press), 213; Robert Post, "Reconciling Theory and Practice in First Amendment Jurisprudence," *California Law Review* 88 (2000): 2355, 2363.

119. Scott Smallwood, "Inside a Free-Speech Firestorm," *The Chronicle of Higher Education*, February 18, 2005 (quoting Churchill, *Some People Push Back: On the Justice of Roosting Chickens*).

120. Smallwood, "Inside a Free Speech Firestorm," A1; Michelle York, "Professor Is Assailed by Legislature and Vandals," *New York Times*, February 3, 2005, B6.

121. "AAUP Releases Statement on Professor Ward Churchill," February, 4, 2005, available at www.aaup.org/newsroom/press/2005/churchill.htm.

122. Thomas Brown, "Is Ward Churchill the New Michael Bellesiles?," The History News Network, available at http://hnn.us/articles/10633.html, March 14, 2005.

123. Stanley Fish, "On Balance," *Chronicle of Higher Education*, April 1, 2005, available at http://chronicle.com/jobs/2005/04/2005040101c.htm.

124. Laurence H. Summers, "Remarks at NBER on Diversifying the Science and Engineering Workforce," January 14, 2005, available at www.president.harvard.edu/speeches/2005/nber.html.

125. Summers, "Remarks."

126. Stanley Fish, "Clueless in Academe," *Chronicle of Higher Education,* February 23, 2005, available at http:chronicle.com/jobs/2005/02/2005022301c.htm.

127. Harvard Standing Committee on Women, quoted in Fish, "Clueless in Academe."

128. Rebecca Winters, "Harvard's Crimson Face," *Time,* January 31, 2005, 52.

129. "The Revenge of Ellen Swallow," *New York Times,* February 20, 2005, E8.

130. Camille Paglia, "Academic, Heal Thyself," *New York Times,* March 6, 2006, A25.

131. Ellen Goodman, "Summer's Teachable Moment," *Boston Globe,* February 24, 2005, A11 (quoting unnamed pundits on political correctness); George Will, "Harvard Hysterics," *Washington Post,* January 27, 2005, A19; Ruth R. Wisse, "Gender Fender-Bender," *Wall St. Journal,* January 21, 2005, A8.

132. George Neumayr, "Professors of Stupidity," *American Spectator,* February 11, 2005, available at www.spectator.org/dsp_article.asp?art_id=7755.

133. Alan Dershowitz, *ABC News, Nightline,* "The Crimson Controversy," February 21, 2005; Richard Freeman, quoted in Fish, "Clueless in Academe."

134. Dershowitz, *ABC News, Nightline.*

135. Rick Levin, "Q&A," *Yale Alumni Report,* March–April, 2005, 23.

136. Summers made three public apologies. Winters, "Harvard's Crimson Face," 52.

137. Alan Finder, Patrick D. Healy, and Kate Zernike, "President of Harvard Resigns, Ending Stormy 5-Year Tenure," *New York Times,* February 22, 2006, A19.

138. Barbara Grosz, quoted in Goodman, "Summer's Teachable Moment," A11.

139. See Deborah L. Rhode, *Justice and Gender* (Cambridge, MA: Harvard University Press, 1989),290; Edward Clark, *Sex in Education* (New York: Houghton Mifflin, 1873), 31–60.

140. John Hennessy, Susan Hockfield, and Shirley Tilghman, "Women and Science: The Real Issue," *Boston Globe,* February 12, 2005, A13.

141. See, for example, Natalie Angier and Kenneth Chang, "Gray Matter and Sexes: A Scientific Gray Area," *New York Times,* January 24, 2005, A1; Alan Ginsburg, et al., *Reassessing U.S. International Mathematics Performance: New Findings from the 2003 TIMSS and PISA* (Washington, DC: American Institutes for Research, 2005), 18–21; Erin Leahey and Guang Guo, "Gender Differences in Mathematical Trajectories," *Social Forces* 80 (2001): 713.

142. Angier and Chang, "Gray Matter," A1; Virginia Valian, "Raise Your Hand If You're a Woman in Science," *Washington Post,* January 30, 2005, B01; Piper Fogg, "Harvard President Wonders Aloud About Women in Science and Math," *Chronicle of Higher Education,* January 28, 2005, A12.

143. Valian, "Raise Your Hand If You're a Woman in Science," B01; Ginsburg et al., *Reassessing U.S. International Mathematics Performance,* 18–21; Carol B. Muller and Sally K. Ride, letter to the editor, "Women, Science and Harvard," *New York Times,* January 21, 2005, A22; Angier and Chang, "Gray Matter," A1; Steven J. Spencer, Claude M. Steel, and Diane M. Quinn, "Stereotype Threat and Women's Math Performance," *Journal of Experimental Social Psychology,* 35 (1999): 4.

144. Hennessy, Hockfield, and Tilghman, "Women and Science," A13; Goodman, "Summer's Teachable Moment," A11.

145. Valian, "Raise Your Hand," Bo1; Virginia Valian, *Why So Slow? The Advancement of Women* (Cambridge, MA: MIT Press, 1999); J. Scott Long, ed., National Research Council Panel for the Study of Gender Differences in the Career Outcomes of Science and Engineering Ph.D.s, *From Scarcity to Visibility: Gender Differences in the Careers of Doctoral Scientists and Engineers* (Washington, DC: National Academy Press, 2001); Yu Xie and Kimberlee A. Shauman, *Women in Science: Career Processes and Outcomes* (Cambridge, MA: Harvard University Press 2003); Lotte Bailyn, "Academic Careers and Gender Equity: Lessons Learned," *Gender, Work, and Organizations* 10 (2003): 37.

146. Olivia Judd, "Different but (Probably) Equal," *New York Times*, January 23, 2005, E17; Winters, "Harvard's Crimson Face," 52; "Larry Summers: Harvard's Hit Man," *Time*, April 18, 2005, 104.

147. "Summers and Smoke," *Wall Street Journal*, January 21, 2005, W11; Piper Fogg, "Harvard Committees Suggest Steps to Help Women," *Chronicle of Higher Education*, May 27, 2005, A8, A9 (discussing initiatives and pledge of $50 million).

148. Bollinger, *Cardozo Lecture on Academic Freedom*.

149. David Lodge, "Prologue," *Small World* (New York: Macmillan, 1984).

150. Getman, *In the Company of Scholars*, 232.

151. Hazard Adams, *The Academic Tribes* (Urbana, IL: University of Illinois Press, 1988), 79.

152. Emily Toth, *Ms. Mentor's Impeccable Guide to Women in Academia* (Philadelphia: University of Pennsylvania Press, 1997), 190.

153. Brooks, *Bobos in Paradise*, 171.

154. Brooks, *Bobos in Paradise*, 175.

155. Toth, *Ms. Mentor's Guide*, 54. See also Getman, *In the Company of Scholars*, 232.

156. Toth, *Ms. Mentor's Guide*, 189.

157. Fran Lebowitz, *The Fran Lebowitz Reader* (New York: Vintage, 1994), 192.

158. Mrs. Patrick Campbell, quoted in Michele Brown and Ann O'Connor, *Hammer and Tongues* (London: J.M. Dent and Sons, 1986), 119.

159. P.G. Wodehouse, *The Girl in Blue* (New York: Simon & Schuster, 1971), 100–01.

160. Toth, *Ms. Mentor's Guide*, 49, 66, 67.

161. Larissa McFarquhar, "The Dean's List," *New Yorker*, June 11, 2001, 21, 64.

162. Stanley Fish, "Wrong Again," *Texas Law Review* 62 (1983), 299; "Still Wrong After All These Years," *Law and Philosophy* 6 (1987): 401.

163. William Major, "The Conference Paper, Reconsidered," *Chronicle of Higher Education*, March 27, 2006, C1.

164. See Thomas H. Benton, "Conference Man Returns to the MLA," *Chronicle of Higher Education*, January 31, 2005, available at http://chronicle.com/jobs/2005/01/20050103101c.htm.

165. Valerie Steele, chief curator at the museum of the Fashion Institute of Technology and editor of *Fashion Theory*, maintains that academics are the worst-dressed middle class occupational group in America. Alison Schneider, "Frumpy or Chic? Tweed or Kente? Sometimes Clothes Make the Professor," *Chronicle of Higher Education* (1998); Valerie Steele, "The F Word," *Lingua Franca*, April, 1991, 16. See also Regina Barreca, "Why We Look So Bad," *The Common Review* 2 (2003).

166. Barreca, "Why We Look So Bad."

167. Neil Rudenstine, *Pointing Our Thoughts* (Cambridge, MA: Harvard University Press, 2001), 369.

168. Daniel S. Hamermesh and Jeff E. Biddle, "Beauty and the Labor Market," *American Economic Review* 84 (1994), 1174; Jeff E. Biddle and Daniel S. Hamermesh, "Beauty, Productivity, and Discrimination: Lawyers' Looks and Lucre," *Journal of Labor Economics* 16 (1998): 172; Daniel S. Hamermesh and Amy M. Parker, *Beauty in the Classroom: Professors' Pulchritude and Putative Pedagogical Productivity*, NBER working paper no. 9853 (July 2003).

169. Hamermesh and Parker, *Beauty in the Classroom*.

170. James M. Lang, "RateMyBuns.com," *Chronicle of Higher Education*, December 1, 2003, http://chronicle.com/jobs/2003/; Gabriela Montell, "Do Good Looks Equal Good Evaluations?" *Chronicle of Higher Education*, October 15, 2003, available at http://chronicle.com/jobs/2003.

171. Dorothy Sayer, *Gaudy Night* (London: Victor Gollanez, 1972), 55.

172. Anna Quindlen, "And Now, Babe Feminism," *New York Times*, January 19, 1994, A21 (quoting Christina Hoff Sommers).

173. Ms. Mentor (Emily Toth), "What to Do When You're Summoned for an On Campus Look-See," *Chronicle of Higher Education*, October 23, 1998, available at http://chronicle.com/jobs/v45/i10/45iomentor.htm.

174. Id., Ms. Mentor (Emily Toth), "What Should You Wear?" *Chronicle of Higher Education*, February 1, 2002, http://chronicle.com/jobs/2002/022002020102c.htm.

175. Michael O'Donaghue, "How to Write Good," in William Novak and Mosche Waldokis, *The Big Book of New American Humor* (New York: HarperPerennial, 1990), 34.

176. Schneider, "Frumpy or Chic?" (quoting Gallup).

177. Schneider, "Frumpy or Chic?" (describing a presentation by Gallup).

178. Ms. Mentor (Emily Toth), "You Only Think You're Unique," *Chronicle of Higher Education*, December 16, 2002, available at http://chronicle.com/jobs/2002/12/2002/121601c.htm; Steele, "The F Word," 16; James M. Lang, "Looking Like a Professor," *Chronicle of Higher Education*, July 27, 2005, http://chronicle.com/jobs/2005/07/2005072701c.htm.

179. Paul Johnson, *Intellectuals* (London, Wiedenfeld and Nicolson, 1990), 230.

180. Tom Kuntz, "How to Succeed in Business Without Really Dressing," *New York Times*, November 30, 2003, E9.

181. Randall Jarrell, *Pictures from an Institution* (London: Faber & Faber, 1954), 57.

182. Lang, "Looking Like a Professor."

183. For examples, see Barbara Ehrenreich, *Bait and Switch: The (Futile) Pursuit of the American Dream* (New York: Metropolitan Books, 2005).

Chapter Six

1. Woody Allen, "My Speech to the Graduates," reprinted in *Hail to Thee, Okoboji U!: A Humor Anthology on Higher Education*, ed. Mark C. Ebersole (New York: Fordham University Press, 1992), 286.

2. Grayson Kirk, president of Columbia, Kingman Brewster, president of Yale, and Arthur Trottenberg, assistant dean of Harvard, quoted in "The Impending Financial Crisis of Higher Education," *Time*, June 23, 1967, 78.

3. "The Impending Financial Crisis," 78.

4. Kelly Field, "U.S. Panel Hears Pleas from College Presidents for More Student Aid," *Chronicle of Higher Education*, March 31, 2006, A28; Association of Governing

Boards of Universities and Colleges, *Renewing the American Presidency* (Washington, DC: Association of Governing Boards of Universities and Colleges, 1996), 2; Werner Z. Hirsch and Luc E. Weber, eds., *Challenges Facing Higher Education at the Millenium* (New York and Oxford, International Association of University Presses, 1999); James J. Duderstadt, *A University for the 21st Century* (Ann Arbor, MI: University of Michigan Press, 2000), 26–27.

5. Ryan C. Amacher and Roger Meiners, *Faulty Towers: Tenure and the Structure of Higher Education* (Oakland, CA: The Independent Institute, 2004), xi; John S. Brubacher and Willis Rudy, *Higher Education in Transition*, 4th ed. (New Brunswick, NJ: Transition, 1997), 422.

6. Charles Miller and Cheryl Oldham, *Setting the Context: Issue Paper by the Secretary of Education's Commission on the Future of Higher Education* (Washington, DC: United States Department of Education, April 4, 2006), available at www.ed.gov/about/bdcomm/list/hiedfuture/reports.html.

7. Arthur Levine, "How the Academic Profession Is Changing," *Daedelus* 126 (1995): 1, 4.

8. Duderstadt, *A University for the 21st Century*, 13–15.

9. Peter Drucker, "The Next Information Revolution," *Forbes ASAP*, August 24, 1998, 46, discussed in Clark Kerr, *The Uses of the University*, 5th ed. (Cambridge, MA: Harvard University Press, 2001), 210.

10. Stanley O. Kienberry, "The University and the Information Age," in Hirsch and Weber, *Challenges Facing Higher Education*, 56, 59.

11. Warren Bennis and Hallam Movius, "Why Harvard Is So Hard to Lead," *Chronicle of Higher Education*, March 3, 2006, B4.

12. For a sample, see Richard P. Chait, ed., *The Questions of Tenure* (Cambridge, MA: Harvard University Press, 2002); Matthew W. Finkin, *The Case for Tenure* (Ithaca: NY: Cornell University Press); Erwin Chemerinsky, "Is Tenure Necessary to Protect Academic Freedom?" *American Behavioral Scientist* 41 (1998): 638.

13. Cathy A. Trower, "What Is Current Policy?" in Chait, *The Questions of Tenure*, 32, 43.

14. Richard P. Chait, "Why Tenure? Why Now?" in Chait, *The Questions of Tenure*, 6, 19–20; Richard P. Chait, "Gleanings," in Chait, *The Questions of Tenure*, 309, 310.

15. American Association of University Professors (AAUP), "The Annual Report on the Economic Status of the Profession," *Academe*, March–April 2005, 21, 25; AAUP, *Statement on Contingent Appointments and the Academic Profession* (Washington, DC: AAUP, 2003), 1. For other figures and problems in their calculation, see Joe Berry, *Reclaiming the Ivory Tower: Organizing Adjuncts to Change Higher Education* (New York: Monthly Review Press, 2005), 4.

16. Roger G. Baldwin and Jay L. Chronister, "What Happened to the Tenure Track?" in Chait, *The Questions of Tenure*, 125, 127.

17. Allen Sanderson, Voon Chin Phua, and David Herda, *The American Faculty Poll* (New York: TIAA-CREF and National Opinion Research Center, 2000), 35.

18. Chait, "Why Tenure? Why Now?" 15–16.

19. Piper Fogg, "Chronicle Survey: What Presidents Think: Presidents Favor Scrapping Tenure," *Chronicle of Higher Education*, November 4, 2005, A31.

20. Donald Kennedy, *Academic Duty* (Cambridge, MA: Harvard University Press, 1998), 138.

21. Finkin, *The Case for Tenure*, 104; Roger G. Baldwin, Jay L. Chronister, *Teaching Without Tenure* (Baltimore: Johns Hopkins University Press, 2001), 21–26; American Council on Education, *An Agenda for Excellence: Creating Flexibility in Tenure-Track Faculty Careers* (Washington, DC: American Council on Education, 2005); Harvey Brooks, "Current Criticism of Research Universities," in *Research Universities in a Time of Discontent*, eds. Jonathan R. Cole, Elinor G. Barber, and Stephen R. Graubard (Baltimore: Johns Hopkins University Press, 1994), 241, 243.

22. Kennedy, *Academic Duty*, 97; Chait, "Why Tenure? Why Now?" 13.

23. For women's disproportionate family responsibilities, see Elizabeth M. O'Laughlin and Lisa G. Bischoff, "Balancing Parenthood and Academia: Work/Family Stress as Influenced by Gender and Tenure Status," *Journal of Family Issues* 26 (2005): 79, 95. For women's disproportionate representation in non-tenure-track positions, see AAUP, *Statement on Contingent Appointments*, 2; AAUP, "Annual Report on the Economic Status of the Profession," 29; Robin Wilson, "Where the Elite Teach, It's Still a Man's World," *Chronicle of Higher Education*, December 13, 2004, A1.

24. American Council on Education, *An Agenda for Excellence*, 4; University of California at Berkeley, UC Faculty Family Friendly Edge, *Leaks in the Academic Pipeline for Women* (2003), available at http://ucfamilyedge.berkeley.edu/leaks.html.

25. Virginia Valian, *Why So Slow? The Advancement of Women* (Cambridge, MA: MIT Press, 1998), available at http://jenson.stanford.edu/uhtbin/cgisirsi/dAbkf-ziAE4/320060208/13; Olga Bain and William Cummings, "Academe's Glass Ceiling: Societal Professional-Organizations, and Institutional Barriers to the Career Advancement of Women," *Comparative Education Review* 44 (2000): 495.

26. For the lack of data, see Ralph Brown and Jordan Kurland, "Academic Tenure and Academic Freedom," in *Freedom and Tenure in the Academy*, ed. William Van Alstyne (Durham, NC: Duke University Press, 1993), 332; Henry Rosovsky, *The University: An Owners' Manual* (New York: Norton, 1990). For the survey, see John Immerwahr, *Taking Responsibility: Leaders' Expectations for Higher Education* (New York: National Center for Public Policy and Higher Education, 1999), 22.

27. Kennedy, *Academic Duty*, 41; Finkin, *The Case for Tenure*, 175.

28. Trower, "What Is Current Policy?" 54; Amacher and Meiners, *Faulty Towers*, 80.

29. Chait, "Why Tenure? Why Now?" 12, Amacher and Meiners, *Faulty Towers*, 80. See also Thomas J. Tighe, *Who's in Charge of America's Research Universities? A Blueprint for Reform* (Albany, NY: State University of New York Press, 2003), 125–27, 121.

30. Amacher and Meiners, *Faulty Towers*, 80.

31. Rosovsky, *The University*, quoted in Kennedy, *Academic Duty*, 131.

32. Mortimer B. Zuckerman, "The Cambridge Question," *U.S. News and World Report*, April 10, 2006, 76.

33. Stuart Palmer, *The Universities Today* (Lanham, MD; University Press of America, 1998), 240; Chait, "Why Tenure? Why Now?" 14–15.

34. James Axtell, *The Pleasures of Academe* (Lincoln, NE: University of Nebraska Press, 1998), 227.

35. Richard P. Chait, "Does Faculty Governance Differ at Colleges with Tenure and Colleges Without Tenure?" in Chait, *Questions of Tenure*, 93.

36. Amacher and Meiners, *Faulty Towers*, 5–6, 24–25.

37. For academic freedom, see Finkin, *The Case for Tenure*, 191–97; for criticism, see Chait, *Does Faculty Governance Differ?*, 93.

38. Chait, "Gleanings," 312; William T. Mallon, "Why Is Tenure One College's Problem and Another's Solution?" in Chait, *Questions of Tenure*, 246, 269. See also Philip G. Altback, "How Are Faculty Faring in Other Countries," in Chait, *Questions of Tenure*, 162, 170 (noting that traditions of academic freedom are fairly well established in other Western industrialized countries, even those without tenure systems, although the protections are narrower).

39. John Tierney, "Free Harvard (or Not)," *New York Times*, March 4, 2006, A13; Richard Thomas, letter to the editor, *New York Times*, March 9, 2006, A22.

40. Axtell, *The Pleasures of Academe*, 233.

41. Suzanne Lohmann, "Darwinian Medicine for the University," in *Governing Academia*, ed. Ronald G. Ehrenberg (Ithaca, NY: Cornell University Press, 2004), 71, 89.

42. AAUP, "Annual Report on the Economic Status of the Profession," 26; Baldwin and Chronister, *Teaching Without Tenure*, 116; Judith M. Gappa and David W. Leslie, *The Invisible Faculty* (San Francisco: Jossey-Bass, 1993), 106–107; Cathy A. Trower, "Can Colleges Competitively Recruit Faculty Without Tenure?" in Chait, *Questions of Tenure*, 182, 215.

43. Berry, *Reclaiming the Ivory Tower*, 8.

44. Baldwin and Chronister, *Teaching Without Tenure*, 127–29; Gappa and Leslie, *The Invisible Faculty*, 189–200; Anne Matthews, *Bright College Years* (New York: Simon & Schuster, 1997), 179; AAUP, *Statement on Contingent Appointments*, 2–4.

45. Lawrence Douglas and Alexander George, "Personals," *Chronicle of Higher Education*, November 25, 2005, B12.

46. James Hynes, *The Lecturer's Tale* (New York: Pantheon, 2001), 63.

47. For discussion, see Thomas Sowell, *Inside Higher Education* (New York: Free Press, 1993), 226.

48. AAUP, *Statement on Contingent Appointments*, 2–3; Berry, *Reclaiming the Ivory Tower*, 9–11.

49. For time disparities, see Ernst Benjamin, "Reappraisal and Implications for Policy and Research," *New Directions for Higher Education* 123 (2003): 79–113; AAUP, *Statement on Contingent Employment*, 3. For poorer outcomes, see Karin Fisher, "Growing Use of Adjunct Professors May Mean Poorer Education for Students, Says Conference Speaker," *Chronicle of Higher Education*, November 7, 2005, available at http://chronicle. com/daily/2005/11/2005110705n.htm (discussing findings by Ronald G. Ehrenberg, director of the Cornell Higher Education Research Institute, indicating that increased use of non-tenure-track instructors correlates with lower graduation rates at public comprehensive institutions).

50. Gappa and Leslie, *The Invisible Faculty*, 102.

51. Gappa and Leslie, *The Invisible Faculty*, 192, 196.

52. Gappa and Leslie, *The Invisible Faculty*, 233–34; Baldwin and Chronister, *Teaching Without Tenure*, 146–58; see also AAUP, *Statement on Contingent Appointments*, and AAUP, *The Status of Non-Tenure-Track Faculty* (Washington, DC: AAUP, 1993).

53. Baldwin and Chronister, *Teaching Without Tenure*, 7, 146–58. Gappa and Leslie, *The Invisible Faculty*, 247–51.

54. Berry, *Reclaiming the Ivory Tower*, 17–48.

55. Trower, "Can Colleges Competitively Recruit Faculty Without Tenure?," 188–219.

56. Chait, "Gleanings," 315–16; Charles T. Clotfelter, "Can Faculty Be Induced to Relinquish Tenure?" in Chait, *Questions of Tenure*, 221, 240.

57. Chait, "Gleanings," 316; Clotfelter, "Can Faculty Be Induced to Relinquish Tenure?," 230.

58. Chait, "Gleanings," 317; Clotfelter, "Can Faculty Be Induced to Relinquish Tenure?," 241.

59. Mallon, "Why Is Tenure One College's Problem and Another's Solution?," 269. See also Altbach, "How Are Faculty Faring in Other Countries?," 160.

60. Chait, "Does Faculty Governance Differ?," 93.

61. Chait, "Gleanings," 320. See also David Margolick, "The Trouble With America's Law Schools," *New York Times Magazine*, May 22, 1983, 20, 36.

62. Amacher and Meiners, *Faulty Towers*, 55–58; Mallon, "Why Is Tenure One College's Problem and Another's Solution?," 269.

63. Matthews, *Bright College Years*, 116.

64. Vickie Schray, *Assuring Quality in Higher Education: Key Issues and Questions for Changing Accreditation in the United States: Issue Paper by the Secretary of Education's Commission on the Future of Higher Education* (Washington, DC: United States Department of Education, April 4, 2006), available at www.ed.gov/about/bdcomm/list/hiedfuture/reports.html. See also Peter T. Ewell, *Accreditation and Student Learning Outcomes: A Proposed Point of Departure, Council for Higher Education Accreditation Occasional Paper* (Washington, DC: Council for Higher Education Accreditation, September, 2001).

65. Cary Nelson and Stephen Watt, *Academic Keywords: A Devil's Dictionary for Higher Education* (New York: Routledge, 1999), 36.

66. Brent D. Ruben, *Pursuing Excellence in Higher Education* (San Francisco: Jossey Bass, 2004), 37–38. See also Donald E. Heller, "State Oversight of Academia," in Ehrenberg, *Governing Academia*, 30, 56.

67. Clara M. Lovett, quoted in Welch Suggs, "Colleges Face New Demands for Accountability, Conference Says," *Chronicle of Higher Education*, March 21, 2005, available at http://chronicle.com/prm/daily/2005/03/2005032101n.ht. For faculty resistance, see Charles Miller and Geri Malandra, *Accountability/Assessment: Issue Paper by the Secretary of Education's Commission on the Future of Higher Education* (Washington, DC: United States Department of Education, April 4, 2006), available at www.ed.gov/about/bdcomm/list/hiedfuture/reports.html.

68. Ruben, *Pursuing Excellence*, 17, 155–60; Baldridge National Quality Program, available at www.quality.nist.gov/index.html

69. Ruben, *Pursuing Excellence*, 18.

70. Suggs, "Colleges Face New Demands for Accountability."

71. Tighe, *Who's in Charge of America's Research Universities?*, 125–27.

72. Tighe, *Who's in Charge*, 130. See discussion in Chapter Three and Alexander W. Astin, "To Use Graduation Rates to Measure Excellence, You Have to Do Your Homework," *Chronicle of Higher Education*, October 22, 2004, B20, available at http://chronicle.com/prm/weekly/v51/i09/09b02001.htm.

73. Derek Bok, *Our Underachieving Colleges* (Princeton, NJ: Princeton University Press, 2006), 327.

74. Sanderson, Phua, and Herda, *The American Faculty Poll*, 32 (finding that only 6 percent of faculty thought that post-tenure review affected performance); Faculty Advisory Council Initial Report, *The University of Texas System Faculty Satisfaction Survey: June 2003* (Dallas: University of Texas, 2003), available at www.utsystem.edu/news/2003/

BORAug2003-Presentations/FACSurvey.ppt (finding that faculty generally do not believe that performance reviews have improved teaching or productivity).

75. Ruben, *Excellence in Higher Education*, 13. See also William Aumlo, "Public Policy and Accountability in Higher Education: Lessons from the Past and Present for the New Millenium," in Donald G. Heller, *Affordability, Access, and Accountability* (Baltimore, MD; Johns Hopkins University Press), 155, 174–185.

76. Schray, *Assuring Quality in Higher Education*.

77. Levine, "How the Academic Profession is Changing," 5.

78. William James, quoted in Clark Kerr, "Knowledge Ethics and the New Academic Culture," *Change*, January–February, 1994, 9, 11.

79. Peter Smith, *The Quiet Crisis: How Higher Education Is Failing America* (Bolton, MA: Anker Publishing, 2004), 139–40; Miller and Malandra, *Accountability/Assessment*.

80. Rubin, *Excellence in Higher Education*, 108.

81. Tighe, *Who's in Charge*, 137.

82. Ruben, *Excellence in Higher Education*, 386.

83. Alain de Botton, *Status Anxiety* (New York: Pantheon, 2004), 108.

84. de Botton, *Status Anxiety*.

85. For discussion of alternatives, see Jeffrey Evans Stake, "The Interplay Between Law School Rankings, Reputations, and Resource Allocation: Ways Rankings Mislead," *Indiana Law Journal* 81 (2006): 229; Eric Dash, "Top Colleges, Rated by Those Who Chose Them," *New York Times*, October 20, 2004, 9; Christopher Avery, Mark Glickman, Caroline Holby, and Andrew Metrick, "A Revealed Preference Ranking of U.S. Colleges and Universities," National Bureau of Economic Research working paper no. 10803 (Washington, DC: National Bureau of Economic Research, September, 2004).

86. Charles Miller, *Accountability/Consumer Information, Issue Paper by the Secretary of Education's Commission on the Future of Higher Education* (Washington, DC: United States Department of Education, April 4, 2006), available at www.ed.gov/about/bdcomm/list/hiedfuture/reports.html; Kelly Field, "New Database Would Customize College Rankings," *Chronicle of Higher Education*, April 7, 2006, A34.

87. George R. Goethals and Cynthia McPherson Frantz, "Thinking Seriously About Paying for College: The Large Effects of a Little Thought," in *New Thinking on Higher Education*, ed. Joel W. Meyerson (Bolton, MA: Anker Publishing, 1998), 15.

88. Adam Smith, *The Theory of Moral Sentiments*, eds. D. D. Raphael and A. L. Macfie (Indianapolis: Liberty Classics, 1982 [1759]), Liii 2.1, 50.

89. de Botton, *Status Anxiety*, 292.

90. Axtell, *The Pleasures of Academe*, 233.

91. William James, *The Principles of Psychology, Volume I* (Cambridge, MA: Harvard University Press, 1981), 296.

92. Gary Marx, "Reflections on Academic Success and Failure: Making It, Forsaking It, Shaping It," in *Authors of Their Own Lives*, ed. Bennett M. Berger (Berkeley, CA: University of California Press, 1990), 260, 271.

Bibliography:
Selected Academic Novels and Humor

Adams, Hazard. *Home*. Albany, NY: State University of New York Press, 2001.

Aldridge, John W. *The Party at Cranton*. New York: David McKay, 1960.

Amis, Kingsley. *Lucky Jim*. New York: The Viking Press, 1965 [1953].

Bellow, Saul. *Ravelstein*. New York: Penguin, 2001.

Brace, Gerald Warner. *The Department*. New York: Norton, 1968.

Bradbury, Malcolm. *The History of Man*. Boston: Houghton Mifflin Company, 1976.

Bradbury, Malcolm. *Eating People Is Wrong*. London: Secker & Warburg, 1976.

Byatt, A. S. *Possession*. New York: Random House, 1990.

Carter, Stephen L. *The Emperor of Ocean Park*. New York: Alfred A. Knopp, 2002.

Cather, Willa. *The Professor's House*. 1925; reprint New York: Vintage, 1990.

Coetzee, J. M. *Disgrace*. New York: Viking, 1999.

Cornford, F. M. *Microcosmographia Academica: Being a Guide for the Young Academic Politician*. 4th ed. Cambridge: Bowes & Bowes, 1949.

Crews, Frederick. *Postmodern Pooh*. New York: North Point Press, Farrar, Straus, and Giroux, 2001.

Cross, Amanda (pseudonym of Carolyn Heilbrun). *Death in a Tenured Position*. 1981; reprint New York: Ballantine, 1988.

Davies, Stevie. *Four Dreamers and Emily*. New York: The Women's Press, 1996.

DeLillo, Don. *White Noise*. 1985; reprint New York: Penguin, 1986.

Ebersole, Mark. *Hail to Thee, Okoboji U!: A Humor Anthology on Higher Education*. New York: Fordham University Press, 1992.

Edson, Margaret. *Wit: A Play*. New York: Faber and Faber, Farrar, Straus and Giroux, 1999.

Eliot, George. *Middlemarch*. 1871; reprint New York: Norton, 1977.

Galbraith, John Kenneth. *A Tenured Professor*. Boston: Houghton Mifflin, 1990.

Gardner, John. *Mickelsson's Ghosts*. New York: Alfred A. Knopp, 1982.

Gilbert, Sandra M., and Susan Gubar. *Masterpiece Theatre: An Academic Melodrama*. New Brunswick, NJ: Rutgers University Press, 1995.

Goldstein, Rebecca. *The Mind-Body Problem: A Novel*. New York: Random House, 1983.

Grudin, Robert. *Book: A Novel.* New York: Random House, 1992.

Harris, Sidney. *Can't You Guys Read? Cartoons on Academia.* New Brunswick, NJ: Rutgers University Press, 1991.

Hymes, James. *Publish and Perish: Three Tales of Tenure and Terror.* New York: Picador, 1997.

Jarrell, Randall. *Pictures from an Institution.* London: Faber and Faber, 1954.

Jarvis, Robert M., Thomas E. Baker, and Andrew J. McClurg. *Amicus Humoriae: An Anthology of Legal Humor.* Durham, NC: Carolina Academic Press, 2003.

Lodge, David. *Small World: An Academic Romance.* New York: MacMillan, 1984.

Lodge, David. *Changing Places: A Tale of Two Campuses.* Bath, England: Chivers Press, 1986.

Lodge, David. *Home Truths, a Novella.* London, Secker & Warburg, 1999.

Lurie, Alison. *The War Between the Tates.* New York: Random House, 1974.

Lurie, Alison. *Love and Friendship.* New York: Macmillan, 1982.

Mann, Heinrich. *The Blue Angel.* New York: Frederick Ungar, 1997.

Maveety, Nancy. *The Stagnant Pool: Scholars Below Sea Level.* New Orleans: University Press of the South, 2000.

McCarthy, Mary. *The Groves of Academe.* New York: Harcourt, Brace, 1952.

McNally, John (ed.). *The Student Body: Short Stories about College Students and Professors.* Madison: University of Wisconsin Press, 2001.

Nabokov, Vladimir. *PNIN.* London: Heinemann, 1957.

Nelson, Cary, and Stephen Watt. *Academic Keywords: A Devil's Dictionary for Higher Education.* New York: Routledge, 1999.

Orwell, George. *Essays.* Edited and introduced by John Carey. New York: Alfred A. Knopf, 1968.

Parks, Tim. *Europa.* London: Seeker and Warburg, 1997.

Phelan, James. *Beyond the Tenure Track: Fifteen Months in the Life of an English Professor.* Columbus: Ohio State University Press, 1991.

Prose, Francine. *Blue Angel.* New York: HarperCollins, 2000.

Reed, Ishmael. *Japanese by Spring.* New York: Macmillan, 1993.

Roney, Lois. *Academic Animals: A Bestiary of Higher-Education Teaching and How It Got That Way.* Philadelphia: Xlibris, 2002.

Roth, Philip. *The Professor of Desire.* 1977; reprint New York: Vintage/Random House, 1984.

Roth, Philip. *The Human Stain.* London: Jonathan Cape, 2000.

Russo, Richard. *Straight Man.* New York: Random House, 1997.

Sarton, May. *Faithful Are the Wounds.* New York: W.W. Norton, 1985.

Sayers, Dorothy L. *Gaudy Night.* 1936; reprint New York: Avon, 1968.

Shields, Carol. *Swann.* New York: Penguin, 1987, 1990.

Showalter, Elaine. *Faculty Towers: The Academic Novel and Its Discontent.* Philadelphia: University of Pennsylvania Press, 2005.

Smiley, Jane. *Moo.* New York: Knopf, 1995.

Snow, C. P. *The Masters.* London: Macmillan, 1951.

Toth, Emily. *Ms. Mentor's Impeccable Advice for Women in Academia.* Philadelphia: University of Pennsylvania Press, 1997.

Wodehouse, P. G. *The Girl in Blue.* New York: Simon and Schuster, 1971.

Professor X. *This Beats Working for a Living: The Dark Secrets of a College Professor.* New Rochelle, NY: Arlington House, 1974.

Index